★ ★ ★

REMEMBERING THE FREE BIRDS OF

SOUTHERN ROCK

LYNYRD SKYNYRD

REMEMBERING THE FREE BIRDS OF
SOUTHERN ROCK

Gene Odom

WITH

Frank Dorman

40% ALC. BY VOL. (80 PROOF)

BROADWAY BOOKS   NEW YORK

BROADWAY

Broadway Books titles may be purchased for business or
promotional use or for special sales. For information, please
write to: Special Markets Department, Random House, Inc.,
280 Park Avenue, New York, NY 10017.

PRINTED IN THE UNITED STATES OF AMERICA

BROADWAY BOOKS and its logo, a letter B bisected on the
diagonal, are trademarks of Broadway Books, a division of
Random House, Inc.

Visit our website at www.broadwaybooks.com

First edition published 2002.

BOOK DESIGN BY JUDITH STAGNITTO ABBATE/ABBATE DESIGN

Library of Congress Cataloging-in-Publication Data

Odom, Gene, 1948–
    Lynyrd Skynyrd: remembering the free birds of Southern
rock / Gene Odom with Frank Dorman.—1st ed.
        p. cm.
    Discography: p. 203
    ISBN 0-7679-1026-5
    1. Lynyrd Skynyrd (Musical group)   2. Rock musicians—
United States—Biography.   3. Odom, Gene, 1948–
I. Dorman, Frank.   II. Title.

ML421.L96 O37 2002
782.42166'092'2—dc21
    [B]   2002023080

10 9 8 7 6 5 4 3 2 1

To my daughters, Melissa Jean and Christina Diane. My grandchildren, Jacob, Courtney, Tyler, and Cody. To my former wives, Brenda and Lori. And to Ronnie Van Zant, Allen Collins, Steve and Cassie Gaines, and Leon Wilkeson, who are no longer with us.

—G.O.

To my wife, Jeanne, and our son, Francis Paul.

—F.D.

CONTENTS

CONTENTS

Nineteen years have passed since I wrote a small book intended as a tribute to Lynyrd Skynyrd, titled *Lynyrd Skynyrd: I'll Never Forget You,* and I had hoped that someone would follow up with a full-length book that would cover the band's story in greater detail. But since that hasn't been done, I decided to have another go at it. In *Lynyrd Skynyrd: Remembering the Free Birds of Southern Rock,* although I haven't recounted band members' family lives, I have otherwise tried to provide accurate information that, in some instances, has not been told, and in others, corrects oft-repeated accounts that sprang from imperfect memories. I have relied upon my own memories of events in which I was involved, and on those of persons who were present for major events in the life of the band, with corroborative evidence that confirms their stories. To the extent that my account of the plane crash differs from those of other survivors, all I can say is that I have written it as I remember it, and if my memory serves me ill, I apologize. I only wish that Ronnie Van Zant could tell the story himself. If he were alive today, I bet he would tell it in verse.

★ ★ ★

REMEMBERING THE FREE BIRDS OF
SOUTHERN ROCK

If you've ever rolled over in a car you know why time is measured in moments. Everything happens so fast. An airplane crash is different. A lot of time can pass before you actually crash, and all the while you're falling, powerless to stop and certain that death is near. And when the end finally comes, only the dead find peace.

A plane crash changed my life. Up until then, things had been going pretty well. I was flying around the world with my closest friends, with a backstage pass for every thrilling performance of one of the foremost rock and roll groups in the world, the Lynyrd Skynyrd band. Then a plane crash took it all away. It took my best friend and my left eye, it robbed me of my livelihood, and for years it nearly drove me insane because I couldn't stop feeling that I could have kept it from happening. I was Ronnie's security guard, and I had clearly failed.

Through years of torment I lived with the knowledge that if I hadn't awakened him before we crashed, Ronnie Van Zant might still be alive or at least he might have died in his sleep. Instead, he drew his final breaths in a blur of confusion and fear, not fully knowing what was happening. Those last few minutes in the air were the longest bits of time I will ever remember. Nor can I ever forget the anxiety most of us felt as we left the ground on that warm October day in 1977. Lakeland, Florida, had been the third stop on the ill-named "Tour of the Survivors," and we were flying up the coast to Greenville, South Carolina. I still have nightmares about it.

Just as we left the runway the starboard engine backfired, the bang so loud I thought it had blown apart. Staring out the window I could see it was still intact, but long orange flames were pouring from the engine as the plane continued to climb. We were all terrified. Of the twenty-four passengers on board, nine were members of the band. There were Ronnie Van Zant, the leader, guitarists Allen Collins, Gary Rossington, and Steve Gaines, bass player Leon Wilkeson, drummer Artimus Pyle, pianist Billy Powell, and two vocalists, Cassie Gaines, and Leslie Hawkins. We were a bunch of Southern country twenty-somethings, out on the lark of our lives and flying on top of the world.

"There's fire shooting out from the right engine," I yelled to the two pilots. "You have to turn around and go back." Scared nearly out of my mind, I ran to tell them as soon as I saw it, but neither man seemed fazed as they focused on the gauges in front of them.

"There's nothing wrong," one of the pilots said.

"I'm telling you there's something wrong," I answered. "I saw flames coming out of the engine."

"There's nothing wrong. Go back to your seat and stay put 'til we're in the air."

And so I returned to my seat. What else was I to do? What can anyone do in a situation like that? The pilots are in charge of the aircraft, they know what they're doing, and if they're not afraid, the passengers shouldn't be concerned.

When we landed in Greenville, South Carolina, I wanted to kiss the ground. During the unsettling flight from Florida the starboard engine had backfired several more times, each backfire sparking a spasm of fear that we managed to overcome with nervous laughter and the faith we had placed in our pilots. On one of these occasions, twelve thousand feet in the air, the engine spewed

LYNYRD SKYNYRD

out a ten-foot torch of fire that lasted for several minutes, offering each of us an unforgettable look at our very serious problem.

That first fiery blast, alone, should have been reason enough for us not to re-board the plane when we left Greenville the next day, especially for Ronnie, who disliked flying more than any of us. Everyone had misgivings, but Ronnie chose to stay with the plane that had brought us, and rather than follow our instincts, the rest of us followed the course that had always been right before; we followed the leader. No one had sense enough to do what we all knew made sense.

"C'mon, let's go. If it's your time to go, it's your time to go," I remember Ronnie saying as he stepped aboard the plane for our final flight together. Most veteran air travelers will never experience the frightening sight of a flaming engine outside their window, but anyone who has ever flown can imagine how all of us felt that day. Because everyone has felt the prick of panic when something doesn't feel right in an airplane.

Ronnie and I had talked about it. At one time or another, whether in takeoff, mid-flight or landing, a subtle sensation takes hold of you and, rightly or wrongly, you feel certain that something is wrong. You glance at the other passengers to see if anyone else has noticed, but all appear to be reading or resting or talking as if they're still in the airport lounge. You study the flight attendants' faces for any sign that something's amiss, but they're absorbed in their work, seemingly unaware that all aboard are in peril. Surely the pilots know, you think, but you don't allow your fear to overcome your reason, because beneath your suspicion there's the comfort of knowing that the pilots are in full control of the situation.

Years later, while headed for takeoff in a big passenger jet, I had the distinct impression that the plane didn't have enough speed to get off the ground. We were moving very fast at that point, but a wrenching feeling in my gut told me we weren't going to make it. I looked around at everyone else, but no one seemed to notice. Suddenly, at great relief to me, the plane began to slow down, and the pilot's voice came over the intercom to announce, matter-of-factly, "We've had a little technical problem, so we're going to go back and try it again." It was all I could do to keep from leaving the plane right then, but I knew that the pilots knew what they were doing. And on that flight they were right. But all of us heard the engine backfire that day as we left Lakeland, and all of us saw the flames, and none of us could ignore the fact that something was wrong with our airplane.

When we leased it, the Convair 240 had been a trusted name in aviation since 1947. Originally designed to carry forty passengers, it was the first pressurized, twin-engine airliner ever built, and it later became the plane of choice among VIPs, including John F. Kennedy, whose "Caroline" was the first private aircraft ever used by a presidential candidate. With a touch of historical irony, a CV-240 later played a role in the space program, which President Kennedy had christened with a speech in 1962. After the space shuttle Challenger exploded in 1986, a CV-240 was modified so that NASA could test an emergency escape hatch for future shuttle missions.

The Convair 240 was created to replace the aging Douglas DC-3 for medium-range passenger service. Of the five hundred and seventy-six CV-240s that were built, commercial airlines and freight carriers bought almost a third; the Navy and the Air Force acquired the rest. Almost seventy-five feet long, with a wingspan of ninety-one feet, nine inches, Lynyrd Skynyrd's CV-240 could reach an altitude of sixteen thousand feet and travel twelve hundred miles on a full tank of fuel. Its maximum speed was three hundred and fifteen miles per hour, but it normally cruised at two-forty, pushed through the air by a pair of eighteen-cylinder, twenty-four-hundred-horsepower engines that hummed along steadily and faithfully until that otherwise beautiful day in the fall of 1977.

We had chartered the plane in Addison, Texas, from the L&J Company, a subsidiary of Falcon Aviation, which employed the

flight crew. Walter Wiley McCreary, our thirty-four-year-old captain, was fully qualified and properly certified and had logged six thousand, eight hundred hours of flight time, including sixty-eight hours in the Convair. His junior by two years, the first officer, William John Gray, Jr., also was duly credentialed.

Les Long had been our pilot on previous tours, with McCreary along as co-pilot, but two weeks before our final tour began, he had left his job with Falcon Aviation. I'll never know if Long's presence would have made a difference that day. I'll always wonder if he would have made the same mistakes that McCreary and Gray made.

I went to the cockpit several times during the flight from Lakeland, almost every time the engine backfired. But each time I did, McCreary and Gray assured me there was nothing to worry about and that everything would be all right. Like arrogant doctors who talk down to their patients, they felt their judgment shouldn't be questioned.

The next morning, after a rousing concert performance, the usual "after work" partying, and a few hours of sleep in a motel bed, I showered and headed straight for the pilots' room. It didn't take an aeronautical engineer to know the starboard engine was ailing, and none of us wanted to have to endure another frightening ride. The flight crew had already left for the airport when I knocked on their door, and when I got to the plane they were working on the engine. We were scheduled to fly to Baton Rouge, Louisiana, that afternoon.

"What's wrong with the plane? That was a helluva trip comin' up here."

"The magneto's been missing a little bit," Gray said, as if a magnet-driven generator were the only problem. "We're going to have a mechanic fly to Baton Rouge to take a look at it."

"Baton Rouge? That's crazy. Why don't you have him fly here?"

"No reason to. It's just something we need to fix so the engine'll run better."

"But that big ball of fire."

"It's really not as bad as it looks," McCreary said. "Besides, even if an engine shuts down, which it won't, we can fly this plane on one engine." It didn't make any sense to me, but, after all, they were flying the plane, and their lives were on the line, too. Once again, arrogance triumphed over ignorance.

"I hope it won't come to that," I said. "I care an awful lot about these people."

"I understand," he said. "We feel it's safe to fly. The mechanic will be waiting for us, and we'll start working on it as soon as we land." And so we talked for a while longer. I was certain we'd have to make other travel arrangements, but McCreary and Gray persuaded me otherwise. I went back to the motel and started knocking on doors to wake up the band as I usually did when we toured. Our limo drivers didn't show up, so we rode to the airport in taxicabs instead—twenty-four people with luggage; the sound and light equipment had already left in a truck. I cautioned the pilots one last time, and they assured me the plane was fine.

It was two minutes past four in the afternoon when we left the Greenville Downtown Airport on October 20. The weather was nice, a balmy sixty-two degrees under a partly cloudy sky with no chance of rain. The plane took off without a hitch, it seemed, but shortly afterward the starboard engine started skipping, the way an automobile engine does when it's missing a cylinder and it ends up being towed. The engine wasn't recoiling or spouting flames as it had the day before, but it was obviously laboring, and it seemed to be working harder the farther we flew.

Every time I complained to the pilots my voice got louder.

"You should've gotten it fixed back in Greenville. This just ain't right," I said, which was finally more than McCreary wanted to hear.

"Everything is under control," he said loudly, clearly annoyed with me. "Now, please, just go back and let us fly the plane."

Occasionally glancing out the window to look at the troubled engine, we saw the sun pass peacefully over the horizon, and we knew Baton Rouge was near. Within the plane it was dark now, the

passengers barely distinguishable as fading silhouettes. It was the only time any of us who were awake felt a sense of complete calm, and there lay Ronnie on the floor, soothed into sleep by a sedative. Suddenly our reverie was broken as both engines started sputtering, first one, then the other, alternating back and forth like twins with asthma desperately struggling to breathe. Billy Powell, the band's piano player, later described that singular terrifying moment in words you could weigh in a spoon: "I heard the pilot say, 'Oh, my God,' and the right engine went out." Some of us were playing poker at the time. The much-needed distraction instantly lost its appeal in the wake of McCreary's prayer.

Leaving a pile of cash and a winning hand I sprang from my seat in the back of the plane and ran to the cockpit, where I was stunned to see the unmistakable look of absolute fear in both of the pilots' faces. They'd been playing a different game for much higher stakes, and now I knew they'd lost. I knew we weren't going to make it.

"What the hell's going on?" I asked, more terrified than curious.

"We've got fuel problems," McCreary called out over his shoulder, his confidence obviously shattered. "We're going to have to make a crash landing. Get back in your seat."

Nothing in life prepares you for a statement like that. It was like hearing a sentence of death, and I wasn't ready to die. Even though my heart was pounding madly, the life seemed to drain from my body, seeping out through the soles of my feet like sand through the stem of an hourglass. Anger and fear enveloped me in the same intense instant. Shaking uncontrollably, at once I was enraged at the pilots and desperately afraid for my life. My worst nightmare was coming true. Rushing back into the cabin with panic gripping my throat, somehow I yelled out the pilots' alarm and quietly cursed the men while others were cursing the plane. I remember hearing Leslie Hawkins, from her second row seat in the center section, calmly telling me to get in my seat and buckle up. Sweet Leslie, who always seemed at peace with herself, said later that she had assumed the crash position with her head between her legs and recited most of the Lord's Prayer in silence.

They say your life passes before your eyes just before it ends. Only one small fragment of mine did. For some strange reason I flashed back to 1968 and the day I was driving Ronnie to our jobs at his brother-in-law's auto parts store. He'd practiced with the band all night and hadn't slept, so he was asleep on the floor of the delivery truck next to where I sat at the wheel. We were heading west on Interstate 10 in Jacksonville when the truck's left rear tire blew out, sending us swerving across the pavement on two wheels. As Ronnie regarded the road from a rather confused perspective, the truck spun round and round like a carnival ride, veering off the highway and onto the grassy median where it finally came to rest. Unable to speak or stop my legs from shaking, I sat for a minute while Ronnie picked himself up in a daze. When he finally spoke, he said it was the best piece of driving he'd ever seen.

For some inexplicable reason that's what flashed across my mind at that particular frightful moment. It was an odd thought to have right then, but it smothered my anger and diverted my fear with an awareness that Ronnie was asleep on the floor of the airplane and it was up to me to keep him alive. We were falling at a fairly normal angle, it seemed, so I thought seatbelts might save us. When I reached Ronnie, I jerked him up from the floor and got him into a seat, ignoring his groggy complaints.

"Man, just let me sleep," he said. Still standing, I buckled his seat belt and yelled into his face. "The plane's gonna crash; put your head down."

Then we hit the trees.

LYNYRD SKYNYRD

CHAPTER 1

REDNECK

Early in the fall of 1976, the world's top rock and roll artists gathered in Hollywood to celebrate their success. The occasion was *Don Kirschner's Annual Rock Awards,* a nationally televised show to honor the best of the artists who had appeared on Kirschner's weekly television show, *Rock Concert.*

Practically everyone who was anyone in the rock music business had come to the grand old, flamingo pink Beverly Hills Hotel that evening, along with a smattering of TV and movie stars whose presence seemed almost obligatory in a town that once had been ruled by film. Among the musical set were Rod Stewart, flanked by a flock of beautiful women, Peter Frampton, whose *Frampton Comes Alive* album would sell eight million copies that year, and the rising songstress Patti LaBelle. Few and barely distinguishable by comparison, the stars of film and television included twelve-year-old Tatum O'Neal, an Oscar winner for her role in the movie *Paper Moon;* and sixteen-year-old Mackenzie Phillips, who had appeared in *American Graffiti.*

EIGHT-YEAR-OLD RONNIE VAN ZANT GAVE THIS SCHOOL PHOTO TO OLLIE MAE HAMNER AND HER HUSBAND, CLAUDE, FOR WHOM RONNIE WOULD WRITE THE SONG "THE BALLAD OF CURTIS LOEW." (HAMNER)

In the 1970s, the billboards that towered above Sunset Boulevard promoted record albums, not movies, and the biggest cinema star in the building that day wasn't even there for the show; she was having dinner. Hoping to see the luminaries of rock step from their limos and stroll through the entrance of the world-famous hotel, a large group of spectators was surprised to see her emerge from the lobby. Walking slowly but proudly on the arm of a younger man, this living fossil from Hollywood's golden age was the once glamorous Mae West, whose eighty-four zestful years had so distorted her face that no one would have recognized her if hotel staff hadn't announced her name. Minutes later, in the starkest of contrasts came the arrival of one of the greatest divas of the day, the dazzling, ever-radiant Diana Ross, who held the crowd's gaze as if she were actual royalty. Aglow in the warmth from a score of popping flashbulbs, she responded through bright, beaming eyes and her famous, self-conscious smile, seemingly confident that everyone had come just to see her.

Inside the hotel auditorium, where admission was by invitation only, hundreds of formally attired guests settled into their seats to hear some of the year's top performing acts. The emcee was Alice Cooper, who started things off with a well-rehearsed temper tantrum that segued into a strange, wonderfully choreographed number in which dancers dressed as spiders moved across the stage while Cooper's band played. It was big-time show business at its creative best. The aristocracy of the recording industry were being entertained, having come to honor the year's top performers, the *crème de la crème,* the ones who had sold the most records. Only in Technicolor dreams could you conceive of a Cinderella setting more unlikely than was set that night for a good ol' boy from Jacksonville, Florida. Wearing a smile as wide as a Southern drawl as he walked toward center stage, Leon Wilkeson, bass guitar player for the Lynyrd Skynyrd band, accepted the Golden Achievement award for what truly was a remarkable level of accomplishment for a bunch of musical misfits. It was a moment filled with irony.

Leon always enjoyed wearing odd hats, but for this gala affair he'd chosen an entire ensemble, and I'm sure that Hollywood's smart set wondered how he'd managed to get past the hotel doorman in the godawful get-up he wore. It was a tuxedo, but it wasn't the traditional James Bond look. The pants and jacket were the customary flat black, but cut with a western flair. The shirt was appropriately white but ruffled from neck to navel. And if that weren't enough of a fashion faux pas in this discerning crowd of sophisticates, all dressed to the nines, Leon added his own fanciful touch, a white cowboy hat and boots, and a wide leather belt with a pair of pearl-handled pistols in cream-colored holsters. These were unexpected accessories for a musician from a band that didn't perform Western tunes, especially when one of their top hits, "Saturday Night Special," is still the most strongly worded anti-handgun pop song ever written.

But regardless of how anyone may have felt about Leon's attire that evening, it was decidedly more fitting than his usual garb; besides, show business people can wear whatever they want, and he was just having fun. In fact, after the show he danced with Mae West. Leon's outfit simply affirmed the Southern maxim: you can take the boy out of the country, but you can't take the country out of the boy. That's a nice way to say what is often expressed in a single word, a word someone uttered quietly in the back of the auditorium when Leon rose to claim the award.

"Redneck."

For anyone who doesn't understand what a redneck is, I should explain. The term originated before the turn of the last century, when most Americans worked on farms and got sunburned necks from being outdoors all day. City dwellers tended to look down on uncultured country folks, and the label was custom-made. If you call a man a redneck today, you're also calling him ignorant, but that "ain't no big thing" if you're a redneck, too. In that case, you're both just good ol' boys wherever you live in this country, although a Southern drawl will usually leave no doubt. Jacksonville, Florida, was where the original Lynyrd Skynyrd band members grew up, and most of its residents' forebears had moved there from the rural areas of Northeast Florida and Southeast Georgia. And for Jacksonville, you didn't get any more country than the Westside.

Despite the magic of the moment when he stood on that stage in Hollywood, Leon was still just a redneck from the Westside of Jacksonville, Florida, and he never pretended to be otherwise. I'm the same way, and so was my best friend, Ronnie Van Zant, the founding father, chief songwriter and singer, and undisputed leader of Lynyrd Skynyrd. Ronnie had asked Leon to accept the award that night at the Beverly Hills Hotel because Ronnie avoided the limelight when he wasn't on stage, and besides, getting dressed up wasn't his style, not even for a prestigious award. For Ronnie, it was jeans and a T-shirt and maybe a hat, unless it was cold, and that's all it would ever be.

To understand Lynyrd Skynyrd, you have to understand Ronnie Van Zant, who, at the peak of his success, was still the same person he was when he started out. Except for his extraordinary talent and the musical skills of the boys in the band, all of us and the people we grew up with were average rednecks. Like the rest of the folks who lived in our part of town, it was manual labor that put bread on the table, just as it had for every other generation before us. Ronnie's father, Lacy Van Zant, made his living hauling goods up and down the East Coast in a big rig truck, and his mother, Marion Virginia "Sister" Hicks Van Zant, worked nights in a donut shop. Her grandfather had called her "Sister" as a child, and the nickname stuck. Lacy and Sister met near the end of the Second World War when he was home on leave from the U.S. Navy and she was just fifteen. They started dating when he left the service two years later, and one of their favorite outings was sitting in a car listening to the radio and singing along with the music. After a year-long courtship, Lacy and Marion began a marriage that would last fifty-three years, and together they would raise six children: the oldest was Jo Anne, Lacy's daughter from a previous marriage, followed by Ronnie, Donnie, Marlene, Darlene, and Johnny.

Lacy was always a good provider, but Sister was the glue that held the family together, especially with Lacy out on the road so much as a truck driver. Sister was a friendly person, generous with everyone she met, but she had a firm side, too, and she was never shy about standing up for what she felt was right, especially if it involved her family. Their house was always open to everybody in the neighborhood, and anyone who ever visited the Van Zants never failed to notice the genuine respect the children had for their parents, and the politeness their kids always showed for each other and for other people.

Lacy and Sister made their home a happy place for their children to grow up in. It was a close, loving family in which the kids were encouraged to enjoy life, to be happy about themselves as individuals, to be proud of who they were in spite of their humble station in life, and to live the American dream without being afraid to fail. It was in this nurturing environment that Ronnie developed his one great dream and all of the confidence he would ever need. The boy loved both of his parents, and as the oldest son of a man who let him be himself, he revered his father. Lacy stressed the value of education, and Ronnie tried hard to be a good student, serving on the school safety patrol in the sixth grade, and sometimes making the honor roll in his upper grades. But just a few credits short of finishing, he withdrew from school toward the end of his senior year.

Leaving high school was a decision Ronnie always regretted, and later in life he confessed that, despite his success, he felt he had failed to live up to his father's expectations. This wasn't true, of course, because Lacy's love for his son was boundless, and yet this feeling followed Ronnie for the rest of his life. It drove him to succeed, and even after he'd done that, it drove him to excel. Many years later, Ronnie told a reporter, "All I can preach is school. That's where power lies, . . . If I can come out of [Shantytown], you can do it. I made a bad mistake. You gotta have education." He'd put platinum record albums on his father's wall, "but never a diploma," he said.

Ronald Wayne Van Zant was born January 15, 1948, in Jacksonville, Florida, and he lived near the outskirts of town on the city's Westside. The Van Zants' home was at the corner of Mull Street and Woodcrest Road. I lived on Mull Street just a few houses away, in a rough, blue-collar area that Ronnie called "Shantytown." He'd heard it called that by the mother of one of his friends, Jim Daniel, who lived in a different neighborhood. Ronnie found it amusing at the time, but the truth was clear to see. The houses were simple structures built mostly of concrete block or wood. Some had missing windows and doors, and some had no electricity. Most streets were paved, but there were dirt roads, too, and one of them distinguished our neighborhood in a way that only a redneck could appreciate. Not really a road, it was a racetrack; and if there is one sport that rednecks enjoy more than all the rest it's stock car racing. Every Saturday night and on many a Sunday afternoon this oval-shaped circle of sand became redneck heaven, and in our neighborhood, if you weren't at the races you felt them anyway, their thunderous roar so loud it rattled windows and smothered conversation in every house. Just three blocks from where Ronnie and I lived, at the corner of Ellis Road and Plymouth Street, Jacksonville's Speedway Park was a metaphor for where our lives would lead: most of us would ride in a circle going nowhere while one of us rode to glory.

For the biggest races at Speedway Park, more than six thousand people would pack the place to capacity, filling the wooden grandstands, the pits, and the infield. Everyone who sat in the bleachers knew they'd be showered with dirt when the cars went past, even in the top rows. But the dirt hardly ever reached Ronnie, our friends, and me, because whatever the admission price was, we couldn't afford it. We watched the races from just outside the fence, perched in the tops of the trees that circled the track. Some races we didn't watch, but we often went there anyway, hoping for a chance to make a little money. Every once in a while a tire would come flying over the fence, and whoever grabbed it first would try

to hide it, scheming to sell it later to one of the race car owners, but not to the one who'd lost it.

Few people know it, but Ronnie wasn't the first major recording artist from Jacksonville to watch the races from outside the fence at Speedway Park. Charles Eugene "Pat" Boone, whose parents had hoped to name their first child "Patricia," was born in Jacksonville in 1934 and went on to sell more records during the 1960s than everyone but Elvis Presley. A descendant of Daniel Boone, he appeared in a number of hit movies, including *State Fair* and *Journey to the Center of the Earth*; he had fifteen hits in the Top 10, including "April Love" and "Love Letters in the Sand," which stayed on the charts for thirty-four weeks; and he still holds *Billboard* magazine's all-time record of two hundred consecutive weeks on the charts with more than one song. Pat Boone was two years old when his family moved from his mother's hometown to Nashville, Tennessee, but on numerous occasions over a period of many years, while visiting relatives in Florida the Boones enjoyed going to Speedway Park. Although they could have purchased tickets (Boone's father was an architect/builder; his mother was a registered nurse), like so many others they preferred viewing the action close-up where they could feel the ground shake as the cars roared past, so they sat in custom-made "bleachers" set up in the beds of pickup trucks at the start of the back straightaway.

Speedway Park was the fastest half-mile dirt track in the nation because it was a "big half-mile." Measured on the inside, it was five-eighths of a mile around, which meant that drivers could reach higher speeds than they could manage on a standard half-mile course. Drawing thousands of fans from all over northeast Florida and southeast Georgia, Speedway Park was part of the National Association for Stock Car Auto Racing's (NASCAR) Grand National circuit, which later became the Winston Cup series. All of the famous drivers raced there. Richard Petty, Tiny Lund, Junior Johnson, Fireball Roberts, Bobby and Donnie Allison, David Ezell, Cale Yarborough, Lee Roy Yarbrough, and Wendell Scott.

One of the nation's top drivers, Lee Roy Yarbrough had his best year in 1969 by winning the Daytona 500 and two other major events. Yarbrough lived in our neighborhood, one block from the track, and starting in the early '60s Ronnie and I used to hang around while he worked on his car in the yard beside his house. We were probably ten years younger than Lee Roy, but he seemed to enjoy our company. Lee Roy was a real-life local sports hero for us, and as Ronnie got older and he began to think about his future, he used to say that he was going to be the most famous person to come out of Jacksonville since Lee Roy Yarbrough.

Less noticed at the time, and overlooked for many years afterward, was Wendell Oliver Scott, the only African-American ever to win a Grand National stock car race, and Ronnie and I were there when he did. Born in Danville, Virginia, in 1921, Scott drove a taxi and hauled moonshine whisky before he got into organized racing. At the age of forty, having won one hundred and twenty races and a state championship in lower-division races, he scraped together enough money to enter NASCAR's top-level circuit, the Grand National, in 1961. During his twenty-two years on the premier racing circuit, from 1961 through the early '70s, Scott competed in almost five hundred races, finishing among the top ten drivers one hundred and forty-seven times while earning the respect of his fellow racers who, like their fans, were all white. Some drivers helped him out by giving him spare parts when they could, but for Scott it was a mixed bag. On December 1, 1963, Scott took the checkered flag in his only win in a major race, a one-hundred-mile event at Jacksonville's Speedway Park.

"Somethin' ain't right here," we heard one man say, but Ronnie's response was quiet and cool. "Lee Roy don't mind racing with him, and if he can beat Lee Roy he deserves to win." I thought a little differently about black people after that, and I began to realize that Ronnie saw things in a different light than most of the rest of us. Scott took his victory lap around the track, but the winner's trophy was awarded to another driver, which

NASCAR officials later blamed on a scoring error when they finally gave Scott the credit he deserved. "Everybody in the place knew I had won the race, but the promoters and NASCAR officials didn't want me out there kissing any beauty queens or accepting any awards," Scott said years afterward. But that was NASCAR, and Jacksonville, and the South, and much of America at that time. That was the atmosphere in which we were raised.

At least for a while in the early 1960s, becoming a champion stock car driver was more than a notion for Ronnie, and his father did nothing to discourage him. Lacy Van Zant had given Ronnie a Corvair when he was old enough to drive, but one day Lacy surprised everyone in the neighborhood when he bought Ronnie a real "muscle car," a brand-new, red 1965 Ford Mustang coupe with a 289-cubic-inch engine and a three-speed stick shift mounted on the floor. Ronnie liked to race that car, but too many mishaps put it out of commission. It was broad-sided once, sending Ronnie to the hospital to confirm that his ribs were bruised and not broken; it was rear-ended and knocked into a ditch by a '57 Chevy he'd just beaten in a race; and a third crash totaled it for good. In 1966 Ronnie bought a real race car, an old, beat-up, dirt-track racer with just one seat and a roll cage, and with three or four guys piled inside (including my brother, Richard) he rolled it over. Not long afterward, Ronnie was in his Mustang racing another car when they came upon a stalled vehicle in the middle of the road and wound up crashing into each other. That was pretty much the end of Ronnie's racing career.

Speedway Park was closed in 1973, just as Lynyrd Skynyrd was cutting their first record album. Neither of those events had seemed possible once. Ronnie's music is played today on radio stations all over the country and before the start of NASCAR races, but all that remains of the track are those trees we climbed and an empty field of weeds. The abandoned speedway serves as another metaphor for what most of us from our neighborhood have become. Nothing special, just plain folks. But one of us became something more than just a weed. One became a brilliant flower, and the rest of us felt a little bit better about ourselves because he did.

To come from our neighborhood and really become somebody was like winning the lottery without ever buying a ticket. Even the best of luck wouldn't have been enough. But Ronnie had something better than luck. He had a strength of will that few people possess, and once he knew what he wanted to make of his life, he pushed himself and the people he needed until his dream came true. Long before any of Ronnie's friends recognized his passion for success, there was one thing that no one had ever failed to notice about him. Ronnie was tough, both physically and mentally.

His mother said he was one of the meanest boys in a neighborhood that sent even meaner boys to prison. Standing five-foot-seven when he was fully grown, solidly built and muscular, Van Zant inherited his mean streak from his father, who told him that fear would defeat most opponents, especially if they knew he would never give up. For boys who lived in our section of the Westside, fighting was a normal part of growing up. We settled our scores with our fists, and for most of us it didn't take long to figure out whom you'd want to confront and whom you wouldn't. Ronnie took on almost all comers. It seemed as if he were always looking for a fight, and some people thought he was just plain mean. But for Ronnie it wasn't as simple as that. He simply enjoyed fighting, and it never mattered how big the other guy was or how formidable, with very few exceptions. Even so, Ronnie wasn't a true "tush hog," as we used to call them. I don't remember the origin of that label, but it was reserved for only the roughest characters who inhabited the Westside. Unlike them, Ronnie always had a purpose when he fought. Either he had a score to settle, which was usually a conflict he'd instigated, or he'd offer to fight just to see who'd win. Tush hogs were different. They fought for no reason at all, with little or no provocation, and with no sense of decorum. And tush hogs always won, because theirs was never a fair contest. A tush hog's only purpose was to hurt somebody, and he never hesitated to pick

LYNYRD SKYNYRD

up a club or a bottle, or a knife or a gun or a chain, if that's what it took.

Ronnie never had a problem with any of the tush hogs. He was too smart for that, and besides, he and I hung around two of the roughest guys the Westside ever produced: my brother, Richard, and Richard's closest friend, Junior Bullard. Richard was arrested more than forty times in his life, mostly for assault and battery. He died in the Duval County jail at the age of thirty-five, officially recorded as a suicide, although an officer's choke hold seemed a more likely cause. Junior Bullard was a mean-as-hell tush hog who once shot a man in the back, leaving him paralyzed for life. After serving seven years in prison for that offense, Junior came back to town and killed a man. The Duval County Sheriff's Department made a big mistake in sending a female officer to arrest him— violent men often respond more calmly to women authority figures than to males, but Junior apparently didn't know that. He grabbed her gun, stole her car and then fled on foot, only to surrender later when a metal spike pierced the sole of his shoe and emerged through the top of his foot. Found guilty by a jury of his peers— cases like Junior's really stand that phrase on its head—he was sentenced to life in prison.

Ronnie used to say that the only people from Jacksonville who'd ever made a name for themselves were Lee Roy Yarbrough and Junior Bullard, and that he was going to make a name for himself, too. When Ronnie entered high school, it became more apparent to him than ever before that some kids didn't live like we did. Back then, Robert E. Lee High School was one of Duval County's top-rated schools, and many of its students came from some of the wealthiest families in town. Their clothes were much finer than ours, and their behavior was decidedly more refined, all of which made a considerable impression on Ronnie, who once remarked, "Man, I gotta be better than this; I can't go to prison." In the eyes of the kids from nicer neighborhoods, tough guys on the Westside were "hoods," and Ronnie didn't want to be a hood anymore.

One thing Ronnie always loved was fishing, his all-time favorite pastime. It's a form of recreation that everyone can afford, if you don't get carried away with it; and even when he could afford the best that money could buy, a simple bass boat was always good enough for Ronnie. As soon as we were old enough to ride a bicycle beyond our neighborhood, our idea of a good time was to head for the Cedar River a mile and a half away, both of us on the same bike. Carrying bamboo poles and burlap bags to hold the "croakers" we'd catch, one of us pedaled while the other rode on the handlebars, bound for our favorite spot on the east bank of the river, in the shadow cast by the bridge on San Juan Avenue. It was peaceful there, near the American Legion Post, and, except for the sounds of veterans coming and going and cars passing above us, it was quiet.

You can throw a rock across the Cedar River, its flow barely apparent as it slowly empties into the St. Johns River, which is more than a couple of miles wide in some places. As boys we never traveled farther than that fishing hole, but whenever we watched a cork or a stick float away we wondered where it would go after it drifted through the heart of the Westside, past the high-priced riverfront homes of Ortega, Avondale, and Riverside, beyond the downtown buildings, around the bend and past the bluffs at Fort Caroline, through the rock-pile jetties at the river's mouth at Mayport, and out into the vast Atlantic Ocean. We knew only the Westside then, and our main concern was mullet, which were so easy to catch it was almost like stealing. We'd catch more mullet than our families could eat, and we'd carry them home in croaker sacks. As "Robin Hoods of the river," we'd go around the neighborhood giving out fish to families who were always glad to get them. Looking back on it, I know we enjoyed showing off our catch, but I clearly remember that Ronnie took pleasure in sharing the wealth with others, including the one black family that lived on the edge of our neighborhood. We knew the kids, who were about our age, but we never associated with them. They were black and we were white; that's just the way things were.

On Sundays in the early '60s, boys used to come to Ronnie's house to watch the first fishing show on television, *Gadabout*

Gaddis, the Flying Fisherman. We were teens by then, and we were hooked on largemouth bass. Bass fishing is absolutely the most pleasurable form of freshwater fishing you can do, and for Ronnie it held a special charm, because seeing one of those fighting fish break the surface of the water—the big ones can eat bullfrogs—dancing on their tails at the end of a nylon line, mouth opened wide, trying to shake out the hook, is a thrill you can't believe unless you've done it. It makes a man feel like a boy again, and the greatest thrill of all is catching a trophy bass. Some guys fish for years without ever landing a lunker, but Ronnie was fortunate. In 1977, the same year he finally bought the '55 Chevy pickup truck he'd always wanted, he finally caught a bass that weighed more than ten pounds. Ronnie had already made a trophy-size splash in the world of music by then, but he got as much pleasure from catching that bass as he did from making gold records. On one of our last fishing trips together, we drove down to Lake Delancey in the Ocala National Forest, about ninety miles south of Jacksonville, passing between Gainesville, where Tom Petty had started his climb up the rock and roll ladder, and Hawthorne, the home of Bo Diddley, the celebrated rhythm and blues man. But Ronnie was focused on fish that day, not music, and when he got that lunker into the boat, we jumped up and down and hugged each other, yelling at the tops of our lungs. I had never seen him happier.

As younger sportsmen, when we weren't catching mullet we were shooting squirrels. Sharing a .22-caliber rifle, we bagged small game in a wooded lot and always shared with our neighbors. We never shot any pigeons, but we did shoot a lot of bottles and cans. There was just something about killing a bird in flight that never appealed to Ronnie. Taking target practice in the woods one day, Ronnie had the scare of his life. Across the road from the woods lived a middle-aged black woman named Alberta, who passed the time drinking when she wasn't doing her job as a housemaid. Aiming at bottles and cans, Ronnie bet me that he could hit a beer can three times in a circle the size of a dime. Taking his shots, he handed me the rifle and walked toward the target and immediately started screaming, "Jesus Christ, I've killed Alberta." I ran over to see her lying still on the ground beneath Ronnie, who was visibly shaken. Then it dawned on me. There was no blood, and the smell of alcohol was in the air. Alberta had passed out from drinking. I shook her and asked, "Are you all right?" and she woke up just enough to answer, "Give me my bottle." We laughed, but I could see that Ronnie was still upset at the thought of killing a fellow human being.

That was Ronnie. The only time he wanted to hurt anybody was when he was fighting. As an adolescent, he dreamed of becoming a championship boxer, and he made a crude but determined start at it. As fighter, trainer, manager, and promoter, Ronnie hosted boxing matches in a circle he drew in the sand at the school bus stop. Equipped with two pairs of boxing gloves, one for himself and one for his opponent, he took on anyone who was up to the challenge. An early indication of the high regard that Ronnie had for himself was the "V the G" he painted on the fuel oil tank beside his house, which his friends could see from the school bus windows. "Must have been put there by some of my followers," he said, noting that the initials stood for "Van the Great." But his closest friends, who called him "Wicker," turned it around on him, saying it really meant, "Van the Goat." They were accustomed to hearing Ronnie and Lacy boasting and telling tall tales, and knew it was all in fun.

Lacy and Ronnie were a father and son who were also friends, and one of the interests they shared was following the career of the greatest boxing sensation the world would ever see, a brash young rebel by the name of Cassius Clay. When Clay won the heavyweight crown from Sonny Liston in Miami in 1964, Lacy, who was in Miami at the time, brought Ronnie the *Miami Herald* sports page recounting the action. Now, it might seem only natural that an adolescent, would-be boxer like Ronnie would pattern himself after someone like Clay, but this was an especially troublesome time for America, and especially in the South. In 1964, just down

the highway from Jacksonville, Martin Luther King, Jr., was arrested in St. Augustine for trying to be served in a restaurant. The year before, Jacksonville's schools had been ordered to begin desegregation, but in 1964 its mayor, Haydon Burns, won praise from the Ku Klux Klan for vowing to enforce discriminatory Jim Crow laws. In the rioting that followed, people were beaten, black churches were firebombed, cars were overturned, and hundreds of people, mostly blacks, were arrested. In 1964, most of Duval County's five hundred thousand residents were blue-collar workers, and old ways were slow to change. In 1966, Ronnie's senior year, only two black students were enrolled in Robert E. Lee High School.

Through all of the racial turmoil, Ronnie continued to admire Clay, because for Ronnie, he was more than just a black man; he was a man, and Ronnie respected him. And when the champ was widely rebuked for becoming a Muslim and opposing the Vietnam War, Ronnie's regard for him never wavered. But what's more telling than Clay's influence on Ronnie as a boxer is that Muhammad Ali, as Ali came to call himself, was also something of a poet, which struck a nerve in his young fan. If an urge to write had been growing in Ronnie's psyche, then it was Muhammad Ali who brought it to the surface, awakening the lyricist within. Self-proclaimed as "The Greatest of All Time," the boxer filled the sports pages with phrases like, "Float like a butterfly, sting like a bee," and Ronnie read them all, relishing the fact that Ali derided his opponents with wit, and then he knocked them out. Only Ronnie's closest friends were aware of his newfound interest, because poetry was only for girls and "sissies," certainly not for a Westside boy who loved to fight. But when Muhammad Ali proved that you could do both, poetry suddenly became acceptable even for "real" men.

There are many examples of Ronnie asserting himself in less violent ways than fisticuffs during his youth, which typically involved standing up for his principles, just as Ali had done. In what was considered a rather outrageous act in high school, Ronnie once stood up to a much feared and reviled physical education instructor, which for ninety-nine percent of the student body was just unthinkable. Finding crap in the shower one day, the coach made the whole class walk around the track until someone confessed to the crime. Ronnie had been in the assistant principal's office during this entire episode, but when he joined the class at the track, the coach told him he had to walk with everyone else even though he clearly wasn't a suspect. Ronnie refused, and the assistant principal backed him up. Incidents like these raised eyebrows around the campus and enhanced Ronnie's growing reputation.

It seemed that everyone knew at least something about Ronnie back then. They knew he loved boxing and fishing and baseball, and football until he broke his ankle at junior varsity football practice (repairing it required pins, which later kept him from being drafted into the Army). But his life as a poet was a secret. Ronnie kept a notebook under his bed for the times he felt like writing, and whatever his private thoughts were, all that he shared with his closest friends were the jottings he'd done for amusement, such as his banter with his friend, Bill Ferris, who could match him verse for verse (Ferris and another classmate, Jim Daniel, were the only ones who went to college). Bill first noticed Ronnie in the fourth grade, when he saw him fighting on the playground at Hyde Park Elementary School. An adult broke it up, but Ronnie got another lick in, and the grown-up shouted, "Don't you hear me?" to which Ronnie replied, "I'm deaf, I'm deaf," playing on the word "deaf." He was fighting a serious fight, but as was almost always the case, he was also having fun.

Bill hit a home run in a game some time later, and Ronnie showed his own maturity by introducing himself and congratulating Bill. They soon became friends, and a few years later they were exchanging comic verses. Ronnie wrote humorous, off-color rhymes about his friends, and he and Bill swapped rhymes about their favorite pro football teams (Ronnie's was the Green Bay Packers),

LYNYRD SKYNYRD

which was good mental exercise for a future songwriter. Working in an auto parts store in 1968 and 1969, Ronnie demonstrated a remarkable ability to remember parts numbers. Later, his keen memory would show itself in his knack for composing lyrics, melodies, and other elements of musical composition, all in his head, without ever having to write anything down. Ronnie would simply tell his band members what he wanted from them, and then make them play it over and over, if necessary, until they got it right.

Ronnie had always loved to sing. His first grade teacher punished him for singing "Ricochet Romance" and "Beer Drinkin' Daddy" on the first day of school, and years later, in high school, he was still crooning, walking the halls singing songs like "Woolly Bully" by Sam the Sham and the Pharoahs, "Little Red Rooster" by the Stones, "Little Black Egg" by the Night Crawlers, and "Sloop John B" by the Beach Boys. Lee High School was fertile ground for future songwriters, and one of the best was Mae Boren Axton, an English teacher who helped shape the rock and roll landscape from her home on Dellwood Avenue. In 1955, she and Tommy Durden wrote Elvis Presley's first single for RCA Records, "Heartbreak Hotel" (Elvis was listed as co-author), which became the No. 1 single of 1956 and launched Elvis onto the world stage. Mrs. Axton passed on her talent to her son, Hoyt, a 1960 Lee High graduate who became a singer, actor, and songwriter whose work included "The Pusher" for Steppenwolf and "Joy to the World" for Three Dog Night.

Ronnie had thought about making a living in music, but as serious as he may have been at the time, he really sharpened his focus on May 8, 1965, when he felt the second jab of the one-two punch that would shape his approaching ambition. That day, seventeen-year-old Ronnie and Bill Ferris went to see the Rolling Stones perform in the Jacksonville Coliseum—the opening acts were the Sir Douglas Quintet and Bobbi Martin. Interestingly enough, only half of the coliseum's eight thousand seats were filled, which reflected the fact that Jacksonville wasn't quite ready for the Stones.

Eight months earlier, twenty thousand fans had seen the Beatles in the Gator Bowl football stadium, but the Stones had a different image. Seemingly crude and unkempt by comparison, they made the Beatles look tame. The Rolling Stones didn't wear uniforms, unlike every other band before them, and wore their hair longer than any other Top 40 recording artists ever had. It was even rumored that they didn't bathe. And if that weren't enough for parents, their music was also troubling. In the wake of Beatles songs like "I Want to Hold Your Hand," the Stones evoked stronger, more physical images with tunes like "Let's Spend the Night Together." Their music had a rough, earthy quality that made grown-ups long for simpler days, like the mid-1950s when Elvis Presley had come to town. Worried that the sight of his swinging hips might corrupt their children's morals, city leaders had summoned a board of censors to review Elvis's act before they would let him perform in public. Ten years later, faced with the affront to decency the Stones were bringing to town, they gladly would have welcomed Elvis back instead. But rock was rolling on, and nothing would ever stop it.

One reason for the poor turnout for the 1965 concert was the fact that no Stones records had ever been played on Jacksonville's only rock and roll radio station, WAPE. With fifty thousand watts of power, the "Big Ape" boomed out the strongest AM signal in the Southeast, sending its distinctive ape call—"Ahhh-yeee-ahhhh"— up the eastern seaboard as far as the Carolinas. If it didn't play on the Big Ape it wasn't rock and roll, and for some reason the Ape hadn't played the Stones.

As Ronnie watched the Stones that night, he couldn't have imagined that the Stones would pack the Gator Bowl on their next visit to town, in 1975, and that one of Ronnie's two younger brothers, Donnie, would open the show with his band, .38 Special. Nor could he have imagined that in 1976 his own band would open for the Stones before at least a quarter of a million fans in Knebworth, England. And for someone who especially loved stock car racing, baseball, and football, it was completely inconceivable for Ronnie that one day his music would greet fans of NASCAR

racing, major league baseball, and professional football. For a dreamer who is willing to work hard to make sure his dream comes true, extras like that are the icing on the cake.

Bill and Ronnie really enjoyed seeing the Stones, but for Ronnie the experience was transforming. That night he went from pondering a career in music to steeling himself to a dream and vowing that he'd make it come true. That night Ronnie made up his mind. He would become Mick Jagger, Jacksonville-style, and from that moment on, whatever thoughts Ronnie had ever had of becoming a boxer he would channel into music.

CHAPTER 2

"I'M YOUR NEW LEAD SINGER"

As serious as Ronnie became about his life's calling, he would always find time for girls. Marie Darsey, now Mrs. Marie Harris, recalls meeting the future star near the end of her sophomore year at Lee High School. "He was a sweet, caring person, and he was very funny," not at all the young ruffian some others had come to know, she said. Before their first date, Marie was out of town visiting relatives when she received a letter from Ronnie. On pink stationery, he wrote, ". . . I have been working about four days out of each week. On the days I have off I just want to be alone. I promise to get in touch with you as soon as you come home. I would really love to have a date with you. I think you are very, very cute. I really crave red hair . . ." In typical Ronnie fashion, he suggested that she remind a mutual acquaintance about a fight in the school lunchroom, probably because Ronnie had won the fight.

"I never knew him as a tough guy," Marie said. "He was always singing, always happy," and he loved the Rolling Stones. "He could

FIRST-GRADER ALLEN COLLINS APPEARED TO HAVE HIS EYES ON A PRIZE. (STRUNK/BULLARD)

sing all of the lyrics to every song in the order they appeared on the record album," she said, and he seemed very confident when he told her, "I'm gonna meet 'em one day."

"Ronnie was always singing. When he walked down the hall at school, he was singing. When we went to a movie, he'd sing all through the whole show. When I'd answer the phone, he'd already be singing," Marie said, noting that when Ronnie sang to her over the phone, he sometimes strummed a guitar. "His mom would yell, 'Ronnie, get off that damn phone.' " On a typical date, Ronnie took Marie to the drive-in movie, where they smooched long past midnight while Rock Hudson and Doris Day beamed from the big screen. "He even took me to see *Mary Poppins*, if you can believe that," she said, adding that he was "a good kisser."

In addition to being "suave and gallant" around her, he was thoughtful and polite around others as well, and "a very generous person, heart and soul," she said, recalling that once, when she and a girlfriend had prepared an unappealing dinner for their dates, instead of complaining, Ronnie cheerfully suggested they go play putt-putt golf, and he paid for all of them, with money he'd earned bagging groceries.

Marie might be the first person ever to hear a statement from Ronnie that he would repeat many times throughout his life, a premonition that may have driven him to develop his talents to the fullest extent possible while he had the ability to do so. "I won't live to be thirty years old," he told her, and he seemed to really believe it. Although they remained friends for as long as he lived—Marie and her husband, Dean, went to Lynyrd Skynyrd concerts, and Ronnie blew straws at her, just as he'd done in school—she had to give him the brush off at one point, because Ronnie was seeing someone else. It was another girl in school, Nadine Ensco, who soon became pregnant, which led to a brief marriage and a beautiful daughter, Tammy Michelle. As it would be for most teenage boys, Ronnie was not at all prepared to be either a husband or a father at that time, but he was beginning to get serious about music.

Of everything Ronnie had tried, music had brought him the

most enjoyment, and once he'd seen a young Mick Jagger on stage in control of a band with thousands of paying fans, the die was cast. But for the fact that he loved it, music was not a likely career choice for Ronnie. He couldn't read notes on a page, he couldn't play an instrument (he'd learned a few chords, but his hands were too small to play a guitar well), and his voice wasn't at all what you'd expect to hear on the radio. I don't know if anyone ever advised him against a career in music—nobody who knew him would have dared—and I don't know if Ronnie ever seriously considered the possibility that he might fail. For Ronnie Van Zant, embarking upon a career in music was almost like boxing. He was pretty sure he could win, he was determined to keep trying until he'd won or discovered that he couldn't, and he knew that if you lose a battle, you can always fight another day. And so this son of a truck driver overcame his shortcomings by combining his greatest personal resources: a hidden talent for song writing, the fury of his fists, and the sheer strength of his will. At the age of eighteen, Ronnie Van Zant took charge of a group of younger boys, and in nine grueling years molded them into a rock and roll band worthy of being called "America's Rolling Stones." Their story together began in the summer of 1966, when guitarist Gary Rossington and drummer Bob Burns were not yet fifteen years old, and guitarist Allen Collins was about to turn fourteen.

Except for Ronnie, the original members of the group that would become Lynyrd Skynyrd were attending Jacksonville's Lake Shore Junior High School in 1966. Half of its students lived on the Westside, whose inhabitants ranged from poor to middle class; the other half lived on the Westside, too, but not as far west. They lived in the neighborhoods of Riverside, Avondale, and Ortega, where most of Jacksonville's wealthiest families lived. This same social structure also described Robert E. Lee High School, where Ronnie went to school. "Ortegans" resided in the areas that bordered the river, and guys like Ronnie lived on the other side of the tracks. Allen would later attend Nathan Bedford Forrest High School in the Westside, which generally was considered a redneck, working-class school. Having played only a minor role in the Civil War, Jacksonville compensated by naming several schools after Confederate generals.

At Lake Shore Junior High there were two fledgling rock and roll bands: the Squires, who were Ortegans with nice guitars, good equipment, and fine clothes, and the Mods, who had decent guitars and poor equipment, and whose only claim to fashion was the Beatle boots they had scrimped and saved to buy. One day in the spring, a "Battle of the Bands" was held in the school cafeteria, and the Mods won, with rhythm guitar Allen Collins, lead guitar Donnie Ulsh, drummer James "JR" Rice, and bass player Larry Steele, who had been Allen's best friend since they were both five years old. (Allen wrote in Larry's 1966 junior high yearbook, "Yea, Mods. To my bass player: wouldn't have another. Yea, rhythm!") The Mods weren't all that much better than their competition, but the Squires lacked a good lead singer. And then they found one, or, rather, he found them.

It was about this time that Ronnie began his transformation from a tough-guy hoodlum looking for fights, to a tough-minded artist looking for something better in life. And, interestingly enough, the catalyst for his conversion was a sucker punch that landed on a young musician. Jay Zienta was walking home from school one night when Ronnie and my brother, Richard, pulled up beside him in Ronnie's car and stopped, and Ronnie got out. Jay hardly knew Ronnie at the time, so he was surprised to discover that, for no apparent reason, Ronnie was about to punch him in the face. Jay turned just in time and caught a fist in the back of his head, and Ronnie got back in his car and drove off. The next morning, Jay walked up to him and asked, "Why'd you hit me last night?" and Ronnie answered, "Was it you I hit? Sorry." "You shouldn't go around hittin' people like that," Jay said, and then, as if nothing had happened, Ronnie started talking about music. "Aren't you in a band?" Ronnie asked. Jay said that his band was called the Kicks, and he asked Ronnie if he could play guitar. Ronnie said he couldn't, and Jay asked, "Well, can you sing?" As if

LYNYRD SKYNYRD

this were a point of honor with Ronnie, he looked Jay squarely in the eyes and answered emphatically, "Yeah, I can sing!" Then Jay said something that must have struck a chord in Ronnie's pysche: "Well, you ought to get a band together."

In retrospect, Ronnie may have targeted Jay for two reasons: no doubt, he was showing Richard how tough he was, but he may also have been a little jealous and resentful that Jay was a musician and he wasn't. But whatever his motivation had been, very soon afterward, in typical Ronnie fashion, he walked into a Squires practice session and boldly announced, "I'm your new lead singer." Practically everyone on the Westside knew who Ronnie Van Zant was, so this was an offer the Squires felt they couldn't refuse. And so, the stage was set for a rematch, although this time the Squires called themselves Us, with Ronnie Van Zant on vocals, Steve Rosenbloom on drums, Ricky Dashler on guitar, and Jimmy Parker on bass. With Ronnie involved, and especially with him allied with the "rich kids," which his fellow students could hardly believe, the interest level was high for Round Two of the "Battle of the Bands."

Wanting to size up the venue ahead of time, Ronnie drove to the school, where he met Larry Steele. "It was the first time I ever saw somebody advancing a gig," Larry said, noting that this was only the first of many valuable lessons he would learn from Ronnie Van Zant. School had been out for about an hour, and no one was there as Larry anxiously awaited the arrival of a street fighter he'd pictured as being large and tall. "When I saw him, I couldn't believe it; he was no bigger than I was, all smiles, and the nicest guy you'd ever want to meet. I remember thinking, nobody's gonna believe how nice this 'stone killer' really is." But Ronnie was also very serious, and Larry noticed a certain forceful quality about him. "When you looked into his eyes, you got the feeling he was six-foot-six and weighed two-twenty-five," he said.

The Mods, who were now Ronnie's rivals, wanted to be competitive, but money was a problem. One day, forced to attend a pep rally in the junior high gym, Allen and Larry and JR sat together and talked about the public address system they'd like to have. The next day in the library, they noticed that the very system they wanted was right there, sitting on a wheeled pushcart by a window. With larceny in mind, they went to the school that Saturday night, more fearful than when they'd planned their caper, and mindful that just across the street a family was having a cookout. That made breaking the window undesirable, so Larry and JR pried it open and accidentally pushed the cart away from the window. Unaware that Allen had walked around the building and entered with ease, Larry held JR by his heels while he reached for the only thing close enough to grab, a Shure microphone. Every light in the library and the cafeteria suddenly went on, and they saw Allen standing across the room, calmly eating an ice cream sandwich he'd "found." In a panic, Allen grabbed the mic stand with the Shure mic and handed it to JR, who handed it to Larry, and they all took off running down the street.

As the end of the school year approached, so many tickets were sold for the "Battle of the Bands" that it had to be moved to a larger facility, the gymnasium of what then was Forrest High School, and today is J.E.B. Stuart Junior High. Finally, the contest began, with both bands playing their best covers of Stones, Animals, Byrds, and Bob Dylan songs, and when it was over, Us had won. But the real winner was Ronnie, who scored well overall and especially on "Paint It Black" and "Little Red Rooster" by the Stones. "Allen and I swore that we won on the music, but Us won by an audience vote, no doubt because of Ronnie," Larry said. "The girls loved him. He was good looking, and he was cool."

Ronnie enjoyed the victory, which he and Allen would debate in jest for years, but Ronnie already had sensed that, except for bass player Jimmy Parker, perhaps, Us didn't have what it took to take him where he wanted to go. All the talent he needed lived fairly close by, and the best among them, then, was a tall, skinny youngster with a surfer haircut and a cherry red Gibson Melody Maker, whom he'd first seen play at the Green Street Youth Center. Born July 19, 1952, Larkin Allen Collins, Jr., was the son of Larkin and Eva Collins, who divorced when Allen was ten years old. He and

his sister, Betty, lived with their mother in a modest, concrete block home on Barlad Street, about three miles south of Ronnie's home, and one day, at the age of twelve, Allen came home filled with excitement. His friend down the street, Donnie Ulsh, had shown him how to play three chords on a guitar, and Allen wondered, "Momma, will you buy me a guitar?" The next day she drove to a music store and bought the first of the five electric guitars that she would buy for her son during the next few years. One of the first was a $99 Truetone hollow body with three pickups that came with an eight-inch amp; another was the red Melody Maker with two pickups. Allen and Donnie Ulsh played through Donnie's Gibson Invader, which was a lot of amp at that time, and for a PA system, the boys used Allen's Truetone amp and his little speaker with a University outdoor horn wired to it (JR Rice, bass player for the Mods, said he'd "found" it in a church). In mid-1965, Allen got a Fender Super Reverb amp and Larry got a Fender bass; for Christmas, Larry got a Fender Bassman amp to match Allen's Super. The Mods were finally starting to look cool.

Eva bought Allen a $500 Les Paul gold-top that he loved, but soon he had to have a Gibson Firebird like the one he'd seen Eric Clapton play with Cream on "The Ed Sullivan Show." One night after practice, with his brand-new Firebird, Allen joined Larry Steele and their girlfriends (Allen's was his future bride, Kathy Johns) for an outing in Stockton Park to smoke some weed, drink a little whisky, and enjoy a magnificent moonlight view of the St. Johns River. Everyone must have been lost in the moment, because later, when Allen drove Kathy's Chevy Nova away from the park, no one remembered that he'd left his guitar leaning against the bumper. The weight of the car and four stoned teenagers broke the neck of the otherwise sturdy Gibson, putting Allen into a state of shock that lasted until he was able to have it repaired.

The guitars and the amplifiers Eva purchased were not small sacrifices for a single mother raising two children. When Allen's father moved out of their house, Eva, who hadn't worked in eleven years, had to support her family, so she went to work at the Swisher cigar factory on the north side of town. It was a job she would keep for the next fifteen years, and in 1965 she took a second job just a few miles from home, at the F.W. Woolworth's store in the Roosevelt Mall, where she worked for seventeen years. Between jobs, she was usually home between 4 and 5 o'clock every day, and she worked most holidays to earn extra money. When Allen was fourteen years old, he let his hair grow almost to his shoulders, which put him in a minority of only a few youths in all of Jacksonville with hair that long. He hid his locks under a baseball cap when he mowed his mother's lawn, so her neighbors wouldn't criticize her for being overindulgent. But one day, his father made him get a crew cut, which devastated Allen and began an estrangement that would last for many years. When Allen withdrew from high school in his senior year to focus on music, he said to his mother, "Momma, this is my thing. When I make it big, I'm gonna buy you everything money can buy."

"His whole heart was in the guitar," said Eva, who remembers that while she was away at work, Allen was usually working, too, using every opportunity to learn how to play the guitar. This was often in her living room with his friends from school, Gary Rossington and Dorman Cogburn. One night, Allen's fellow Mods couldn't find him, so they went to see his mother at Woolworth's, where she worked until 9 o'clock. She didn't know where he was, either, but it turned out that he was asleep in his bedroom the whole time. No one had thought to look there, because Allen never seemed to sleep, often staying up for two days at a stretch. During this time, Allen befriended Dean Kilpatrick, who'd moved from New York and ended up living in Allen's mother's home like one of the family. Dean would become an artist, but he would spend most of his time traveling with the Lynyrd Skynyrd band, as a personal assistant and friend.

Like most of the boys, Allen played baseball in the summer of 1966, but when he wasn't on the diamond he was practicing his guitar. On Saturdays the Mods didn't practice enough to suit Allen. Donnie couldn't practice at all, and Larry and JR preferred to prac-

tice only in the afternoon, so Allen and Gary Rossington often spent Saturday mornings teaching each other whatever they'd learned the week before. Gary Robert Rossington, who was born December 4, 1951, had begun his musical education playing drums with Bob Burns. Taking an interest in the guitar, he started making payments on a Sears Silvertone, which his sister's boyfriend, Lloyd Phillips, helped him learn to play while he waited for Carol on their dates. At Lake Shore Junior High, Gary's friendship with Allen grew stronger with their mutual love of the instrument, and the two of them became practically inseparable as they taught themselves to play like their heroes. By focusing on their dream and practicing nearly all of the time, they became a dynamic duo who would influence many a future guitarist.

While Allen and Gary practiced on Saturday mornings, Larry and JR enjoyed their weekly morning bus ride downtown to Jacksonville's largest music store, Marvin Kay's MusiCenter, to gaze at brand-new equipment they couldn't afford. Formerly a men's clothing store, Marvin Kay's had a three-sided mirror the boys would check to see how their hair looked from the back. There were probably not more than a dozen males in all of Jacksonville with long hair then, if that many, so it was important to look as cool as you could. Returning from downtown late one morning, Larry and JR found Allen's amplifier missing from JR's house, where he'd left it the night before. Thinking Gary might have borrowed it to practice at Bob Burns's house as he often did, JR phoned Bob, who told him that Allen had quit the Mods. "Larry's gonna whip your ass!" JR said. It was a threat that might have worked if Ronnie hadn't also been at Bob's house that day, having left Us to start a new band. With me along for the ride, Ronnie drove to JR's house to confront Larry. He said, "Larry, the way I look at it is this. You've got a really good guitar player in Donnie Ulsh. You've got Allen, and he ain't that good. Gary ain't that good, either. Now, I'll take Allen and I'll take Gary, and between the two of 'em I can make a good guitar player out of 'em. Now, don't that make sense?" It was an offer Larry felt he couldn't refuse, and thus, a band was born.

In the weeks and months before Allen left the Mods, Gary Rossington and Robert Louis "Bob" Burns, Jr. had been playing together, calling themselves Me, You and Him, with Larry Junstrom on bass. One day Gary and Bob went to a Little League baseball game to watch Ronnie play, and Ronnie knocked a line drive that struck Bob in the head and knocked him unconscious. Ronnie ran to see if Bob was all right, and when the game was over the three of them went to the carport of Bob's house to make music, hacking away at songs like "Last Time" by the Stones and "Gloria" by Them. A few weeks later, while riding around in Ronnie's car they saw Allen Collins riding his bike. Ronnie yelled for him to stop, but Allen was afraid of Ronnie, so he veered off the road and pedaled into a wooded lot. The next day, while Allen was pitching in a sandlot baseball game, Ronnie and I pulled him off the mound and told him he'd found a new band. That was the day he left the Mods.

The first time Ronnie and Allen and Gary and Bob performed together in public, it was on the back of a flatbed truck for a festival in a church parking lot. Lacking a regular bass player at the time—Bob wanted Timmy Jerrell to play, but he had no equip- ment—they let Billy Skaggs stand in as they kicked off their set with a Byrds version of "Hey Joe." A week or so later they were joined by Jimmy Parker, formerly of the Squires and Us, who was a great guy and very funny. They moved their practice sessions from Bob's house to a garage apartment on a service road beside Inter- state 10, calling themselves the Pretty Ones, and then the Noble Five. They also practiced in Ronnie's parents' living room, and in a mobile home on their property, which today is enclosed by a tall wood privacy fence that Lacy Van Zant built after Lynyrd Skynyrd became famous. What began as a trickle of slowly moving cars filled with fans quickly became a flood of gawkers, many of whom parked and walked up to the house for a closer look. It was the only aspect of Ronnie's stardom that didn't appeal to Lacy, who had done all he could to help his son reach the top, including buying Bob Burns his first set of drums for the Noble Five, purchasing their first trailer to haul equipment and later a Chevy station wagon.

The Noble Five played for teen parties and dances in the Green Street, Southside, and Brad Tredinnick youth centers, and Woodstock, the only one with an actual stage. The idea was to play these small venues until they became good enough for the Westside Teen Club, the Cedar Hills Youth Association's "Sugar Bowl," the Friday Musicale, and the Good Shepherd Church, all of which had stages. During this time the boys used to play at least five Yardbirds songs a night. Allen liked to jump up and do windmills like Pete Townshend, which he could do without missing a note, displaying a showmanship that everyone else in the band lacked. For the next couple of years, they always ended their shows with Cream's version of the Robert Johnson tune, "Crossroads."

Ronnie's friend, Jim Daniel, remembers the Noble Five's first recording effort, which was Ronnie's first serious attempt at song writing. "Chair With A Broken Leg" was sort of an anti-war song, and Jim recorded it on a reel-to-reel tape deck in "Aunt Viola's Sound Studio"—Ronnie's aunt's house and not an actual studio. Ronnie, Allen, Gary, Bob, and Jimmy Parker were on that tape, but it's long gone now. Jim Daniel was the band's first "manager," helping them book gigs wherever he could and watching the fun when the music stopped. He remembers them getting into a big fight with some boys after they played for a dance in the Woodstock Youth Center auditorium, and two nights later there was a repeat performance at a graduation party dance they played for Lee High School seniors in 1967. Jim also recalls more peaceful engagements, such as the one at his own school, South Georgia College, in Douglas, Georgia, later that year.

Back when the Mods were still together, before they were good enough to play at Good Shepherd Church, Allen, Bob, Larry, and JR sometimes had gone to Good Shepherd on Friday nights to hear other bands. This usually triggered a thirst for more than musical knowledge, so the boys would walk to a drinking establishment at 2517 Edison Avenue that was shaped like a large concrete jug. The

Little Brown Jug catered only to black folks who were old enough to drink, but a black man by the name of "Shaky," who lived nearby, would go to the Jug and buy them a six-pack of Colt 45 malt liquor with their money and keep a bottle for himself. The Jug, which was torn down and replaced in the early '70s, inspired a line from Ronnie in the song, "Gimme Three Steps," although he'd never actually been inside.

Sometimes Jimmy Parker wouldn't show up when the Noble Five rehearsed, so one night Ronnie asked Larry Steele to fill in for him. The next morning they learned that Jimmy had been killed in a traffic accident. Larry Junstrom, who had been playing with a group called the After Five, became their bass player shortly afterward, and for the next four years the founding members of the group that would become Lynyrd Skynyrd stuck together, adding keyboardist David Knight for a brief period, but otherwise never breaking up and re-forming or constantly changing personnel as every other band in town did regularly.

Bill Ferris, who became the first "roadie" for the Noble Five, remembers sharing the driving with Ronnie—they were the only ones old enough to have a license—when they hit the road for a gig at the annual Forest Festival in Perry, Florida, a small North Florida town where vestiges of old Southern culture still linger (in 2001, a tavern owner lost his beverage license for keeping separate bars for whites and blacks; someone from out-of-town had complained). What the "liberal" youths from Jacksonville encountered back then was an intolerance for "long-haired hippies." Having a bite in a local eatery after the show, Ronnie and the boys had to beat a hasty retreat to avoid a brawl with a bunch of older, larger rednecks.

Figuring their odds of becoming successful were slim, the Noble Five changed their name to the One Percent, practicing most of the time at Larry Junstrom's house on Edgefield Street, but sometimes rehearsing in Allen's mother's living room, which she encouraged, often begging them to play "Proud Mary" by Creedence Clearwater Revival. This they gladly obliged her, and in return, on Sundays when she wasn't working, Eva often made them cookies.

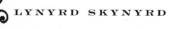

She remembers Ronnie as "a generous young man who never met a stranger . . . Every night when I got home from work, Ronnie would be the first one out the door to greet me, and he always gave me a kiss. He was sweet and lovable," she said. Arriving home from work one weekday to find her front yard filled with girls, she said, "There's a bunch of 'em today. You boys must be doin' good!" Larry Steele and Donnie Ulsh were also doing well, having formed the Malibus and then the Male Bachs after Allen had left the Mods. Soon the One Percent and the Male Bachs were among the city's best "garage bands," and as good groups eventually do, they needed a better place to practice. What they found was absolutely perfect, Art Eisen's Comic Book Club at 318 West Forsyth Street downtown. In return for letting them rehearse, Eisen made them his regular house bands and paid them a modest salary. For musicians, it was the biggest game in town. All of the best out-of-town bands played there, and for the next eight months or so, that's where the One Percent and the Male Bachs honed their skills, which came pretty naturally with the long hours they put in.

Every night until 11:30 the Comic Book Club was a teen club—the placecards at every table read, "Dear Customer: You are stamped when you come in so that you may re-enter the Club the same night for a small fee of five cents. This is to discourage loitering in front of the Club. We must enforce our minimum, which is a partially filled glass in front of you at all times. No alcohol allowed. Thank you: The Management." After closing for an hour, the place would re-open as a bottle club that rocked 'til the wee hours. One night the One Percent would play the teen club and the Male Bachs would play the bottle club, and the next night they'd switch. For a while they took turns playing all night long just to see who could outlast the other, playing ten hours a night, six nights a week and sometimes seven. On weeknights, when the club was usually empty, Larry Steele often jammed with the One Percent, either trading or sharing vocals with Allen and Gary while Ronnie saved his voice for the weekends. "We sounded like hell, but you wouldn't know who was causing it," Larry said.

During its years in business (it became a parking garage in 1975), the Comic Book Club and its predecessor, the Beach-comber, hosted all of the best bands in the region, including Bob Seger, the Cardboard Bachs, the Night Crawlers, and some groups that would evolve into the Allman Brothers Band: the Allman Joys, which became the Hour Glass, both of which featured Duane and Gregg Allman; My Back Yard, with former Hour Glass bass player Pete Carr; the Second Coming, featuring Carr and future Allman Brothers Band members Berry Oakley and Dicky Betts on bass and guitar, organist Reese Wynans, who would play with Stevie Ray Vaughn, and lead guitar Larry Reinhardt, who would join Iron Butterfly; and Larry Steele's favorite band, the Bitter Ind (for "Individual"), featuring future Allman Brothers Band drummer Butch Trucks, future Cowboy member Scott Boyer on lead guitar and vocals, and bassist David Brown, who would play with Boz Skaggs. The Bitter Ind changed its name to the 31st of February to avoid a trademark conflict with New York's Bitter End nightclub. (Incidentally, in the summer of 1965 at the Westside Teen Club, Larry had seen a band called the Vikings, which had the first singing drummer he'd ever seen. It was Butch Trucks, a graduate of Jacksonville's Englewood High School.)

Ronnie was very familiar with the Allman Joys, who in the early part of 1967 were coming to the Comic Book Club for a two-night gig under their new name, the Hour Glass, with the One Percent opening for them on Friday and the Male Bachs opening on Saturday. Recognizing their talent, Ronnie told Larry Steele, "They'll either make you want to work hard, or they'll make you want to quit. When you hear these guys, you're gonna forget all about the Bitter Ind. Now, remember I told you this."

The Hour Glass had become almost famous, having opened shows in Los Angeles for the Doors, the Grateful Dead, the Jefferson Airplane, and other bands of note. But as good as they were, they were very impressed with the One Percent that Friday night, when they played several brand-new songs the Hour Glass had just recorded. The One Percent played as well as they'd ever

played, but when the Allmans started their first set with Moby Grape's "Can't Be So Bad," everyone in the place was awestruck, and especially all of the aspiring young musicians who'd come from miles around to hear them. When Larry looked over at Ronnie to see his reaction, Ronnie just grinned. The Hour Glass were rumored to have been paid something like $1,800 for their two-night engagement, a figure that amazed the younger boys. But Bob McClain, who managed the club, predicted the Allmans would lose it all in poker, as they'd done on each of their previous visits. Sure enough, they did and had to borrow money to get out of town. Gregg Allman literally lost his shirt.

While both the One Percent and the Male Bachs kept working harder and getting better, the boys in the One Percent never seemed to stop practicing, and this continued into the following year as they kept their friendly rivalry going in clubs throughout the city. A favorite venue was the Forest Inn on Lake Shore Boulevard, which had been a bottle club where ex-servicemen brought their girls to dance in the 1940s. Painted turquoise-green, the Inn had good acoustics, and the bands could practice whenever they wanted within walking distance of their homes. The only problem was police who'd arrest long-haired kids if they caught them without a driver license or other identification. Once, when the cops came in the front door Bob Burns went out the back and ran home to hide, scampering through the swamp behind the building that housed country music radio station WQIK.

Just as they had as the Noble Five, the One Percent always worked hard for everything they got. While other bands would squander their earnings and complain that they could improve if only they had better equipment, Ronnie and the boys saved their money, borrowed when they had to, and bought better equipment. It was a lesson from Ronnie that Larry hadn't fully absorbed at the time. A couple of years earlier, when Ronnie was about to borrow from his father to buy new equipment, his dad was injured in a traffic accident and received a sizable insurance settlement. Knowing the Van Zants had come into some extra cash, Larry asked

Ronnie, Why not use the opportunity to buy even better equipment than he had planned? and Ronnie's answer surprised him. "Because we have to pay it back. You always have to pay back what you owe. I'm sure we can afford to pay back the money for the stuff we're going to buy, but I'm not sure we can afford to pay back more than that." With that kind of thinking, and that kind of leadership, the One Percent was the first Jacksonville band to own Super Beatle speakers, just like the Allmans used, and they were the first local group to have Marshall stack amplifiers.

In 1968, with money saved from playing at the Comic Book Club, the One Percent bought a green Ford Econoline van with jalousie windows and hit the road for their longest venture from home, a summertime trek to St. Louis, Missouri. Performing in Gaslight Square and listening to blues bands was a valuable learning experience, and just making the trip enhanced their reputation among their Jacksonville fans. Ronnie knew when he planned the trip that the more you perform locally, the less seriously you're taken by local fans. He knew that traveling made for good publicity, of which more would follow in 1970 when the newly named Lynyrd Skynyrd hooked onto a tour of Southern college campuses with Strawberry Alarm Clock, whose members included guitarist Ed King and Jimmy Pittman, a Clapton-style guitarist who'd played with a number of bands at the Comic Book Club, and whom Allen and Gary had tried to emulate.

Ronnie is the reason the One Percent worked as hard as they did to improve. Back when they were the Noble Five, if it were up to the others, they'd have spent a lot less time practicing than they did. Unlike Ronnie, they often preferred to sit around smoking pot and making each other laugh, and Bob Burns was the funniest among them—once, for a school history assignment, a straight-faced Bob stood in front of his class and talked about the great "Gangus Rufus," whom he'd made up just for the occasion. Ronnie didn't smoke much pot back then, if any, and it was all he could do to keep from punching the others for getting too stoned to practice. But as the group got better and expectations were higher, Ronnie

never hesitated to impose swift, severe punishment to keep his boys in line. He would tolerate a few minor infractions for a while, and then he'd reach a breaking point and explode with his powerful fists. As the years went by, the boys would often strike back, but they always took his abuse. They understood his vision for their future, they believed he could make them succeed, and they instinctively knew that he would. From a practical standpoint, they also saw that he heard all of the music around him very clearly, he was always right about how they could sound better, and he was the only one who could make them work hard enough to succeed. It was a part of the band that would last throughout their career.

Allen, who was wild by nature, presented a constant "parental" problem for Ronnie, who often chided his young guitarist for goofing off. "If it wasn't for me," he'd say, "you'd still have your head in a glue bag." In junior high school, Allen had signed up for wood shop so he could sniff wood glue every day—that's what he said, and that's what he did. On one such occasion, having passed out on the floor, he fell over when the instructor opened a door he'd been lying against. The substance he was abusing was toluene, a solvent used in glues, lacquers, and paints. Inhaling too much of it causes unconsciousness and sometimes death, which Allen surely didn't realize. But it was an early sign of the self-destructive behavior that he would exhibit throughout his life, either with drugs or alcohol or automobiles, often in dangerous combinations when he clearly knew what could happen. It was also during his adolescence that Allen began drinking too much. After teen dance gigs he sometimes stayed up until 4 or 5 o'clock in the morning and got too drunk on beer and too hungover to be able to roll and throw newspapers to the sixty or seventy customers on his pre-dawn paper route. Allen always seemed happy and carefree in those days, but his behavior often betrayed that image.

A few weeks before Christmas in 1968, by which time Larry Steele had left the Male Bachs to form Black Bear Angel with David Knight and Jimmy Dougherty (lead singer in the Allen Collins Band many years later), a guy by the name of James

Silverman sent Ronnie and Larry written invitations to a meeting at the Forest Inn, where he hoped to entice them to join the "Sacrana Rock Family," a three-band package he would manage. He'd already signed the third group, the King James Version, which featured Dru Lombar, who would join Grinderswitch and Dr. Hector and the Groover Injectors; Buzzy Deloach on keyboard; Scotty VanWinkle on drums; and a precocious young bass player by the name of Leon "Thumper" Wilkeson, who bore a certain resemblance to Thumper Rabbit in the cartoon movie, *Bambi*. On the appointed evening, both bands arrived to find the normally empty stage filled with an impressive display of expensive musical equipment. After the King James Version performed to show what they could do, Silverman told the boys what he could do for them. He said all of the right things, and everyone thought it was a golden opportunity—everyone but Ronnie, who quietly surmised that Silverman would benefit from the arrangement, but not the bands. Both groups said they would perform their first engagement as a "family" that coming Friday night, but the One Percent didn't show up, electing, instead, to practice.

"Ronnie was his own man. He didn't do anything because he thought somebody else wanted him to do it," Larry observed. It was another lesson from Ronnie. The One Percent didn't sign up for the scheme, but the following year, as Lynyrd Skynyrd, they did play a couple of gigs with Black Bear Angel and the King James Version while those two bands were playing for Silverman. Not long afterward, Larry learned that Ronnie's assessment of Silverman was probably correct. Following a gig near Jacksonville, Black Bear Angel thought Silverman hadn't paid them their due, so the next morning Larry liberated an appropriate amount of cash from a clothes dresser in Silverman's apartment while he slept in the bed beside it.

CHAPTER 3

LET LEONARD BE LYNYRD

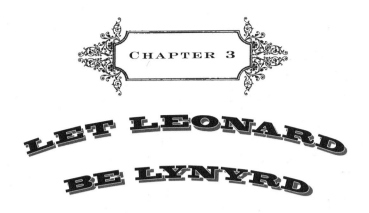

Among all of the many artists who influenced Lynyrd Skynyrd in their formative years, those who had the most immediate impact, perhaps, were Duane and Gregg Allman, who spent a lot of time in Northeast Florida. The Skynyrd boys caught their shows many times, most often in Daytona Beach, where the Allmans had gone to high school, or in Jacksonville's Comic Book Club, or sharing the stage with them at free, outdoor shows in Jacksonville's public parks. The Allmans stood head and shoulders above all of the other bands in the region, and it was obvious they would become major stars. Just seeing them close-up was a thrill for Ronnie and the boys, but in the early spring of 1969 they actually met them and became fairly well acquainted. Ronnie's new girlfriend and future wife, Judy Seymour, was living with two friends, Mary Hayworth and Allen's pal, Dean Kilpatrick, in a large, two-story Victorian house in Jacksonville's Riverside area, the "Green House," which today is one of the most distinctive structures on a very attractive avenue. Just a few houses away, future Allman bassist Berry Oakley

ORIGINAL DRUMMER BOB BURNS IN JUNIOR HIGH, BEFORE HIS HAIR TOOK OFF. (BASFORD)

and his wife lived in another tall Victorian, the "Gray House." It was there, on the living room floor, that Allen and Gary asked Gregg Allman, a frequent visitor, how he managed to come up with original songs, and Gregg had said it was simple: just make up your mind to do it, and don't get up 'til it's done. In March, all of the young men who would become known as the Allman Brothers Band gathered for a jam session in the Gray House and discovered they had the right personnel and the right sound for a band that would make it big. By the end of the month, they had booked their first public appearance together, a show in the Jacksonville Beach Coliseum, where, because of contractual obligations that affected various members, they were billed as "Duane and Gregg Allman, Berry Oakley, and all the rest, formerly of the Second Coming." Within a few months they all moved to Macon, Georgia, to become major recording artists with Capricorn Records.

The Allmans' success inspired Ronnie at a time when his own band was attracting a new level of interest. In May of 1969, David Griffin, the general manager of Marvin Kay's MusiCenter in Jacksonville, encouraged the One Percent and Larry Steele's band, Black Bear Angel, to record some songs locally in Norm Vincent Studios. Black Bear Angel laid down a couple of long, rambling tunes, but being more marketing oriented, Ronnie chose two shorter songs with radio play in mind: "Need All My Friends" and "Michelle," which Ronnie had written for his daughter from his brief marriage to Nadine Ensco, Tammy Michelle. By the time they finished recording these two rudimentary songs on a black, seven-inch vinyl record, the One Percent had changed their name, which appeared on the locally produced Shade Tree Records label as "Lynard Skynard," the final spelling not having been determined yet.

"Lynyrd Skynyrd" is a rather bizarre appellation that merits some explanation, as previous descriptions have missed some key elements of the story behind the name. In order to fit their rising sense of self-worth, the boys in the One Percent felt the need for a new name, so they started kicking ideas around at bass player Larry

Junstrom's house, where an abundance of humor was often led by the wit of Bob Burns. Based upon something that had happened to Gary at school, the boys had kept a running gag going for more than a year, feigning fear that Leonard Skinner, a physical education instructor at Robert E. Lee High School, would burst through the door and catch them smoking pot.

Reinforcing this idle mirth was Allen, who loved singing nursery rhymes and silly songs of the period, such as "They're Coming to Take Me Away, Ha-Haaa!" by Napoleon XIV (Jerry Samuels), and especially a tune Allen had been singing since 1964: comic songster Allan Sherman's hit, "A Letter From Camp," which also was known by its opening line, "Hello Muddah, Hello Fadduh." It was a boy's lament, begging his parents to come take him home from summer camp, and in one verse, ptomaine poisoning from dinner struck a boy named Leonard Skinner. Once Allen had an actual Leonard Skinner to sing about, he found the song even funnier than before, and he sang it more often.

By the time Coach Leonard Skinner started teaching at Lee High School in 1966, Ronnie and Larry Junstrom had already left Lee, leaving only Gary and Bob to worry about the coach (Allen went to Forrest High.). As fellow long-hairs, what they had feared most at school was enforcement of the dress code imposed by Duval County's new school superintendent. For girls, skirts could be no shorter than two inches above the knees. For boys, socks and tucked-in shirts were required, sideburns had to be above the earlobe, and hair couldn't touch your shirt collar or fall within two fingers of your eyebrows. "The philosophy behind that was, if students were dressed better and looked neater, they'd behave better and study better. It didn't work," Skinner said long after the code was scrapped in 1970, the year that he left Lee. Many teachers sent students to the assistant principal's office for violations, but coaches were high-profile staff back then, and at almost six-foot-two and two hundred pounds, Skinner cut a rather imposing figure. Wearing his standard coach's uniform, which was shorts, T-shirt and tennis shoes, with a coach's whistle hung from his neck, Skinner was on patrol every day, alternating from hall duty to lunchroom duty to study hall duty; and before and after school he had alley duty, watching for wayward behavior in a walkway just off the school grounds.

"I was a very strict coach, very demanding, hard-nosed, and probably not on the list of most popular teachers in those days," Skinner said. "It was very simple. You're either going to control them, or they're going to control you." Healthy and vigorous for his age—he turned sixty-nine in January of 2002—a mild-mannered Skinner concedes today, "I was a little more intense in those days." And on one such day he sent Gary Rossington to the assistant principal, who suspended him from school for wearing his hair too long. Afterward, Ronnie's father accompanied Gary to school (Gary's father had died when he was young) and explained to the principal that Gary had long hair for a rock band in order to help his family. The principal said Gary could wear a wig, but he suspended him again for not already having it cut. Not long afterward, Gary turned sixteen, the age at which a student could withdraw from school, and he dropped out.

Coach Skinner continued to be a source of humor for the boys more than a year later. Goofing around while practicing in Larry Junstrom's house, whenever someone knocked on the door or the phone rang, they joked that it must be Leonard Skinner. Unaware of the gag, their friend, Jim Daniel, who had been out of town for several months, was with them one day when the phone rang. Bob answered it and then hung up. "Who was that?" Jim asked. "Oh, that was Leonard," Bob answered, and then he explained the joke. Whenever the coach's name came up, Allen would sing, "Hello Muddah, Hello Fadduh," and the *coup de grâce* was Bob's merriment in mispronouncing Skinner's name, which he did while the '60s drew toward a close and the boys were wondering what to call themselves. Sharing the Lynyrd notion with Ronnie over the phone one day, Bob hung up and said, "I think we're really gonna do this." That night at a gig in the Forest Inn (it was torn down in 1972),

Ronnie asked the audience what they thought of the idea, and the response was overwhelming. Thus, the name was born.

Having made their first recording, which got some play locally but didn't catch on, the group continued working with David Griffin. In addition to booking Skynyrd and Black Bear Angel for gigs, to showcase their talents Griffin created a "Battle of the Bands" for groups throughout Northeast Florida, to be held in the Regency Square shopping mall in Jacksonville's Arlington area. Promotions for the battle included an appearance on a local morning TV show hosted by Phyllis Fouraker, whom Bob had poked fun at whenever he watched the show. But Bob wasn't laughing when Lynyrd Skynyrd performed on TV, with Ronnie lip-synching "Need All My Friends." When time came for the battle, however, the band chose not to compete for the grand prize, a Marshall public address system, electing instead to take a paying gig. Black Bear Angel also withdrew from the contest, but only because they'd learned from Ronnie the publicity value of not being overly available. After the battle, which was won by the Camelots with Don Barnes, future guitarist/vocalist for .38 Special, Griffin arranged another multi-band battle at the Jacksonville Beach Coliseum, financed by vendors whose equipment was carried by Marvin Kay's MusiCenter. Again, Lynyrd Skynyrd opted for another gig, and the final two bands were the King James Version with Leon Wilkeson, and the eventual winner, Larry Steele's Black Bear Angel.

Two weeks later, those two groups and Lynyrd Skynyrd were booked to perform for the grand opening of the Jacksonville Art Museum, sponsored by the local ABC-TV affiliate at the time, WJKS channel 17, and featuring television stars Frank Sutton, who played Sergeant Carter on *Gomer Pyle,* and Don DeFore and Whitney Blake, who played George and Dorothy Baxter on *Hazel.* After Black Bear Angel played, using equipment supplied by David Griffin, Lynyrd Skynyrd followed, preferring their own gear. When they opened their set with "Walk In My Shadow" from the first Free album, *Tons of Sobs,* Larry Steele was struck with the realization that they were bound for much bigger things. "They kicked our ass!

That's when I knew they were off and running," he said. For their second number, Lynyrd Skynyrd performed "Free Bird" for the first time in public. It was May 9, 1970.

It was a song that had been under development for almost a year, having begun with a question posed by Allen's girlfriend and future bride. For Kathy Johns it was obvious that there would always be another love in Allen's life, and that was music. Watching him practice in his mother's living room one day, she asked, "If I leave here tomorrow, would you still remember me?" Struck by the thought, Allen immediately began trying to fashion a tune that he would return to, again and again, eventually asking Ronnie to write some suitable lyrics. Not long afterward, Allen's mother was making a ham sandwich for him when he asked her a weightier question than Kathy's. "How would you like to have a little grandbaby?" Her response was, "I thought you said she was a virgin," and Allen said, "She was." Ever supportive, Eva told him to call his sweetheart and tell her to "come over here so I can hug her." As "cute as a button," Kathy "always had a friendly smile and a hello," and she would make a fine daughter-in-law. Both of them were eighteen years old when they were married in October of 1970, and soon afterward Allen's mother helped him get a job delivering flowers.

During the time that David Griffin was booking Lynyrd Skynyrd for shows in North Florida in 1970, they were fortunate to attract the attention of someone who would lead them toward a new plateau. In July, 1969, the Allman Brothers had signed with Capricorn Records and its owner, Phil Walden, who had met Duane Allman the year before in Muscle Shoals, Alabama. Hearing there was more talent to be found in Jacksonville, Phil's younger brother, Alan, sent an associate, Pat Armstrong, to observe Griffin's "Battle of the Bands" in the Jacksonville Beach Coliseum (the building was razed in 1992). As a result, Armstrong, who later helped Molly Hatchett develop professionally, invited Lynyrd Skynyrd, Black Bear Angel, and Mynd Garden, with future Molly Hatchett member Dave Hlubek, to audition for him. On the appointed date, Skynyrd arrived at the coliseum first, at 10 a.m., and basically stole the day,

then left for a gig in St. Augustine. Their eventual reward was to acquire the management services of Alan Walden, who would take them on the most exciting adventure of their young lives, the first of several trips they would make to record their own music in a place called Muscle Shoals. (In the music business, "Muscle Shoals" loosely refers to either Muscle Shoals or Sheffield, two small towns roughly two miles apart.)

Founded in 1969 by four of the finest musicians to be found anywhere, Muscle Shoals Sound Studio had already hosted Leon Russell, the Rolling Stones, Boz Scaggs, and Cher by the time Lynyrd Skynyrd arrived in Sheffield, Alabama, in October 1970. With Jimmy Johnson on guitar, Roger Hawkins on drums, David Hood on bass, and Barry Beckett on keyboards, the Muscle Shoals Rhythm Section (Leon Russell called them "The Swampers") was the force that had drawn so many famous artists to this out-of-the-way hamlet in the northwest corner of the state. Originally with Rick Hall's FAME Studios in Muscle Shoals, they'd worked with some of the top rhythm and blues artists of the 1960s, such as Aretha Franklin, Percy Sledge, and Wilson Pickett. Johnson and Hawkins bought a studio at 3614 Jackson Highway in nearby Sheffield, and they partnered with Hood and Beckett to form the first rhythm section in the country to own their own recording, publishing, and production companies, whose impressive array of clients would include Joe Cocker, Paul Simon, Bob Seger, and Rod Stewart. Disappointed to find the studio fully booked when they rode into town, Skynyrd and Walden rented Quin Ivy's nearby Quinvy Studios, where, with engineer and future Quinvy owner David Johnson, they put together a demo tape that would spark a vision of stardom in the halls of Muscle Shoals. Hearing their name for the first time, Barry Beckett's response was, "Leonard who?" but soon an agreement was reached: Jimmy Johnson would co-produce a Lynyrd Skynyrd demo tape with Tim Smith, a Walden-managed singer and songwriter who was under contract to Johnson's production company.

Their mission accomplished, at least for the time being, the band drove the six hundred miles back to Jacksonville to await the first of the many trips they would make to Alabama during the next two years. Still just subsistence artists who were living from gig to gig, the boys were pleasantly surprised to find they'd become local celebrities almost literally overnight, as news of their recent good fortune had beaten them back to town. None of their musical peers had ever been to a major recording studio, and Lynyrd Skynyrd had done it in no less a musical mecca than Muscle Shoals, the "Hit Capital of the World." Booked for an outdoor show on their first day back in town, as they arrived at Greenfield Stables near the Intracoastal Waterway east of town, the band was received as warmly as if they were really the Rolling Stones. While another band was performing, someone recognized Skynyrd's van entering the property, and a buzz immediately spread through the crowd: "It's Skynyrd. Here comes Skynyrd," and when the van came to a stop and the band got out, a cheer went up that drowned out the band on stage. Larry Steele, who would go on to become stage manager and co-writer for .38 Special, remembers it well. "It was a killer entrance," he said. "Another triumphant return for Lynyrd Skynyrd."

As they'd been doing throughout the past year, between trips to Muscle Shoals the band was playing gigs in Northeast Florida and Southeast Georgia. Bob Burns was the only member of the group without a regular, non-musical job at the time—Allen and Gary made hamburger patties at Clark's Meats, where employees could wear long hair—so Bob often hauled their equipment around in a white Ford van, often with Larry Steele along for the ride. On one such trip to Gainesville, Florida, home of the University of Florida Fightin' Gators, after Lynyrd Skynyrd defeated their chief local rivals, RGF, in a "Battle of the Bands" in a union hall not far from the UF campus, they headed for beers in the student Rathskeller, where fellow Westsider Rickey Medlocke was performing with Blackfoot, a band he had formed from Fresh Garbage. The multi-talented Medlocke, who had played the banjo in the first grade and could play almost any instrument, had sung and played mainly percussion in Fresh Garbage and was now singing and playing

rhythm guitar, along with vocalist Jackson Spires on drums, Charlie Hargrett as lead guitar, and Greg T. Walker on bass. Often afterward, Skynyrd and Blackfoot performed together on the UF campus, free of charge, either in the Rathskeller or outdoors on the courtyard of the J. Wayne Reitz student union building. These were fun times. The bands would just show up unannounced on weekend afternoons, trumpeting their presence on a public address system that was really a bass amp they weren't using. Playing separately and then jamming together, Skynyrd and Blackfoot always managed to draw large crowds from all over the campus of 25,000 students, just as the Allmans and Skynyrd had done for free outdoor concerts in Jacksonville's public parks.

With Lynyrd Skynyrd about to begin recording under Jimmy Johnson's tutelage, Bob Burns suddenly left the band (he would return the following year, explaining that his girlfriend had convinced him to leave). This was very good timing for Rickey Medlocke, who was looking for a job. Things weren't going very well for Blackfoot, which had moved its operation to New Jersey, and when Rickey spoke with Allen in June 1971, Allen suggested that he call the boss. Ronnie asked if he still played drums, and Rickey said yes, so he spent a couple of days getting reacquainted with a drum set, drove to his folks' house in Florida, and reported for work. Two weeks later, a slightly revised Lynyrd Skynyrd drove up to Sheffield to make music together. With the Swampers's only studio booked solid during normal business hours, the boys worked long into the night, sleeping in a cheap, truck-stop motel during the day, and playing low-paying gigs when they could get them.

During this time, Lynyrd Skynyrd had rented an old, run-down farmhouse in Jacksonville's Mandarin area for practice sessions. Across the river from the Westside and just to the south, for a brief period the "Mandarin House" off State Road 13 also became a home for Larry Junstrom, who was there one day, alone, when Larry Steele stopped by. The band had fired Junstrom, but he didn't know why, he told Larry. Today, Junstrom says he can't recall details from thirty years ago, but whatever happened, it was a shame, because Junstrom was a very fine bass player who would go on to have a very successful career with .38 Special. Ed King, who would join the band as bassist in 1973, remembers that Junstrom clearly had mastered the instrument when King met the band in 1970. "He was one *hell* of a bass player, even back then. As smooth as they come," King said. On *Skynyrd's First: The Complete Muscle Shoals Album,* Junstrom is given credit for appearing on only one of the songs that was recorded in June-July 1971. And even then, this only official reference to the band's original bassist is rather indistinct. On the liner notes for "One More Time," which was first released in 1977 on *Street Survivors,* the bass player is listed as "Gary T. Walker or Larry Junstrom." With the exception of "Free Bird," which features a bass part Ed King overdubbed in 1975, Walker, who had accompanied Medlocke on a hiatus from Blackfoot, played bass on all of the other 1971 recordings, having overdubbed Junstrom's part as Ronnie had wanted. For all of the songs recorded in 1972, the man on bass was Leon Wilkeson, who, following early fits and starts, would become the definitive source of bottom for a band on its way to the top.

As they would demonstrate for Al Kooper two years later in Atlanta, Lynyrd Skynyrd showed Jimmy Johnson how hard working and well rehearsed they were, prompting both veteran musicians to say how impressed they'd been observing these virtual unknowns for the first time. Johnson coached them to stay in tune, maintain tempo, and play in the right key, which all beginners have to learn. He also taught Larry Junstrom and Rickey Medlocke, and then Leon Wilkeson and Bob Burns, how to make the bass and bass drum work together for a more powerful effect. In 1973, Kooper taught Ed King, who had replaced Leon, how to make the bass work well with Bob's bass drum. Both Johnson and Kooper found all of the band members eager to learn, willing to listen, and quick to apply their schooling. They were hungry high school dropouts who finally had found the right classrooms with the right teachers and the right course of study. And no student of any subject has

ever worked any harder than each of them did to earn the reward they sought.

It would be seven years before fans would hear the original versions of some of the seventeen songs that Lynyrd Skynyrd recorded in Muscle Shoals Sound Studios in 1971 and 1972. Before the plane crash, in 1977, they'd planned to produce an album from those initial efforts, but the project was delayed for a year. By then, *Skynyrd's First . . . and Last* was considered a prized commodity, selling more than a million copies within two months. Only seven of their original songs appeared on the album, but in November, 1998, all seventeen tracks were released on *Skynyrd's First: The Complete Muscle Shoals Album,* including "Free Bird" and "Simple Man," which, like the others, reveal the exceptional musical qualities that attracted each of the band's early financial supporters.

The average listener could be excused for thinking that Eric Clapton, Jimi Hendrix, Paul Kossoff, and other well known guitarists were performing on some of the tunes, because Allen Collins and Gary Rossington were excellent students who had listened to their idols' records for years, and they'd mastered their instruments sufficiently well to defy just about anyone to close their eyes and know who was really playing. After hearing *Skynyrd's First . . . and Last,* some music critics, in fact, said it was as good or better than the group's first two albums, which would follow in 1973 and 1974, and some even called it one of the best of their five studio albums. But regardless of how critics ranked their early work, it's clear from listening to these songs that Lynyrd Skynyrd had a style all their own, that their arrangements were surprisingly rich and varied for such a young group, and that Ronnie's command of his somewhat limited vocal skills was nothing less than remarkable.

Among Ronnie's early influences were the brassy, take-charge sharpness of Mick Jagger, the soulful singing of Paul Rodgers and Gregg Allman, the Oklahoman boogie of Leon Russell, and the wood porch, poor man's blues of Muddy Waters. He had them all down pat, in fact, but rather than merely mimic their wonderful sounds, he clearly discovered the flavor of his own voice, which he seasoned with what some critics confused as being solely "Southern": his fondness for country music, and especially the down-home, sylvan stylings of Merle Haggard. But for all that his fans would love about Ronnie, for Lynyrd Skynyrd the critically essential quality was the always-excellent output of their powerful, gifted guitarists. From the start, Allen Collins and Gary Rossington had been the path to the pot of gold at the end of Ronnie's rainbow. They were the best he could find when he found them, and he never found reason to change. Absorbing the brash new sounds of the Rolling Stones, Blues Magoos, and Yardbirds, Allen and Gary had practiced long and hard to achieve the brilliant virtuosity of Clapton, Hendrix, Kossoff, Jeff Beck, and Duane Allman. Along the way they'd also ingested the throbbing, hard-rock blues of Led Zeppelin, the backwater bayou howl of Creedence Clearwater Revival, and the rambling, hard driving blues of the Allman Brothers.

Borrowing from here and there and blending the pieces together, these two young men—Allen was just shy of his 19th birthday on their first trip to Muscle Shoals, and Gary was five months older—showed that they could be rock stars in their own right, crafting cleverly conceived arrangements and executing them with the precision of polished professionals. With their intuitive stylings and a fire in their fancy fretwork, it was Allen and Gary who initially made Skynyrd's music work. They were integral parts of a tight-knit band that was moving in the right direction, and it was only a matter of time before they would win. But that time had not yet come in 1972, which seems difficult to discern when you hear their music from Muscle Shoals.

Beginning with a somewhat muted version of the solo played by pianist Billy Powell, the first "Free Bird" sounds distinctively different from the subsequent recordings fans would come to love. At seven and a third minutes, it's two minutes shorter than would appear on *Lynyrd Skynyrd: Pronounced Leh-Nerd Skin-Nerd* or *"Pronounced"* some two years hence, and far less generous in spirit.

All things considered, however, it's a fine piece of music, especially on first hearing it, and it's here that Allen and Gary really shine, recording on separate tracks for the first time. Rickey Medlocke offers a light but adequate touch on cymbal and snare, the bass and guitars are crisp and clear, and Ronnie's voice, backed with fine falsetto from Rickey and Tim Smith, is considerably better than you'd expect from a guy who supposedly couldn't sing. But heard as a whole, the band sounds much too controlled, as if this were an audition they had to pass, which, in effect, it was. Closing with a strutting bolero send-up to former Yardbirds guitarist Jeff Beck, this comparative sparrow of a song was surely a hit in the making, but not yet the eagle to come.

(It's been said that Billy joined the band in 1971, after Skynyrd played for a dance at Jacksonville's prestigious Bolles private school. But those are just imperfect memories. In fact, Billy officially joined the band in 1973. But the reference to Bolles is worth noting, because it shows why they couldn't have afforded to add another member during the Muscle Shoals period. Lynyrd Skynyrd played for Bolles on only one occasion, after a football game on October 15, 1971. It was a two-hour gig that paid $200, and Bill Babcock, who still teaches history at Bolles, has a copy of the contract he signed with Ronnie.)

Although it would come to be associated with Skynyrd's fallen leader, "Free Bird" was Allen's musical masterpiece, and he would continue making it better, as he'd been doing off and on for most of the past two years. From a soft, slow-paced melody, he and Gary transformed it into a quiet prelude that progresses into a polyphony of accelerating exchanges so apparently free of restraint you think they might fly apart. That's exactly the sense that Allen wished to convey, as if their spiraling, double-pronged interplay would spin out of control, and for fans of rock and roll it would become the perfect musical encore. Allen and Gary had been playing together for years by the time they entered the studio. They'd rehearsed their wildly soaring solos so meticulously, and they could play them so fast, there was just no way they would ever miss a lick. It was this life-on-the-edge sensation that made the mature "Free Bird" the tumultuous success it became.

Always quiet and shy, Gary developed a natural style of playing that was much in the manner of Ry Cooder and of Paul Kossoff of Free. In fact, it's been said of Gary that he was the only guitarist besides Clapton who could play like Kossoff. Laid back and soulful, he preferred to stand in place, his boyish face hidden in hair, while the wiry, long-legged Allen played the ham, jumping all over the stage with his free arm flailing the air like a windmill. Both highly competitive youths who had thrived on mastering the frills and licks of their idols, once they'd passed their apprenticeship, they became perfect foils for each other, thrusting and parrying in practice until they could play each other's parts so well you had to watch to tell them apart. As craftsmen, their writing styles were so similar you have to read the record labels to avoid guessing wrongly on who should get the credit. Allen and Gary took turns sharing song writing credits with lyricist Ronnie, who always had the final say on what their fans would hear.

One of Gary's first song writing efforts was good enough, to say the least, to appear on Lynyrd Skynyrd's final pre-crash album, *Street Survivors*, which many critics felt was their finest body of work. Released on the *Lynyrd Skynyrd* boxed set in 1991, "One More Time" is the first example of quotation music that Skynyrd was fond of performing. Although original in composition, each of these pieces features carefully measured parodies, either subtly or clearly apparent, of rock and roll legends whose work they had most admired. In this song there's a rhythm that's found in some of Jethro Tull's early work and a guitar solo reminiscent of Clapton. Ronnie's voice is as smooth as it ever gets, and there are a few brief bars of Gary's and Allen's high-pitched *pas de deux* that was Skynyrd's original signature sound.

Rickey Medlocke teamed up with Ronnie to write "Preacher's Daughter," which would wait seven years before its original release in 1978 on *Skynyrd's First . . . and Last*. Actually a revised Blackfoot

song that Ronnie recast with his own lyrics, this fast-paced blues rocker opens with a compelling drumbeat and a steely Jimi Hendrix glissando (Ronnie called Hendrix his "hero"), adding a driving Ted Nugent-like rhythm and a lead that would have made Hendrix proud. But, as always in these musical tributes, it's just enough to make you think, and appreciate, because this music belongs to Lynyrd Skynyrd. Displaying his raspy quality at its best, Ronnie shows he can stretch his vocal cords, and the twin towers of sound, Allen and Gary, close this one out in a running guitar fadeout that sounds like they'd done it a million times before, and they probably had.

Distinctively un-Skynyrd, "White Dove" is nevertheless a very nice song and a fine musical arrangement that is all Rickey Medlocke. Singing lead in falsetto, he's accompanied on this sweet lilting waltz by Randy McCormick on Mellotron and Gimmer Nickols on acoustic guitar, in a telling preview of the tremendous talent Medlocke would bring to the band many years later. Playing both drums and mandolin and singing the lead on "The Seasons," Rickey Medlocke shows his mettle again, with some nice work from Ed King that was added four years later. Two more songs written and sung by Rickey Medlocke close the session in mid-1971. "You Run Around" is otherwise Skynyrd material, a rousing number with plenty of rhythm and a clever change of pace toward the end to hold a listener's interest. "Ain't Too Proud To Pray" is an acoustic piece that's even more surprising to hear on a Skynyrd album than the other Medlocke tunes.

"Wino" is Ronnie's tribute to the big-city blues of Jack Bruce and Eric Clapton in Cream, with Allen and Rickey sharing the credits. As fragile as Ronnie's larynx proved to be throughout his career, he couldn't have sung "Wino" very often in concert, as he alternated from the smoothness of Bruce to a grating yell that almost had to hurt his throat. Allen showed he could work a wah-wah pedal as well as Clapton ever had, and Gary came up with a police cruiser siren sound to close this rocker out. "Comin' Home," which features some nice guitar licks that Ed King would add in

1975, achieves a Neil Young sound as performed by Buffalo Spring-field. Ronnie reaches into the upper range of his voice, offering the fullest measure of what he could offer. The guitar parts seem to honor the Outlaws in finishing this number, with double-stringing on the last few bars in a piece that was nothing special but generally excellent, just the same. In "Lend A Helpin' Hand," Allen and Gary shared songwriting credit with Ronnie, kicking it off with a lick they would return to on *Nuthin' Fancy* in the form of "Saturday Night Special," and sounding as if two Claptons were playing at once. On Gary and Ronnie's "I Ain't The One," Rickey Medlocke starts with a catchy drum solo that sounds as if he'd listened to Paul McCartney's solo album. Ronnie sounds a bit like Johnny Winter in a deep water well on this song, which would reappear on *Pronounced* in a fuller, richer version.

With eleven worthy tracks recorded forever on tape, the boys were optimistic that a record company might jump at the chance to have them. But after six months, Alan Walden had failed to attract a label, in part, perhaps, because most of the songs exceeded the standard three-minute length that radio stations typically preferred—Ronnie had felt the time was right to step outside the conventional norm, as some other groups had done, but his timing was off by a year. So the band kept playing gigs in Florida, Georgia, and South Carolina, and practicing as hard as ever. Still struggling financially, in 1972 the band returned to Muscle Shoals to record six new compositions.

(During a gig at Jacksonville's Friendship Fountain on April 10, 1972, the boys met a guitarist whom Allen would choose to replace him fifteen years later. The warm-up band for Skynyrd was Running Easy, featuring Randall Hall, a seventeen-year-old Forrest High School student. After the show, during which Skynyrd used two drummers, Bob Burns and Rickey Medlocke, Allen introduced himself to the younger guitarist and praised his skills. "Randall, you know you can smoke me," he said. But he would compliment him even more in 1987, when, paralyzed from an auto accident and

unable to play with the new Skynyrd band, Allen asked him to take his place.)

In terms of the caliber of the song writing, the quality of the arrangements, and the draw of the band's distinctive sound, Lynyrd Skynyrd's return to Muscle Shoals was marked by a striking new level of musical maturity that only "One More Time" and "Preacher's Daughter" had reached the year before. Like the tunes they'd tracked the previous summer, the six new songs were original, but unlike the rest, they featured the return of Bob Burns and the addition of Leon Wilkeson, whom Gary had recruited in Jacksonville, and who was now an even better bass player than he'd been for the King James Version. Bob, who had been there from the beginning, knew exactly what was required for every Skynyrd drum part, and Leon would become essentially indispensable to the total Skynyrd sound. Born April 2, 1952, Leon Russell Wilkeson was an unconventional bass player who would provide *the* Skynyrd bass line, at first on his Gibson Thunderbird and later on a Fender jazz bass. As guitarist Tony Bullard remarked rather presciently, shortly before Leon's death in July 2001, "You don't realize how much he adds to the backbone of that band. If you take Leon out of the equation, it just ain't Lynyrd Skynyrd."

The original version of "Gimme Three Steps," which Ronnie and Allen wrote, was first released in 1991, but, except for the pumped up bass and bass drum that appeared on *Pronounced*, the first take in 1972 was surely ready for prime time. It also featured backup vocals from Leon, the only member of the original group who ever even approached a microphone to sing. But as good as this version was, they somehow managed to improve upon it the following year. Had "Sweet Home Alabama" and "Free Bird" not already caught the public's fancy, "Was I Right Or Wrong" might well have become one of Skynyrd's all-time biggest hits. But for some reason this song by Ronnie and Gary wasn't released until *Skynyrd's First . . . and Last* in 1978, having been sweetened two years before with the voices of Cassie Gaines, Leslie Hawkins, and Jo Jo

Billingsley. Featuring a "Gimme Three Steps" grind and a strong guitar solo, this is a great number, in which Ronnie immediately draws you in with an earnest, soft-spoken lament, then really gets you moving with a rousing refrain that makes this exceptional. Coming, as it did, on the final package of original Skynyrd songs, both the lyrics and the music serve as a fitting denouement for the band and a proper epitaph for Ronnie.

Ronnie admired Leon Russell, and in "Down South Jukin' " he and Gary put together a tune that was probably what Russell would have done if he'd written and performed it himself, an uptempo kind of number that the Georgia Satellites might have done years later, but with the kind of feminine touch that Leon Russell liked. While Ronnie did his best impression of Russell, this song might have stood on its own, but Leslie, Cassie, and Jo Jo would enhance it a few years later, as would Ed King, Jimmy Johnson, and Wayne Perkins on guitars, with Ronnie Eades adding another Russell-like, jukin' touch on saxophone.

A tribute to Paul Kossoff and Free, "Simple Man" is probably Ronnie and Gary's best shared composition, on which Ronnie doubles up on vocals, alternating from mezzo piano to mezzo forte. Hearing this crystalline version tells you just about everything you need to know to get at the heart of Ronnie Van Zant. As much as any other song he wrote, this one shows how much Ronnie's determination to succeed paid off, but not merely in making hit records and earning some money. More than anything else, "Simple Man" reflects the fact that he'd succeeded on the merits of what he was trying to accomplish: simply to make the kind of music that people would want to hear. It's top quality work in every way, and anyone who hasn't listened carefully doesn't comprehend how good he was, and how good they all were together.

Sounding like something from the early Free, Allen's "Trust" would be heard in its rough, original version on the boxed set, but it would find better form on *Gimme Back My Bullets* in 1976. It features an homage to Free's Paul Kossoff by Gary and an absolutely stunning bass part that demonstrates unequivocally why

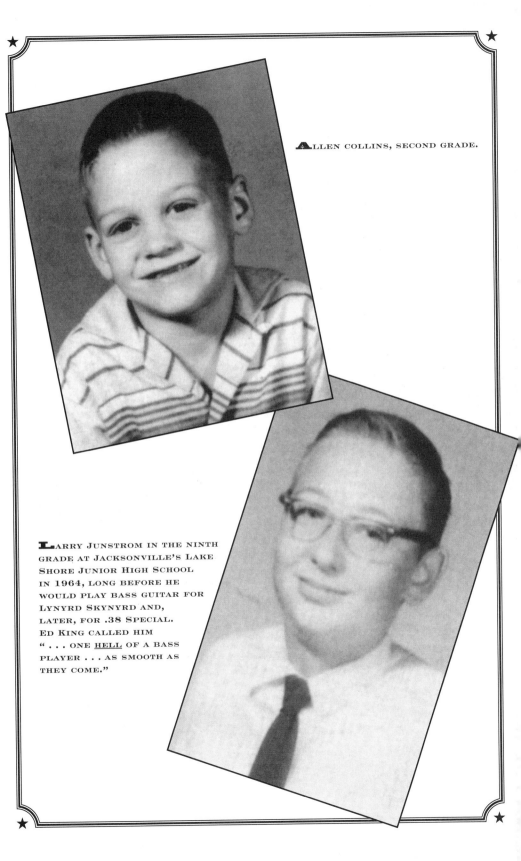

ALLEN COLLINS, SECOND GRADE.

LARRY JUNSTROM IN THE NINTH GRADE AT JACKSONVILLE'S LAKE SHORE JUNIOR HIGH SCHOOL IN 1964, LONG BEFORE HE WOULD PLAY BASS GUITAR FOR LYNYRD SKYNYRD AND, LATER, FOR .38 SPECIAL. ED KING CALLED HIM " . . . ONE HELL OF A BASS PLAYER . . . AS SMOOTH AS THEY COME."

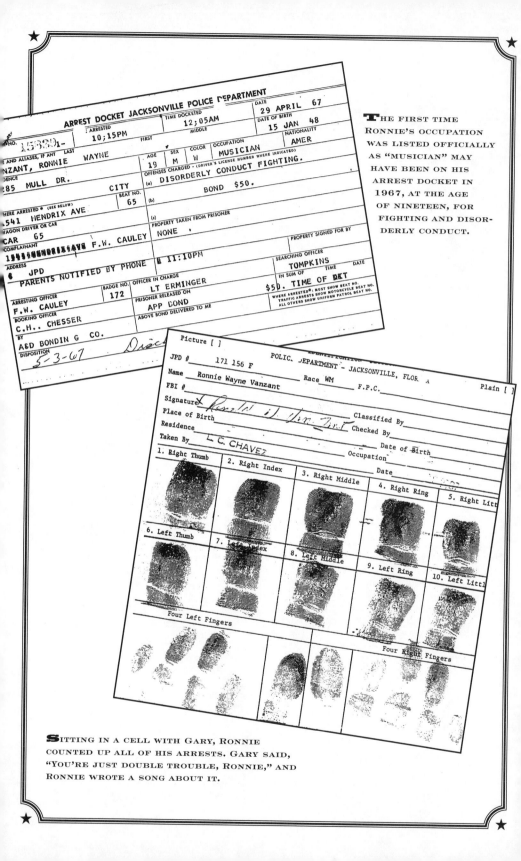

THE FIRST TIME RONNIE'S OCCUPATION WAS LISTED OFFICIALLY AS "MUSICIAN" MAY HAVE BEEN ON HIS ARREST DOCKET IN 1967, AT THE AGE OF NINETEEN, FOR FIGHTING AND DISORDERLY CONDUCT.

SITTING IN A CELL WITH GARY, RONNIE COUNTED UP ALL OF HIS ARRESTS. GARY SAID, "YOU'RE JUST DOUBLE TROUBLE, RONNIE," AND RONNIE WROTE A SONG ABOUT IT.

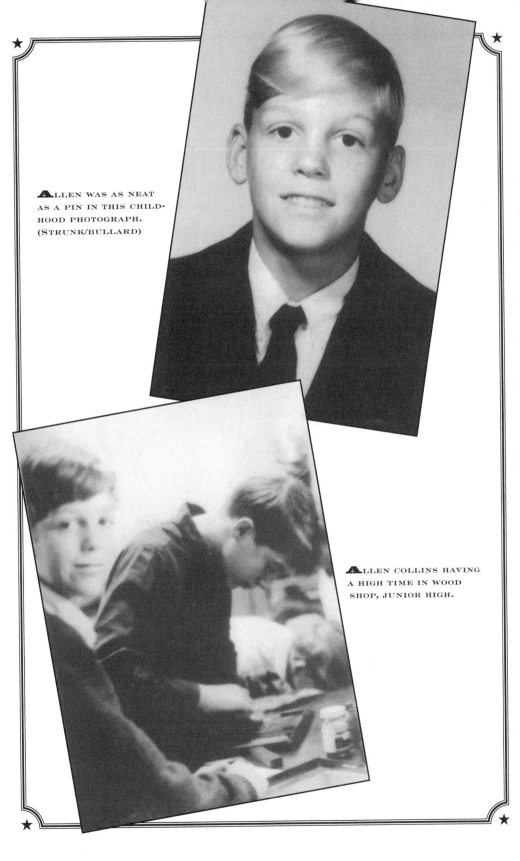

ALLEN WAS AS NEAT AS A PIN IN THIS CHILD-HOOD PHOTOGRAPH. (STRUNK/BULLARD)

ALLEN COLLINS HAVING A HIGH TIME IN WOOD SHOP, JUNIOR HIGH.

Allen

Gary

The

1 %

Ronnie Vanzant

387-3341

Bob

Larry

In 1968, figuring their odds of becoming successful were slim, the Noble Five changed their name to the One Percent. Business card features Ronnie Van Zant, Allen Collins, Gary Rossington, Bob Burns, and Larry Junstrom. (Steele)

Leonard Skinner, pictured in Lee High School's 1969 yearbook, had sent Gary to the assistant principal's office two years earlier for wearing his hair too long.

FOR KATHY JOHNS IT
WAS OBVIOUS THAT MUSIC
WOULD ALWAYS BE THE
OTHER LOVE IN ALLEN'S
LIFE. WATCHING HIM
PRACTICE ONE DAY, SHE
ASKED, "IF I LEAVE HERE
TOMORROW, WOULD YOU
STILL REMEMBER ME?"
(STRUNK/BULLARD)

BASS PLAYER LARRY STEELE, WHO
WAS PRESENT FROM THE START AND
BRIEFLY JOINED THE BAND, SHARES
A JOVIAL MOMENT WITH GARY
ROSSINGTON. (STEELE)

NOT MANY YOUNG ROCK AND ROLL FANS WERE BUYING
HOUSES IN THE MID-1970S, WHEN THIS PHOTOGRAPH WAS
TAKEN, BUT REAL ESTATE PROVIDED A GOOD LIVING FOR
THE FORMER HIGH SCHOOL COACH, LEONARD SKINNER,
FOR WHOM THE BAND WAS NAMED. (LA SALA-DORMAN)

LETTER LEONARD SKINNER RECEIVED
FROM MCA TO CONFIRM HIS PERMISSION
TO USE A PHOTOGRAPH OF A "LEONARD
SKINNER REALTY" SIGN FOR <u>NUTHIN'
FANCY.</u> (LA SALA-DORMAN)

RECORDS, INC

January 30, 1975

Leonard Skinner Realty
1702 Osceola
Jacksonville, Florida 32204

Re: "FOR SALE" SIGN TO BE USED FOR
LYNYRD SKYNYRD

Gentlemen:

The purpose of this letter is to confirm your telephone
conversation with George Osaki, Director of Creative
Services of MCA Records, Inc., regarding our right to
use a photograph of your realtor's sign "Leonard Skinner
Realty", for use as an album cover and/or as part of the
liner for the album tentatively entitled "NUTHIN FANCY",
featuring the performances of LYNYRD SKYNYRD, and/or for
such other uses as we may elect in connection with the
advertisement and promotion of such album.

By asking you to execute and return the enclosed copy of
this letter, we are asking you to and will consider that
you have, upon our receipt of such letter, represented
and warranted that you are the sole and exclusive owner
or otherwise control all rights to the artwork contained
in your sign, and that you agree to indemnify and hold
MCA Records, Inc. harmless of and free from all claims,
liabilities and expenses arising out of any alleged vio-
lation of any such representations and warranties as the
result of the exercise by us of rights granted to us by

AT THE AGE OF EIGHTEEN,
RONNIE VAN ZANT TOOK CHARGE OF
A GROUP OF YOUNGER BOYS, AND IN
NINE GRUELING YEARS MOLDED
THEM INTO A ROCK AND ROLL BAND
WORTHY OF BEING CALLED
"AMERICA'S ROLLING STONES."
(ODUM)

THE HONKETTES (LEFT TO RIGHT): LESLIE
ANN HAWKINS, CASSIE GAINES, AND
JO JO BILLINGSLEY, WHO ROUNDED OUT THE
SKYNYRD SOUND JUST AS RONNIE HAD WANTED.
(SARDOS)

FROM THE TIME HE PICKED
UP A GUITAR AT THE AGE OF TWELVE,
ALLEN WAS DETERMINED TO BECOME
A ROCK STAR. (SARDOS)

RONNIE, ALLEN, GARY, AND THEIR PERSONAL
ASSISTANT, DEAN KILPATRICK, ENJOY A FEW
MINUTES IN THE SHADE DURING A SUMMER-
TIME SHOW. (BULLARD)

RONNIE IN A RARE
MOMENT, PAUSING
FOR A PHOTOGRAPH
WHILE NOT ACTUALLY
PERFORMING.
(GRIFFITH)

NOT YOUR AVERAGE
AMERICAN TOURISTS IN
ENGLAND, BILLY, DEAN,
GARY, AND ALLEN SOAKED
UP THE SIGHTS AND THE
LIQUOR WHEREVER THEY
WENT. (GRIFFITH)

BILLY AND GARY IN SOARBRUCKEN,
GERMANY, OCTOBER 20, 1975.
(GRIFFITH)

ARTIMUS AND BILLY DURING A
QUIET MOMENT IN ENGLAND,
OCTOBER 1975. (GRIFFITH)

WALKING WAS ALWAYS SAFER THAN DRIVING FOR
BILLY, GARY, AND ALLEN, PHOTOGRAPHED HERE ON
A CITY STROLL IN ENGLAND IN 1975. (GRIFFITH)

RONNIE ENJOYED WATCHING GARY AT WORK IN
LONDON, OCTOBER 1975. (GRIFFITH)

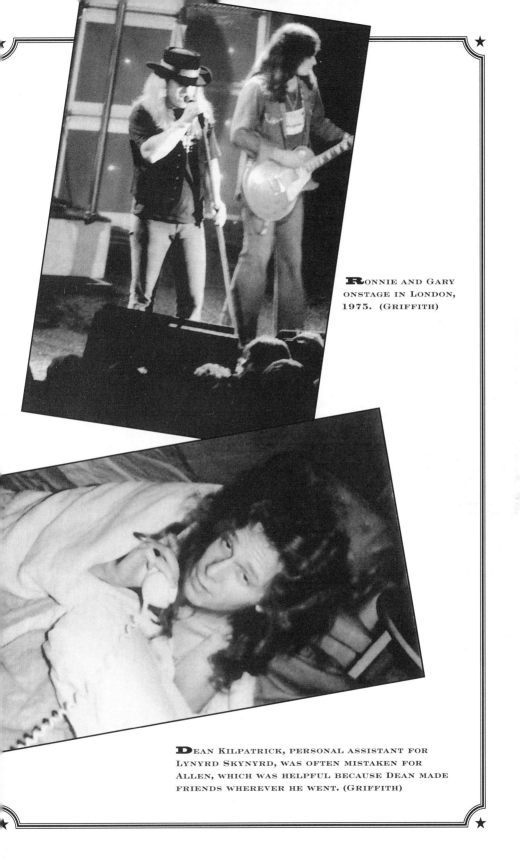

Ronnie and Gary onstage in London, 1975. (Griffith)

Dean Kilpatrick, personal assistant for Lynyrd Skynyrd, was often mistaken for Allen, which was helpful because Dean made friends wherever he went. (Griffith)

GARY ROSSINGTON
AWAKES FROM A CATNAP
DURING TOUR OF ENGLAND,
OCTOBER 25, 1975. IT WAS
BETTER THAN FALLING
ASLEEP AT THE WHEEL OF
A CAR AND CRASHING INTO
A TREE AND A HOUSE.
(GRIFFITH)

ALLEN SHOWED THAT
HIS MANUAL DEXTERITY
EXTENDED FURTHER THAN
PLAYING GUITAR. (STEELE)

THROUGHOUT HIS LIFE, ALLEN
WAS ALWAYS BURNING THE CANDLE
AT BOTH ENDS, AND EVERY COUPLE
OF DAYS IT CAUGHT UP WITH HIM.
(GRIFFITH)

A concert in New York, New York, April 1976, ended on a sour note for Leon. During "Free Bird" in the Beacon Theater, he broke up his guitar and tossed it into the audience, inadvertently slashing the face of a girl in the front row. (Sardos)

Laid back and soulful, Gary preferred to stand in place, his boyish face hidden in hair. (Ross)

Leon was later considered the "fourth guitar" (in the later, three-guitar format). "Trust" offers a very good example of how Ronnie was always striving, and succeeding, to make each song stand on its own. With an intro that hints at "The Weight" by The Band, this song offers subtle changes in pitch and tone, and the spark of a jerky, scraping sound that works the way gimmicks are supposed to work, adding a catchy little something that makes you notice, enhancing without detracting from the whole. Skynyrd knew the value of gimmicks, and in not overdoing them.

"Things Goin' On" is another good juke from Ronnie and Gary, but a slower-hand offering with a nice bit of fretwork from Ed King. It's also another example of how Ronnie's lyrics can make you immediately catch his message by synthesizing a complex issue into a simply stated expression—in this particular example it was powerful people making world-class decisions with no regard for average folks. In a basso profundo voice that's not apparently Ronnie's, with studio tricks provided by Johnson he backs himself up on this song, sounding more like another singer than a low-pitched version of himself.

Ronnie's songs on *Skynyrd's First: The Complete Muscle Shoals Album* ran the gamut of thoughts that young men typically ponder: not wanting to settle down, turning the table on a deceptive female, avoiding a fight after dancing with another man's girl, regret for being unable to reconcile with estranged parents, cruelly chiding a miscreant woman, looking forward to weekend revelry, lamenting the wasted life of a drunk, appreciating a mother's advice, advising a friend to watch out for deception, yearning for home, suggesting help for less fortunate people, observing life's "haves" and "have nots," and avoiding marriage if you're not the prospective father. (On November 18, 1972, Ronnie would enter into his second marriage, one that would last, to Judy Seymour, whom he'd met in 1969.)

Why this album didn't sell when Alan Walden shopped it around was probably just bad timing. But what this package lacked in timing, it more than made up for in a singular requisite quality that all great groups possess—musical intelligence, which abounds on these recordings. Uncommon for a group of young musicians especially, there's a rich variety of sounds here, a surprising range of vocals, and an interesting assortment of lyrics, all combined in smart musical arrangements with well-timed instrumental teasers that are guaranteed to please the most discriminating ears. These boys clearly knew what they were doing.

Serendipity sometimes smiles on those who are well prepared, but there is also random misfortune. For Lynyrd Skynyrd, one such hapless instance occurred when one of the demo tapes was somehow wound on a reel the wrong way, so that not all of the tracks could be read by a tape player. The result saw some of the band's best work distorted, prompting dismay and utter disgust. Upon hearing it for the first time, without realizing a mistake had been made, Ronnie was overcome with all-too-human emotion. Stung by what he thought was betrayal from a man he'd come to regard as a friend, the leader of the band blamed Jimmy Johnson, who was equally offended at this unexpected challenge to his integrity and his friendship. The following year, while playing "Simple Man" for Al Kooper as Skynyrd worked to make *Pronounced,* a studio engineer discovered it was just an innocent mistake. Shocked and chagrined, Ronnie called Johnson right away to apologize, and one year later he made more amends when he wrote the band's biggest hit song, "Sweet Home Alabama," in which he honored the Swampers.

CHAPTER 4

"AMERICA'S ROLLING STONES"

Even when Lynyrd Skynyrd was still testing the waters as an unknown opening act at concerts, very few bands were thrilled at the thought of following them in performance. In the language of show business, they were a tough act to follow. Regardless of who was headlining, Skynyrd's attitude was to grind the main act into pulp before they'd even begun to play. And that is virtually what they did with a revved-up, blues-rock boogie that was the essence of musical excitement. Stunned by the quality and the intensity of their performance, without any pointless props, first-time fans would soon discern the dynamics of their appeal. Some people attributed Skynyrd's success to the driving rhythms and the dazzling virtuosity of their fiery guitars, and the pounding, percussive forces of an outstanding bass and a power-packed set of drums. Others commended the well-crafted musical arrangements they always performed with precision and passion. But stirring within

GARY ROSSINGTON WAS FOURTEEN YEARS OLD IN THE SUMMER OF 1966, WHEN THE CORE OF THE FUTURE SKYNYRD GOT TOGETHER IN BOB BURNS'S GARAGE. ELEVEN YEARS LATER, GARY WAS SIGNING AUTOGRAPHS IN ALTAMONTE SPRINGS, FLORIDA, THREE DAYS BEFORE THE PLANE CRASH. (ODUM)

the music there was also something else: honest, true-to-life lyrics about plain, ordinary people, sung in a straightforward way. Singing as if he were seated beside you sharing his innermost feelings, Ronnie Van Zant conveyed a sincerity that truly set him apart and completed their perfect package. Lynyrd Skynyrd's global renown was a product of these three exceptional elements—a mass of incomparable sound, a singular composition and style, and frank, blue-collar lyrics sung straight from a man's heart.

Watching him walk on stage toward the close of his stellar career and knowing him as I had since childhood, I was often struck by the fact that Ronnie was really even there. He had absolutely no formal musical training, he couldn't really play an instrument, and yet, there he was, night after night, standing in the spotlight at the center of the stage, surrounded by a wealth of musical talent. And for a genre of music based on guitar, Ronnie was blessed with not one but two, and for many years three, absolutely superb guitar players. It was truly a wonderful experience to witness this scene repeated again and again in concert halls and sports stadiums all over the world, which even Ronnie couldn't have envisioned when he'd started assembling a band a decade earlier. But he might have had an inkling. Once he'd recruited Allen Collins from the Mods, Ronnie had remarked to Larry Steele that neither Allen nor Gary Rossington could play very well. This was true at the time, as they were just learning, but what Ronnie didn't mention was the potential he'd seen in this pair of rock star wannabes. Although some prompting from Ronnie would be needed from time to time, both teenage talents were earnest about learning to play, and both would become great guitarists. But in Allen there were qualities that came without any coaching. As Ronnie had noticed right away, Allen had a natural sense of rhythm, which every good rock band needs, but there was something else about Allen that Ronnie couldn't have appreciated at the time: his perfect sense of pitch. You can play an instrument well without these intrinsic traits, but with natural rhythm and perfect pitch you can make a good band that much better, and that's what Allen did.

Another dynamic that would prove fortunate for Ronnie and his new band was the fact that Allen and Gary had been learning to play together for almost as long as they'd owned their first guitars. Allen learned a little from his neighbor, Donnie Ulsh, and Gary learned a little from his older sister's boyfriend, but they mainly learned from each other and taught themselves, listening to the radio and playing the same records over and over, until they could duplicate what they heard. Unable to afford new records, most of their "platters" came from the bargain bin at Woolworth's, where Allen's mother was employed, and they usually practiced in her living room because she was usually away at work, where she avoided hearing the same notes, the same licks, and the same songs repeated so many times that she might have lost her mind. Eva remembers coming home one night after Woolworth's closed and warning the boys they'd have to wind it down. Toward their later teen years, when they helped themselves to beers from her refrigerator, their practice sessions sometimes lasted longer than Eva would have liked, with the volume too loud for too long. "You boys'll have to keep it down after 9 o'clock," she'd say, and at 10 she'd return, "You boys, cut it down." At 11 she'd cut it off entirely and send young Gary home.

Both Allen and Gary eventually learned how to play everything they wanted to play. It became a sort of contest to see who could accomplish the most, but they were both genuinely happy at the end of every match, knowing they'd played to a draw. Gary could play what Allen played, and Allen could play what Gary played, yet each developed his own style and sound. On his Les Paul, which he named "Berniece" after his mother, Gary embraced a laid back, soulful style of play, with a note-structured approach that would ripen with age but stay true to the roots that it grew from, mainly Ry Cooder, Paul Kossoff in Free, and Eric Clapton in Cream. Allen could play their leads, too, on his chosen tool of the trade, a Gibson Firebird, but he was a natural rhythm man and more inclined toward chords. Allen and Gary became the perfect yin and yang, with individual styles that were both contradictory and complementary at the same time. Unlike the more technically polished men who later took turns as third guitarist, Ed King and Steve Gaines, Allen and Gary were rough and tumble guys who fiddled with frills and notions until a cohesive outline began to form. One would try a verse structure and the other would offer a chorus, and if they could remember these rough sketches later—it might be the next day or a month or more later—it was probably worth keeping. This was how they became so good together, combining their strengths in a symmetry of sound that would take Lynyrd Skynyrd to the first rung of the rock and roll ladder, as *Pronounced* would clearly prove.

Once it became apparent to Ronnie that coming up with lyrics would never be a problem for him, he shifted his focus to the music. At first, Allen or Gary would play something, and Ronnie would say, "I like that. Keep playing that, and I'm gonna sing to it." At other times, he'd come up with a verse and an idea of how a melody might work, and he'd coax a tune from whomever he could reach, or whoever jumped in first. Somehow, despite Allen's and Gary's disparate styles of playing, their writing styles were so similar that it would be difficult to tell who did what if not for the credit on their record labels. Both guitarists worked hard, but Ronnie always wanted to practice longer and harder, which was partly due to the fact that practice sessions were easier for him, since he didn't have to play an instrument. But it was also a sign of his intense desire to succeed, and the nagging feeling he'd always had that his time on Earth was limited, that every minute lost was an opportunity wasted. And so, Ronnie became the taskmaster. Follow his rules, and you'd have no problems, but break them, and he'd break something of yours. The rule broken most often was becoming too inebriated to function, and at one time or another everyone felt Ronnie's wrath for that. "You can get stoned after practice," he'd say, "but if you get stoned before practice I'm gonna beat your brains out." Something else he'd say before he started punching people was, "What do you mean you can't remember your

part? You played it right yesterday!" And for Ronnie, especially, playing music exactly right was always of paramount importance. In Ronnie's view, people go to concerts expecting to hear what they've heard on the radio and on records, and that's what Ronnie wanted to deliver. While other bands might play variations of their songs or drift into rambling jams, Lynyrd Skynyrd set out to play their music precisely the way they'd composed and recorded it—and their fans were glad they did.

By the early part of 1973, most rock and roll fans had never heard of Lynyrd Skynyrd, because they hadn't yet made a record. Even so, they were nearing the brink of the one big break that would carry them into the big time, and one sure sign of this was their ability to land one- and two-week engagements in some of the hottest nightclubs in Atlanta, Georgia, the "New York City of the South." If you could make it there, it could have been said, you could make it anywhere. By contrast, Skynyrd's friendly rock and roll rivals, Black Bear Angel, were still playing in the same old places in Jacksonville, with a new name, Alice Marr, and some new personnel. They were Larry Steele on bass, Ronnie's brother, Donnie Van Zant as lead singer, Bill Pelkey on drums, Don Barnes on guitar, and Billy Powell, who in mid-1971 had played piano on two of the Muscle Shoals demo songs but hadn't yet officially joined the band.

For all who toil in the field of music, being in the right place is just as important as being prepared. For Lynyrd Skynyrd, who had been fortunate to meet Alan Walden, this time the place was Funochio's rock and roll nightclub in Atlanta, where they found a new friend and mentor. Al Kooper was a well known force in the world of rock—he'd written "This Diamond Ring," which had been the No. 1 single in 1965; he'd recorded with Bob Dylan, Jimi Hendrix, and the Stones; he'd been part of the famed Blues Project; and he'd founded Blood, Sweat and Tears. While staying in Atlanta to record his backup band, Frankie and Johnny, Kooper encountered a former acquaintance who managed Funochio's. Lynyrd Skynyrd happened to be playing there one week, and for Kooper it was love at first sound. He liked their songs and he loved their down-to-earth style, something he felt had been missing from contemporary rock and roll. Unlike the technically complicated music that contemporary bands like Yes and Emerson, Lake and Palmer were churning out, Skynyrd's songs were structured simply, and Kooper thought their sharp, heavy sound would be a strong draw for youngsters who were starved for something new that was rooted in old-time rock. Kooper initially found the barefoot Ronnie repulsive, but quickly observed that Ronnie had an oddly compelling presence on stage, where his store of potential energy seemed always about to explode. He wasn't at all theatrical in a conventional sense, but he exuded a powerful confidence that made audiences want to watch him just the same. Kooper listened to the band every night, and on the third night he began joining them on stage for jams. On their last night, Kooper said he'd like to produce a Lynyrd Skynyrd album. Ronnie said he'd ask Walden to consider the proposal, and the band returned to Jacksonville.

Kooper later likened his introduction to Skynyrd to walking into a backstreet bar and discovering the Rolling Stones before they'd ever signed a contract. Meanwhile, Kooper noticed there were a number of other good bands in Atlanta and only one record company interested in Southern bands, Capricorn Records, which was owned by Alan Walden's brother, Phil. Seeing an opportunity, Kooper decided to form a company of his own, Sounds of the South, and he got MCA Records to finance the venture and distribute the records. Off and on for a couple of months or more, Kooper and Alan Walden discussed contract terms, until Ronnie all but sealed a deal himself. Ronnie told me he'd been leery of Kooper at first, but that he gradually came to trust him enough to make a phone call that he hadn't planned to make. When the band's equipment was stolen, Ronnie called Kooper late one night and asked if he could borrow $5,000 to buy what they needed in order to keep their next booking. Kooper gladly sent him the

money, and Ronnie promised to return both the money and the favor.

Ronnie meant what he said, but there was a problem brewing that Kooper knew nothing about. Kooper's contract offer would apply only if Ronnie had a band, and there were serious concerns that the group would soon be minus one member. With Skynyrd standing on the threshold of a dream, Leon Wilkeson wasn't sure that God had wanted him to be a rock star. Torn with internal conflict, he felt that a fast-paced rock and roll lifestyle was incompatible with his faith, and from day to day, the matter of whether or not he'd continue depended entirely upon how much he was drinking. Uncertain about Leon, one Saturday morning back in Jacksonville, Ronnie asked Allen to call Larry Steele to see if he'd like to join the band, beginning that night in St. Augustine. "We'll come by and teach you a bunch of songs, then we'll play tonight, and tomorrow we're going to Atlanta," Allen said, but the trip was put off for a week. During that time Larry rehearsed with the group, and Ronnie and his wife, Judy, picked up Larry in Judy's gold Toyota sedan and took him to Paulus Music Company, where Ronnie told him to choose the best bass amp in the store. "Get plenty of sleep, we're leaving in the morning for Atlanta," he said. Ronnie also asked Billy Powell to join them for the Atlanta gig, but he couldn't make the trip.

On the side of the road at the intersection of Interstates 10 and 75, they picked up Leon, who'd hitched a ride from Orlando. Once they arrived in Atlanta, Leon began teaching his bass parts to Larry, who was on hand in case Leon decided to quit. During their one-week gig in the Headrest nightclub, Leon played with the band every night, after which he and Larry practiced in the bathroom of the room they shared in a Days Inn motel. In the process, they also became drinking buddies, which proved to be a costly mistake for Ronnie, and maybe for Larry as well. Ronnie's mistake was allowing Larry and Leon to run up a tab at the bar in the Headrest, because at the end of the week the band owed the club money. "We weren't just charging drinks for us, we were entertaining other bar guests. Ronnie was furious, but he didn't say much about it," Larry said.

During a rehearsal break, Ronnie and Larry and some of the others were sitting around a table in the bar, when a guy from another band walked up and gave Ronnie a message. "Talked to a friend of yours," he said. "Yeah, who?" Ronnie asked. "Ed King. He said to tell you he'll be seeing you soon." A look of shock came over Ronnie's face because he hadn't wanted Larry to know that he'd also asked Ed to join the band. Glancing over at Larry, hoping he hadn't heard the exchange, Ronnie responded, "Oh, yeah. He's a helluva good musician, ain't he?" Before the week was out, Kooper signed Skynyrd for just $9,000, with Leon still on board, and the band returned to Florida to rehearse for their first recording session together.

Skynyrd got back to town on a Sunday, with plans to rehearse the next day in a one-room wooden cabin they'd rented near Green Cove Springs, south of Jacksonville. They called it "Hell House" during the summer because it wasn't air-conditioned and ventilation was poor, but now it was winter and it was freezing cold because the building had no heat. On Monday, Bob Burns was supposed to pick up Larry in their truck, "Big Blue," but he never showed up. Allen called Larry that night and said they'd decided not to practice. The same thing happened the next day, and on Wednesday, Ed King arrived and officially joined the band—Leon had already quit. A few days later, at a party at the home of Bill Chester, who would soon become a Skynyrd roadie, Ed walked up to Larry and apologized. "I'm sorry about the way things turned out, man," he said. Ronnie told Larry he'd "messed up" by costing the band too much money in Atlanta, but that was probably only an excuse. Ronnie had known how important that Atlanta trip would be, and he wasn't willing to risk not having a good bass player when they needed one the most. So he had asked both Larry and Ed to be there, to be doubly sure that Leon's spot would be filled if he decided to leave the band. Two backups. It was the last important lesson that Larry would learn directly from Ronnie. (Years later, while shucking oysters in Allen's garage on Larry's birthday, Allen summed up the episode in three words: "We screwed you." Then he drove his friend to Marvin Kay's MusiCenter and told him to pick out any bass in the place. Larry chose a Sunburst Fender jazz bass, and Allen paid for it.)

When Ronnie and company returned to Atlanta, Kooper was surprised to learn that Leon had been replaced. This unexpected personnel change might have nixed the deal if Ed were a lesser musician, but he soon proved his worth, and despite Ed's lack of formal musical training, Kooper would come to regard him as something of a musical genius, and his favorite Skynyrd guitarist.

Born September 14, 1949, in Glendale, California, Ed King had no apparent musical inheritance when he decided to play the drums at the age of twelve. But a drum set wouldn't fit the family's pocketbook at the time, so he opted for a guitar instead, and a rented one, at that. "It was cheaper than a set of drums," Ed told me, adding, "Good thing, eh?" The Stella acoustic guitar was very difficult to play, but that wouldn't dissuade a boy who'd been seized with an overwhelming desire to play like the guys he was hearing on the radio. For Ed, this was initially Dick Dale, the king of the surf guitar, and Duane Eddy, whose twangy, bass-heavy instrumentals with inspiring solo riffs elevated the popularity of the electric guitar and influenced lots of boys like Ed, including Carl Wilson, George Harrison, and John Lennon. Eddy figured in no less than fifteen Top 40 hits in the late '50s and early '60s, although his best-known work might be the theme from TV's *Peter Gunn*. Ed also listened to blues-rock legend Lonnie Mack, who influenced Keith Richards, Eric Clapton, Jimmy Page, and Stevie Ray Vaughn. And he learned from the strumming of James Burton, who played for Elvis Presley, and from Pete Townshend, Duane Allman, and Eric Clapton.

"My mother always discouraged my pursuit of music, and I can't blame her, though I did at the time," Ed said. "I knew I had some style and just wanted it *so* bad." And so he persisted, and within five years he was part of a band with real potential, the

Strawberry Alarm Clock. At the age of sixteen, Ed knew what he wanted to do with his life, so he decided to forgo the diploma he would've earned in 1967 to devote all of his time to his music and his band. "I quit at the end of the eleventh grade," he said, adding, "I only did well in English and typing." Ed's calling was clearly elsewhere, and before his eighteenth birthday, his group had recorded a song that became the No. 1 hit in the nation. Neither Ed nor keyboardist Mark Weitz received credit for co-writing "Incense and Peppermints," on which Ed played bass, all the guitar parts, and tambourine, and they were never paid for the effort; all they got was their picture on the cover of *Cashbox* magazine and the benefit of becoming a household name. "We had no idea what was going on," Ed said, noting that the band dissolved into bankruptcy in late 1968 and "totally fell apart." Nobody would've guessed they weren't doing well, though. On their final tour in 1968, they were on the bill with the Beach Boys and the opening act was Buffalo Springfield, featuring Neil Young and Stephen Stills. Stills would join Al Kooper and Mike Bloomfield for their *Super Session* album that year.

There are thieves of every kind in life, and the music business has seen its share. A year or so after they'd broken up, Ed and Mark Weitz discovered that a bogus band was performing under their name, so they re-formed Strawberry Alarm Clock and started touring for themselves. This was a fortuitous decision for Ronnie Van Zant and Lynyrd Skynyrd, who became their opening act in 1970, on a three-month tour of Southern college campuses. During the tour, Skynyrd mainly covered Led Zeppelin, Cream, and Jimi Hendrix, but they also played a couple of original tunes, including "Need All My Friends," which blew Ed King away. He and Ronnie got along well, and Ed told him to call him if he ever needed someone to play either guitar or his favorite instrument, the bass. "Ronnie Van Zant was the only reason I would ever even consider joining the band. He had a quality about him that just reeked of greatness," King said.

When Ed reported to work in Florida, he was struck by the

band's strict practice regimen, which he would have to make his own. They were the only musicians he knew who would get up at 6 a.m. and be at practice by 8, he said, and it made a deep impression on him. Especially under Ronnie's direction, they were extremely well disciplined, with a near-obsession with playing every song exactly right, note for note, every time they played it. Fiercely determined, they had the attitude that if you work harder than everyone else is willing to work, you're bound to succeed. "Inspiration and perspiration," Ed said, and he fit right in from the start, which was good, because within a couple of weeks, on March 26, 1973, Lynyrd Skynyrd entered Studio One in Doraville, in Atlanta's northern suburbs. They taped twenty songs (including "Was I Right Or Wrong?," "Mr. Banker," and "Take Your Time," which would become the "B" side for both of the singles, "Don't Ask Me No Questions" in April 1974, and "Sweet Home Alabama" in June 1974) for Kooper to consider for the first record album they would make together in the weeks ahead. And joining them for the trip was another surprise for Kooper, the band's newest official member, Billy Powell.

William Norris Powell was born in Corpus Christi, Texas, on June 3, 1952. His father, a naval aviator, had died from illness while stationed in Italy, and Billy's mother moved the family to Jacksonville's Westside. She enrolled Billy in Sanford Academy, a military boarding school in Sanford, near Orlando, where he took piano lessons from a teacher who immediately recognized his natural gift for music. Like Allen Collins, Billy had all three of the qualities that every great musician has: virtuosity, a natural sense of rhythm, and perfect pitch. While enrolled in Bishop Kenny High School in Jacksonville, Billy continued his piano lessons, and after graduating in 1970, he enrolled in Florida Junior College in Jacksonville to study music, and he joined the Alice Marr band. About that time he joined his friend, Kevin Elson, as a roadie for Lynyrd Skynyrd. The two of them were thinking of starting their own band when, in the spring of 1971, after a high school gig with Skynyrd, Kevin told Ronnie and the others that Billy could play the piano.

"You gotta listen to him play," Kevin said. Billy sat down at a piano that happened to be there, and he played a part he'd composed for "Free Bird."

Thrilled to learn that a talented piano player was right there in his midst, Ronnie invited Billy to join them that summer for a couple of trips to Muscle Shoals, where Billy played on "Free Bird" and "Comin' Home." Kevin, who was still in high school and would work for the band for many years as sound engineer, also made those trips and played organ in the background. Ronnie told Billy he'd find a place for him in the band when they could afford to add another member, which wouldn't happen for almost two years. In the meantime, Billy had some work to do. Having been trained in classical music, he hadn't yet learned to loosen up, prompting Ronnie to call him an "educated fool." Stung by the criticism, Billy began developing what, for him, was a new approach to the piano. He'd always been able to play by ear, and he could replicate nearly anything that anyone else could play, so now he just pointed his ears in the right direction and the style he was after soon followed. Rounding out this period of self-adjustment, Al Kooper showed Billy how to make his instrument blend more in concert with the guitars. And then he was off and running. It was as if he'd had a barrel of rock and boogie and honky-tonk inside him waiting to get out, and once it did, Skynyrd's overall sound was greatly enhanced.

In the studio, Kooper was pleasantly surprised to learn how remarkably well rehearsed the band was, and to discover their exceptional talent for arranging. Like Ed, he was amazed at how demanding the boys were on themselves during rehearsals. Aside from what he was able to teach them from his own experience, which he relates in his book, *Backstage Passes & Backstabbing Bastards,* Kooper knew he had struck gold with Skynyrd. He did all he could think of to make their debut album succeed, including making three trips to New York City to mix it, and doubling the guitar solos to give them more power and clarity, as he would do on each of their next two albums. Kooper also played a variety of instruments on the album—he's listed as "Roosevelt Cook" in the

credits—and later performed with them on tour, without ever stealing the limelight. In very large measure, the success of Lynyrd Skynyrd can be attributed directly to their association with Kooper. As Ed King has said, "Had it not been for Al, no one would've heard of Skynyrd. He was the visionary behind the band and how it should be presented to the world."

Having composed three new songs to go along with five they'd chosen from the Muscle Shoals collection, Skynyrd spent six weeks recording *Lynyrd Skynyrd*. Kooper hadn't been able to talk them into changing their name, so he felt that a little instruction was necessary so that people would know how to say it. Even so, not everyone got the message. After its release, *Pronounced* was picked up on radio in Europe and Japan, where Skynyrd still has legions of fans. An American who first heard Skynyrd in Europe, Nick Nicoll of Richmond, Virginia, remembers Skynyrd's radio debut in Italy, where he was stationed in the U.S. Navy. On the Armed Forces Radio Network one day, an American deejay, Rita DiMartino opened her "Good Morning, Naples" show with a song from a hot new band she introduced as "Lenny-yard Skinny-yard." She obviously hadn't been to the party for the launch of Kooper's new record label.

To publicize Sounds of the South and its three bands (Mose Jones, Elijah, and Lynyrd Skynyrd), in May, Kooper and MCA hired a Los Angeles-based public relations firm, represented by Sharon Lawrence. Her first order of business was a promotional party in Richard's nightclub in Atlanta, where Mose Jones and Skynyrd would perform for radio personalities and music writers for newspapers and music magazines around the country. Richard's owners put up $10,000 for the event, and MCA and its subsidiary, Sounds of the South, put up $15,000, mainly for catering and travel expenses for out-of-town guests—about one hundred and fifty of the four hundred invitees attended. Mose Jones played first, and then Skynyrd stole the show with a stellar performance that featured what is probably the cleverest gimmick anyone has ever cooked up to impress a record company. Primed for the occasion, Ronnie and

Ed King had written a song that was guaranteed to blow the minds of every MCA executive present, which it did. But aside from being resourceful, "Workin' For MCA" was also one of the strongest rock songs Skynyrd ever produced. Something else about this party is worth noting; it was held under a protective court order barring interference by the police. It was a Sunday, when alcohol couldn't be served, but the club owners felt the law didn't apply to a private affair. Police and the city attorney's office disagreed, so one of the owners, an attorney himself, secured a restraining order. A lot of aspirations were riding on this affair, so it's fortunate that the police were unable to enforce the law. It's hard to imagine a kickoff party for Lynyrd Skynyrd without any alcohol.

The party was a smashing success, and MCA invested $100,000 for a "Who is Lynyrd Skynyrd?" advertising campaign that began six weeks before the album's release. (A few years later, as a joke, Ronnie would don a T-shirt bearing the question, "Who are the Rolling Stones?") With three weeks to go, radio stations started playing cuts from the album, and after its release on August 16, initial sales weren't meteoric but they met Kooper's expectations. And why not? From the slow blues rhythm in "Simple Man" to the cascading guitar solos in "Free Bird," Lynyrd Skynyrd showed the remarkable musical range they would offer on each of their products to come. (It would take a year before *Pronounced* really took off, reaching gold record status in December 1974.)

There was plenty to like about this album, with valuable contributions from Kooper on five of its eight songs. Beginning with "I Ain't The One," his favorite among the songs he'd heard them play, this version introduced Skynyrd's distinctive guitar wailing and had a fuller, richer texture than the original. Billy's light touch on the ivories was a healthy new addition. In another welcome change, two annoying distractions were gone from Ronnie's excellent vocals: the hollow chamber effect from the earlier take and the craggy yowling that strained his throat when he stretched it more than he should have. It's Gary's song, but Allen played the lead, which is an indication of how well these two guitarists worked

together. As was true of all of the original members, they were friends first and musicians second, as Kooper had learned, which accounts for the lack of creative differences that fractured so many other bands. Returning the favor in "Tuesday's Gone," which he wrote for this album, Allen gave Gary the lead and the soul of its mournful mood. Perhaps because he liked it so much, Al Kooper played bass on this one, sang backup harmony, and added a rich orchestral quality on a marvelous machine called a Mellotron. The instrument looked like an electronic organ, but it was really a cache of pre-recorded tapes that could be blended for an assortment of splendid sounds, as the Beatles, the Stones, Led Zeppelin, and other bands had done. But what really made this song work was the solid piano accompaniment that would clearly establish Billy's standing as an integral part of the "new" Skynyrd sound. For only this song, the Atlanta Rhythm Section's Robert Nix played drums.

The *Pronounced* version of "Gimme Three Steps" was much more forceful than the original, with Gary's lead and Allen's rhythm substantially strengthened by Kooper's wise decision to double-record them. The added density of the twin guitars enlivened this bouncing barroom romp, and the beat of a bongo, played by percussionist Bobbi Hall (she had worked with the Doors and would later help Stevie Nicks's solo efforts), was a suitable supplement to Bob Burns's drums. Although some critics panned it for being too comedic, this version became a pretty big hit with fans, and it remains one of their most popular songs today. For a non-musician, especially anyone who is not a musical director, it's difficult to imagine improving upon Skynyrd's initial rendering of "Simple Man," but they did on this record, or, at the very least, they made a fabulous piece of music an unforgettable classic. One almost imperceptible enhancement was the introduction of an organ, which Kooper played, although, as most Skynyrd fans already know, Kooper felt pretty strongly that this song shouldn't have been part of this album. He changed his mind later, but he was adamant at the time. Once he and Ronnie had finally stopped arguing, Ronnie did something that most artists might only think about doing with the producer of their very first record album. He walked Kooper to his automobile (a Bentley is more than just a car), closed the door for him when he got in, and leaned into the driver-side window. "When we're done recording it," he said, "we'll call you." They did, and Kooper returned a few hours later to add the organ part.

Performed at a slightly slower tempo than the original version, this "Simple Man" would become a moving homage, not only to the late Ronnie Van Zant, but to the entire band as well. It's an honest portrayal of a mother's advice to her son, which he wrote after the death of his grandmother. On a number of levels, it was arguably the best song Skynyrd ever recorded, but its origin was as simple as its name—Ronnie made the whole thing up while taking a shower, and, just as he typically did, he remembered it without ever writing it down.

The honky-tonk character that would come to define much of Skynyrd's subsequent work was a great addition to the *Pronounced* version of "Things Goin' On," as Billy's stature grew. With a stronger start and more flourish throughout, its mellow, foot-stomping beat made "Things Goin' On" a perfect choice to follow the somber "Simple Man," although it, too, was a serious song, recalling Ronnie's genuine concern for people of meager means. In another sign of the things that would come from Ed King, Ed played lead guitar on the song that Al Kooper wrote for the album, "Mississippi Kid." Ronnie wrote the lyrics, of course, and he gave co-writing credit to Bob for coming up with the name. "Mississippi Kid" is quiet and understated, much in the manner of Leon Redbone's front porch style of picking and moaning, with Kooper playing along on mandolin and tapping a bass drum for some bottom. The only other instrument was a perfect choice: a harmonica played by Steve Katz, who had played guitar with Kooper's Blues Project and had helped him create Blood, Sweat and Tears. This was the one song Ed didn't play the bass on. Most of the bass parts on the album had been composed by Leon Wilkeson, who, as it turned out, was only sitting this album out, although no one could've said that with any certainty at the time. Not even Leon.

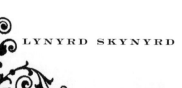

But Ronnie wanted Leon back. Ronnie couldn't play an instrument, but he knew good musicianship when he heard it and felt very strongly that Leon Wilkeson was *the man* for the bass. Ed King felt the same way. A few months earlier, while rehearsing in Hell House before their recording sessions in Atlanta, Leon visited the cabin and took a turn at "Simple Man" while Ed sat back and listened. Ed had never heard the song, but he realized then that Leon was the best bass player he'd ever heard, and he's never changed his opinion. "To this day," Ed told me, "I never, *ever* write a bass part without first asking myself, 'What would Leon play?' He taught me how to re-think the instrument. He was a true original." In fact, on the final two songs they recorded for *Pronounced,* "Simple Man" and "Free Bird," Ed created the parts for his Fender jazz bass after hearing Leon play. He said he'd caught Leon's vision of the style that would work best for Lynyrd Skynyrd. And so, in June, when the band was back in Jacksonville awaiting the release of *Pronounced,* in his own inimitable way, Ronnie sat down beside Ed, who was playing his Stratocaster. He put his arm around him and said, "Ed, . . . you're the worst bass player I ever played with." He was obviously using humor to make his point because he placed great value in Ed and he definitely didn't want to lose him. The next day, Billy and Bob went to see Leon at Farm Best Dairy Products, where he was busy making ice cream. That led to a talk with Ronnie, who said the band needed him, but that Leon would have to make a commitment to stay and work hard. Thus was born a "guitar army," as Gary liked to call it. On the very first day they played together in Hell House, they created "Sweet Home Alabama" and "I Need You," and then they were really off and running.

Lynyrd Skynyrd became one hundred and ten strings of sound: three high-powered, six-string guitars, an awesome four-string bass, and eighty-eight lively piano strings struck by nimble fingers. Now on a Fender Stratocaster, Ed immediately added an element of creativity and spontaneity that Allen and Gary responded to very well. Whereas before, practice sessions had often been tense affairs, with Ronnie yelling and punching and generally keeping everyone off balance and sharper than they would have been, with Ed around, practices grew much more relaxed—at least for a while. Each of the three guitarists had his own distinct style, and they never minded sharing the leads and solos and fills because there was always plenty to go around. Ed (who would later play a Gibson SG Standard, then a Les Paul) generally preferred playing rhythm, but whenever he had an idea he felt strongly about, he jumped in with solos or leads. Once somebody had something started, everything usually fell into place pretty naturally. And now Ronnie had one more collaborator to work with. He sometimes had the words already written and would coax a melody or a rhythm out of one of the others by humming or tapping his finger. Sometimes the guitarists competed for parts, and if every part was good enough to everyone's satisfaction, a place was found for them.

For *Pronounced*, Ed showed more of his range of talent by writing "Poison Whiskey," an upbeat number in which every member of the ensemble shines. At three minutes and eleven seconds long, it's the shortest cut on the record but a very worthy offering. The album ended with "Free Bird," which the Rock and Roll Hall of Fame and Museum would include among its "500 Songs That Shaped Rock and Roll." With Kooper on organ to buttress Billy's piano, and enriched with a much stronger rap from the drums, this version opened with a church-like quality that's akin to the opening bars of "You Can't Always Get What You Want" by the Stones. And then came Allen's memorable lead on his Gibson Firebird, coupled with Gary's counterpart on a Gibson SG (Gary normally played a Les Paul), for a riveting guitar duet rivaling the popular "Layla" by Eric Clapton and Duane Allman. For anyone who sat through a Skynyrd concert for the first time back then, thinking Allen was only a rhythm man, they were in for a real surprise. This classic rock anthem would be played on radio so often over the years that it became a frequent joke that Allen loved and Ronnie would have relished, when fans called out for "Free

Bird" at non-Skynyrd concerts. As was true for every song on the album, Ronnie's voice had matured from the demo tapes of the previous two years, partly because he was constantly trying to improve himself, and partly because he was much more relaxed with an actual recording contract indelibly sealed in ink.

Ronnie always felt that *Pronounced* was Skynyrd's best album. "They're the best bunch of songs we've done, and there's more different kinds of songs on it," he said, referring to the lyrics, the arrangements, and the range of musical stylings. He also liked the fact that most of the music on the album represented several years' worth of hard work, trial and error, hopes and failures, and very little income in the process. Ronnie had always known they would make a record that people would buy, but the others were never as certain. Just before *Pronounced* was released, the band's unofficial publicist, Sharon Lawrence, who was working for Elton John at the time, picked up a copy of the first pressing and took it to Allen Collins, who was struck with amazement that his dream was coming true. They were songs he'd played over and over and over, and now that he could hear them on a real LP that people could actually buy in stores throughout the country, he put it on his stereo and listened for the next four hours. And just like a fan, he played a little "air guitar" while he listened, tapping his foot and focusing on the music so he could discover every flaw. Lawrence told a reporter that Allen was filled with wonderment that this long-awaited day had finally arrived. "I can't believe it," he said. "An album that will go in real record stores everywhere. Do you think anyone will buy it?" Then he smiled and said, "It ain't perfect by a long shot, but it's us, and it's been worth putting up with Al Kooper."

Kooper and the boys had argued about just about everything, from song selection to what key to play in, but that's what people do when they're creating a winning product. Theirs was a working relationship built upon mutual respect. In promoting their first album, Kooper made a clever but ambitious assertion that might well have backfired with any other band. They were "America's Rolling

Stones," he said, and whether or not they were, the comparison worked because Skynyrd delivered the goods. It would be a few years before "both" of the Stones would play on the same bill, but just now another of the world's top acts was about to enter the picture.

CHAPTER 5

"TURN IT UP"

When Lynyrd Skynyrd emerged in the mid-1970s, glitter rock was coming into vogue, disco was about to take off, and progressive, musically complex bands like Yes and Emerson, Lake and Palmer had reached their peak in popularity. Conventional rock, as embodied in bands like the Rolling Stones, seemed to be at a standstill until, like Superman speeding to the rescue, along came "country rock," or "Southern Rock," as it came to be called, to take back the rock and roll landscape. When applied to Lynyrd Skynyrd, the Allman Brothers Band, ZZ Top, the Marshall Tucker Band, and others, the Southern Rock label had a certain appeal, but it was also largely a misnomer, as explained by the gentleman Southern songster, Charlie Daniels, whose songs and fiddle playing are a staple of classic, good American music, Southern in style with an appeal that's universal. "I never saw [Southern Rock] as a genre of music," Daniels told me, adding that, although rock and roll is based in the blues, which is indigenous to the South, and except for hav-

"YOU DON'T REALIZE HOW MUCH HE ADDS TO THE BACKBONE OF THAT BAND. IF YOU TAKE LEON OUT OF THE EQUATION, IT JUST AIN'T LYNYRD SKYNYRD." (ODUM)

ing Southern accents and making hit records about the same time, each Southern Rock band had a unique style and sound. What these bands did have in common was their social, cultural, and economic background, which served as a natural bond that still connects them today.

Lynyrd Skynyrd was "as pure a rock and roll band as you'll ever find," said Daniels, who has maintained friendships among all of the Southern Rock ensembles. "They don't follow trends and fads and styles. They're much in the tradition of the Rolling Stones, not to compare the two, but that kind of purity. They never took on a tangent." Skynyrd has been compared most often with the Allman Brothers Band, who were really a Southern blues band. But in creating an aggressive, raucous style of their own, Skynyrd helped bring rock and roll back as an American art form, and it wasn't hyperbole when Kooper called them "America's Rolling Stones." The Stones were the band that had most fired Ronnie's imagination, and the music they'd charmed him with was really American blues, which most American kids like him had never heard. The Stones had begun their career by borrowing songs from black artists such as Chuck Berry, Solomon Burke, Bo Diddley, Slim Harpo, John Lee Hooker, Robert Johnson, Jimmy Reed, Howlin' Wolf, and Muddy Waters. But instead of refining it for America's white, mainstream music market, as Elvis Presley, Buddy Holly, Pat Boone, and others had done, the Stones elevated the genre without compromising its down-to-earth character, so that white kids were finally exposed to the power and the soul of the blues. And so, when Ronnie was digging the Stones, he was really savoring the same kind of back-to-the-roots music he'd heard from the likes of "Curtis Loew." When he found out what had nourished the Stones, he went to the table himself—the turntable. Ronnie listened, and in 1973 the world would begin to hear the result.

After *Pronounced* was released in August, Skynyrd's first show out of the box was September 16, 1973, in Jonesboro, Georgia, where they began a twenty-concert tour as an opening act for artists who included Dr. John, B.B. King, the James Gang, John

Mayall, and Muddy Waters. Except for a date with Kooper's Blues Project in New York City's Avery Fisher Hall, most of the shows were small town gigs, and most of them were in the South—Macon and Athens, Georgia; Pensacola, Florida; Ruston, Louisiana; Charleston, Clemson, and Greenville, South Carolina; Springfield, Missouri; Passaic and Princeton, New Jersey; Salem, Virginia; and Burlington, Charlotte, Hickory, Wilmington, and Wingate, North Carolina. Slowly but surely, the message was getting out that Skynyrd was a valued commodity. In *Cashbox* magazine a reviewer wrote, "Watch for this band. Tight, mean and rough, they're one of the few rock acts in the business that really get it on." Toward the end of this two-month jaunt, Kooper met Pete Townshend and manager Peter Rudge of the Who, who were preparing for their *Quadrophenia* tour, and he pitched the idea of adding Skynyrd to the show. In another fortuitous moment for Lynyrd Skynyrd, the Who hadn't signed a warm-up band yet, and Skynyrd seemed a good fit. An unbelievable break. But were they up to it?

In Skynyrd's final show before joining the Who tour, they were supposed to open for Focus, a Danish band, in Atlanta's Omni, on November 18. But Focus never showed up, and neither did many fans. The crowd was so small, in fact, that the Omni's management restricted seating to the area behind the stage. Skynyrd ended up playing through the house PA system, facing the rear of the stage for only a few hundred people. It was an inauspicious start for the daunting challenge that lay ahead: thirteen shows that would test their mettle in a string of dates in major metropolitan settings, including Los Angeles, Dallas, Chicago, Detroit, Boston, Philadelphia, Cleveland, and Montreal. The first of these was on November 20, a sold-out gig in San Francisco's Cow Palace, where 18,000 people had paid to hear world renown recording artists, the Who, and not some upstart band from Jacksonville. Skynyrd had never performed for more than a thousand people at a time, if that many, and now they were about to walk out onto a stage in front of more people than any of them had ever seen in one place before. It was reminiscent of Woodstock in 1969, when Crosby, Stills and Nash had appeared in front of a much larger crowd, and Stephen Stills declared, "We're scared shitless."

Now, for a bunch of small-town boys who were about to play the biggest show of their lives, opening for one of the biggest bands in the world, you might think a little nip or two from the bottle might help to calm some nerves, but surely you wouldn't get drunk. However, that's what the Skynyrd boys did, and somehow they managed to pull it off. They'd grown accustomed to drinking a fair bit already, but from that day forward, their alcohol intake would expand to ludicrous levels. Afflicted with a bad case of stage fright before they even got to the Cow Palace, they started drinking early and didn't ease up until it was time to play. The only one who never looked scared was Ronnie, although he let on later that he wasn't quite as calm as he looked. Ronnie was confident. He'd worked hard to get there and knew his band was ready. As it turned out, the drinking probably helped, but that was the wrong lesson to learn from the experience, and habitual, excessive consumption, if not outright alcoholism, would hurt them all in the years ahead.

By and large, Ronnie and the boys found they could handle the liquor and still perform reasonably well, and that's what counted the most. That night in Frisco, some of the Who's fans tossed coins onto the stage to hurry Skynyrd off, but the crowd grew excited at what they were hearing, and when they finished their set something completely unheard of happened: Lynyrd Skynyrd got encores, which no opening act for the Who had ever done. This was more than enough reason for Townshend and company to accept them as equals, which they did, and then something else happened that made it a night to remember. With the audience overly primed by their opening act, which can be troublesome for any headline act, the Who couldn't take the stage on time because Keith Moon, their drummer, had passed out. They were hoping Bob Burns could sit in for him, but by the time Skynyrd had finished, Bob was too drunk to play any more. So the Who appealed to the crowd for help, and someone from the audience volunteered and became a one-night drummer for the Who.

Except for lukewarm responses in St. Louis, Chicago, Detroit, and Philadelphia, Skynyrd was well received in each of the other venues. In Dallas, they came as close as you can get to an encore, when listeners-turned-fans held up their lighters to show their newfound respect. In Atlanta, just nine days after the show where Focus hadn't showed, Skynyrd was back in the Omni again, but this time everything was different. The place was packed, they played facing forward, and the response from the crowd was spirited. In Boston, where something would always seem to go wrong in the years ahead, either on stage or off, just when the audience was thoroughly entranced by the song that would be their perennial closing number, "Free Bird," the air went out of the bag. In the middle of the song, one of the Who's road crew accidentally knocked out the power to Allen's side of the stage. It was a frustrating way to close out a show for a group of perfectionists like Skynyrd, but the next time it happened the result was different.

On New Year's Eve in Atlanta, an "all-night" party with Lynyrd Skynyrd was advertised for the three-thousand-seat auditorium in the Sheraton Biltmore Hotel, with tickets priced at six bucks in advance and six-fifty at the door. It was obvious they'd oversold the show—one estimate put the crowd at five thousand—but the evening went reasonably well until an MCA employee accidentally kicked out the power for the entire stage for a couple of minutes. This time, however, as soon as the power came back on, Skynyrd started right back up on exactly the same note they were on when the power had gone off. That's how tight they were. These guys were definitely not just a show band; but true musicians of the first order.

In January of 1974, only five months after the release of their debut album, Skynyrd flew to Los Angeles to record a second one. And why not? They'd already recorded "Sweet Home Alabama," which they were sure would become a hit, and they'd already performed in concerts all of the other songs that would appear on the second album. In order to work more closely with the folks at MCA, Kooper chose to record the album in the Record Plant in

Los Angeles, where the presence of celebrities was a little unnerving for a bunch of small town rockers. One day, John Lennon, whom they had idolized, walked into the studio and spoke briefly with Kooper, throwing everyone out of whack for a while. None of the band members actually met Lennon, but the newest member of their road crew did. Stage manager Joe Barnes and Craig Reed, who still works for the band as production manager, had just parked the band's twelve-passenger van after a thirty-eight-hour drive from Jacksonville with the band's equipment. As Reed recalled, "I was walking into the studio, and [Lennon] was walking out, and I said, 'Do you know who you are?' He thought that was pretty funny, and we ended up having lunch together in a restaurant across the street." Inside the studio, the band met Stevie Wonder and Jackson Browne, and Don Henley, Glenn Frey and the rest of the Eagles, who were recording *On the Border*. (In the liner notes for *Second Helping* and *On the Border*, mention of "Wotan and Odin, the Fire Gods" is a reference to characters in a pinball game in the Record Plant studio.) Between recording sessions, Skynyrd did a few shows in California, including a gig with Dave Mason at the Whisky a Go Go in LA, where Clint Eastwood was in the audience, and a stadium show in San Diego with the Eagles and Fleetwood Mac.

Toward the end of their recording sessions, the boys and some of their stage crew showed up unannounced at Kooper's rented house and tossed him into the swimming pool. It was his birthday, and none of them wanted to let it pass without bestowing a boisterous show of affection for their friend and mentor. Three days later, anxious to resume the tour, the band hit the highway again for a six-month, cross-country trek with more than seventy scheduled show dates. As an opening act, Skynyrd was a very marketable commodity by then. Their growing base of fans was a source of additional ticket sales for a number of headline acts, such as Savoy Brown and ZZ Top, the Doobie Brothers, Wishbone Ash, Black Oak Arkansas, and Allen's all-time favorite guitarist, Eric Clapton. One such pairing proved to be a bit of a mismatch, though, when fans of Black Sabbath showed they had no interest in anything but the main event. In the Nassau Coliseum on Long Island, New York, some rather vociferous fans surged toward the stage in a move to get Skynyrd off, only to be turned back in dramatic fashion by a mild-mannered Leon Wilkeson, who fired a shot across their bow, so to speak, from a pistol he'd loaded with blanks. The greater insult came when a "Black Sabbath" sign was lighted behind the stage before the band was done.

The first time they headlined a show came in March, when most of the fans who had packed Memphis Stadium had come to see Lynyrd Skynyrd, and not the scheduled main act, Frank Zappa. A true musical genius whose precision-made music always stood firmly on the cutting edge of rock, the great Zappa was too avant-garde to sell out a stadium, so that when he was unable to make the engagement, Skynyrd had no trouble filling the place. It was a telling precursor to the release in mid-April of *Second Helping,* which drew very favorable reviews, most of which called it a better overall product than *Pronounced.* In addition to having a Top 10 hit, the album had several other first-rate songs, offering everything from laid back, porch swing blues to infectious, high-energy rhythms and blistering three-guitar rock, all with consistently solid production levels. Skynyrd was clearly moving forward in both substance and style, as demonstrated most convincingly with the album's first track. For a band that most people would associate with Southern rock, Lynyrd Skynyrd's all-time biggest hit single was really a country pop song.

Ed, Gary, and Ronnie had written "Sweet Home Alabama" in Hell House on the day that Leon had rejoined the band in June of 1973, after *Pronounced* was finished but not yet released. It had begun the day before, with Gary on acoustic guitar, playing the arpeggio part that would end up behind the verse. That night, all of the solos that would help make Skynyrd famous came to Ed in vivid detail in a dream, and the next day they put it all together, along with "I Need You," which also would appear on *Second Helping.* Four days later, they drove to Atlanta just to record "Sweet

Home," which they completed in an afternoon in Studio One. When they returned to Jacksonville, Ronnie, Allen, and Gary took a copy to their friend, Bill Ferris, who remembers how excited they were when they announced, "This is going to be *the one.*" And how right they were. Ed's catchy opening solo would always bring audiences to their feet, and even today, listeners join Ronnie in his quiet call for the band to "turn it up." Had it not been for the controversy over its lyrics, and the fact that northern radio stations were slow to begin playing a song about Alabama, this good-time sing-along might've made it to No. 1. The only significant change made to the original recording was Kooper's decision to round out the sound with two of the finest female backup singers in the business, Clydie King and Merry Clayton, whose voices have adorned the work of Bob Dylan, the Rolling Stones, Elton John, Carole King, Leon Russell, BB King, and many others.

Ronnie sounds like a doleful Steve Miller in "I Need You," a slow, bluesy, "I miss you, baby" kind of song that Ed and Gary wrote. It was recorded late one night after Bob and Kooper had left the studio, thinking the day's session had ended. Allen and Gary doubled on leads and Ed played rhythm and bass. Sitting in for Bob was musician/songwriter Mike Porter, whose one-hundred-plus album credits include Merle Haggard, Vince Gill, and John Hiatt. On Gary's "Don't Ask Me No Questions," Gary soloed while Ed played slide and bass. Kooper played piano and scored an arrangement for horns, which were played by the much-sought-after brass of Bobby Keyes, Trevor Lawrence, and Steve Madiao. Ronnie's lyrics were a reference to his annoyance at being home on break and getting calls from people asking about the band. Ronnie didn't like to talk "shop" while he was home, but if you mentioned fishing, he would gladly converse all day.

On Ed's rocker, "Workin' for MCA," Allen and Gary doubled on leads, Ed played solo and frills, and Leon sang backup and the "wolfman" growl at the start. This was a *tour de force* for Skynyrd, not only because of the occasion for which it was written (after hearing it, MCA signed with Kooper's Sounds of the South), but

also because it gave every band member an opportunity to show off their virtuosity, including some feathery finger drills from Billy that sounded like some of the *Spirit* album from Spirit. Allen wrote the music for Ed's favorite Skynyrd song, "The Ballad of Curtis Loew," on which Ed used a metal slide for his solo, instead of his usual heavy glass. Gary also soloed, while Kooper played piano and acoustic guitar and sang backup. Ed wrote the funky, honky-tonk "Swamp Music," on which he played fills while Gary soloed. Allen wrote the music to Ronnie's cautionary tale about drugs, "The Needle And The Spoon," a pounding rocker on which Allen sounds so much like Clapton, wah-wah pedal and all, that a casual listener might think it was the exalted master himself.

The band ended the album with one of the only five cover songs that Skynyrd ever recorded, an exhilarating send-up of J.J. Cale's "Call Me The Breeze." Only someone who doesn't like music or rhythm and hates to stand up and clap, wouldn't like this classic crowd-pleaser that ranks among Skynyrd's finest work. Ronnie had wanted to do Cale's version, with a slow-hand beat like Clapton had done with "Lay Down Sally," another song by Cale. But instead, Gary transformed it into a rollicking, good-time rocker that would've become their encore if not for "Free Bird." This was good ol' blues-based rock and roll at its best, perked up Skynyrd-style with a honky-tonk piano and a wall of six-string firepower. Cale's lyrics seemed custom-made for Ronnie, and Kooper's brass arrangement for Keyes, Lawrence, and Madiao helped pack it to the brim with sound.

By the time *Second Helping* was finished, *Pronounced* had become the fourth most frequently played album on FM radio, with its eleven-minute "Free Bird" the most popular track. But even so, sales of *Pronounced* could have been better, a problem attributed to its lack of a major hit single. "Gimme Three Steps" hadn't taken off as a single, and a four-minute version of "Free Bird" also had come up short. This made the choice of a promotional single from *Second Helping* all the more important. Ronnie wanted to release "Sweet Home Alabama" as the first single from the album, but Kooper preferred going with "Don't Ask Me No Questions" instead, thinking "Don't Ask" would fall flat if it followed the much stronger song. Released in April, "Don't Ask" failed miserably as a single. "Sweet Home" was issued in June and quickly rose to No. 8 on the charts. It made *Second Helping* a top-selling album, it catapulted sales of *Pronounced,* and it made Lynyrd Skynyrd a household name. What more could you ask of a song?

Now they had two albums to sell, and the pressure to sell them was pronounced. But this was the kind of pressure performers look forward to having when they first hit the road in the world of big-time rock. The glamour of travel, the parties, the girls. Free food. Free booze. Free drugs. People always providing whatever they might ever want and things they would never need. For Ronnie this was entirely unexpected. He was the kind of guy who never really cared about money. If he had cash in his pocket, other people's money wouldn't count. "I can't let a dollar burn a hole in a seventeen-dollar pair of jeans," he said to me once, when I objected to him buying my dinner, again. A self-described "steak and 'taters man," he always insisted that I order the best cut of meat, and he was never shy about sending a slab of beef back to the kitchen if it wasn't what he expected, even if it was mine and I really didn't care. "You ought to get your money's worth," he'd tell me, and then he'd pay for the meal. Harley Lamoureaux, a longtime friend of the band, recalls Ronnie remarking about the irony of finally having enough money to buy whatever he wanted, and yet people wouldn't let him pay. "Ronnie used to tell me that once he got money, everybody wanted to give it to you, and back when he had no money he had to pay full price for everything," Lamoureaux said. Booze? Pot? Cocaine? Uppers? Downers? Rock stars don't have to go looking for any of that stuff. People just offer it and insist that you take it for free, and everyone with the band reaps the rewards. So it's a rolling party, day after day, week after week, month after month, with little time off between shows.

For rock stars, the glamour of touring is all on the stage; everything else is the burden they carry to get there. To help Skynyrd

handle the pressures of travel, the heavier drinking that had begun at the Cow Palace had become a daily routine. Coupled with the strain of being away from home and practically living on a bus they called "The Great White Wonder," alcohol would figure in many instances of internal strife and external conflict. One such incident happened in San Francisco in May. They had stopped at the Orphanage nightclub, and a curious bystander invaded their space by sticking his head into the door of the bus for a look-see. Ronnie, who was drunk, popped him, probably in a knee-jerk reaction to the chance of theft, which had occurred in the past but wouldn't have figured in this particular instance. The blow knocked the guy out of the bus, and when Ronnie stumbled out after him to finish the job, he was immediately set upon by a few of his victim's friends. Gary hopped out to help, but the decision went to the home team, not the visitors. Throughout the years, unless they were clearly outnumbered and not too drunk to realize it, the boys in the band were rarely reluctant to fight. As often as not, they were the ones who started these altercations, which were usually just outlets for blowing off steam from the rigors of life on the road.

The story of rock and roll touring has been told so many times about so many different groups that it doesn't bear retelling here. But anyone who'd like at least a general sense of what it was like for Skynyrd should see the movie, *Almost Famous*, whose writer and director, Cameron Crowe, got to know Lynyrd Skynyrd, the Eagles, Led Zeppelin, and the Allman Brothers Band while traveling with them as a writer for *Rolling Stone* magazine. Except for the details, it's all there in a nutshell, in the story of a fictional band that Crowe based on the groups he followed. Interviewed about the film, Crowe described the late Ronnie Van Zant as "a very honorable guy," and very fittingly, the Skynyrd song he chose for the soundtrack was "Simple Man."

Almost Famous is one of several movies that have featured songs by Lynyrd Skynyrd. In *Forrest Gump*, the Jenny character ponders suicide with "Free Bird" playing in the background. And

"Free Bird" was the final song on the soundtrack of *Duets*. In *Outside Providence*, "Free Bird" plays in the background while a group of teenagers mourn the death of a friend. In *Con Air*, a prison escapee watches his fellow convicts dancing to "Sweet Home Alabama" and says, "Define irony: It's a bunch of idiots on a plane dancing to the music of a band who died in a plane crash." "Tuesday's Gone" was played in *Boys Don't Cry*, and "That Smell" was a very appropriate choice for the cocaine chronicle *Blow*. "That Smell" also was used on television, on a Saturday Night Live sketch in which Will Ferrell portrayed fact-challenged presidential candidate George W. Bush quoting the "poet" Lynyrd Skynyrd for the verse, "Ooh, that smell. Can't you smell that smell?" in regard to the 2000 vote counting mess in Florida.

Looking for a gimmick that would give the group some panache and a rebellious persona, in 1974, MCA came up with the idea of flying a large Confederate banner on stage, playing upon the distinction conveyed by Kooper's Sounds of the South record label and piggybacking on the popularity of the Allman Brothers Band, who were also Southern boys. As if an entire musical genre could derive from a regional dialect, the notion of Southern rock was born and the rebel flag just naturally followed. It seemed like a good idea at the time, but not every prospective Skynyrd fan was happy to see this divisive symbol. For Skynyrd, the "Southern Cross" generated raucous approval from some of their admirers and total revulsion from others. The band members gave very little thought to it, at first, except for the innocent notion that they were a bunch of rebellious rockers from the South. As a bonus gesture that Ronnie considered a "showbiz stunt," in keeping with the spirit of the defiant image that was concocted for the band, on the Torture Tour he strode onto the stage wearing a Confederate officer's coat and hat.

Whatever effect the rebel image would have on audiences throughout America, when *Second Helping* was released in Great Britain in the middle of May, with the rest of Europe to follow, the best marketing tool for Skynyrd was the play they received on the

radio. Following an initial boost from favorable reviews and a fair amount of air play, word-of-mouth praise made Skynyrd a top-selling band throughout Great Britain, France, Germany, Belgium, and Holland. The only problem with *Second Helping,* wrote a reviewer for *Sounds* magazine, was that it "lacks the bone crushing attack of their debut album, . . . although they manage to retain enough freshness and excitement to keep your arse shaking." (Maybe he was disappointed that "Free Bird" wasn't on it.) Another reviewer called it refreshing, yet understated, showing marvelous musical skills and exceptional good taste. Not bad for their second effort, which peaked at No. 12 on the chart.

On the first of June, Lynyrd Skynyrd shared the stage with the Allman Brothers Band for the "Georgia Jam" in Atlanta-Fulton County Stadium, where they performed for more than 61,000 fans, along with the Marshall Tucker Band and Grinderswitch. It was a great way to start off the summer, but toward the end of the month an unfortunate accident would show that for Ronnie, friendship was more important than fame. Allen's wife called him in Cleveland with the sad news that Larry Steele's younger brother, "Bo," had been killed in a traffic accident. Allen told Ronnie, who immediately said, "Pack it up, it's time to go home." The next day, Allen walked into Larry's house and tried to console him in his frank, "tough love" manner. His first words to Larry were, "Are you just gonna sit there feelin' sorry for yourself? You ought to be celebratin' that Bo ain't here in this hell-hole any more with the rest of us. He deserved better, he got better, and there ain't nothin' you can do about it." His message was harsh but his heart was with Larry, and so was Ronnie's, as his prompt decision had proved.

Friendship lay at the heart of another important decision for Ronnie about this time, as he was thinking of making a personnel change. Bob Burns was a solid drummer and a thoroughly nice guy, but Ronnie had always valued him more as a friend than he had for his musical skills, and he was considering hiring a new drummer and keeping Bob on board as a percussionist. However, it was beginning to be apparent that Bob was having some problems that had nothing to do with music. Earlier in the year, Bob had been involved in an automobile accident on Jacksonville's Buckman Bridge, in which the driver of the other car was killed. This very unfortunate incident affected him a great deal, but something else was troubling him, too, and there were not-so-subtle signs that he was gradually coming unwound. Except for the time they'd spent in the studio recording *Second Helping,* Skynyrd hadn't taken a serious break from the road in almost a year. Everyone needed some rest, so the plan for all of August was to do mainly that, while Ronnie recruited a drummer. As it turned out, the man who would replace Bob at the end of the year would begin the process that month by helping to record Skynyrd's next big single, "Saturday Night Special," which would appear on the band's third album. Thomas Delmar Pyle, whom Charlie Daniels had recommended, would prove to be the right choice, although it would be a few months before he was fully up to speed. In August, after rehearsing with the band in a nightclub they'd rented for that purpose, Pyle joined them in Studio One to record the song. They had to get it out right away, because Kooper had secured a place for it on the soundtrack for the Burt Reynolds movie due out that year, *The Longest Yard.*

Born July 15, 1948, in Louisville, Kentucky, Pyle had the gift of natural rhythm, which he says he remembers pondering as a boy, hearing horses hooves and the mechanical throb of a bulldozer he rode with his grandfather. To nurture his budding interest, Pyle's mother bought her nine-year-old son some bongos, and when he was twelve, his father bought him a set of Slingerland drums he recalls today with great fondness. Pyle played in his high school band and emulated his favorite drummers, Ed Shaugnessy and Gene Krupa. After serving in the U.S. Marine Corps, he enrolled in Tennessee Technical College, not far from Nashville, where he acquired the nickname, Artimus. This was supposedly because he was a baby-faced innocent, a la Artemis, the Greek goddess of chastity, although there was also Artemis Gordon to draw upon, a character in the popular TV show, *The Wild, Wild West,* and there's

an Artemus, Kentucky.) Soft-spoken but energetic, Pyle overcame his cherubic face the same way Leon covered up his, by growing a dense, old-growth forest of a beard.

Larry Steele recalls getting a call from Allen while they were in the studio recording "Saturday Night Special," and Allen said they were thinking of changing drummers. "You gotta hear this guy!" he told Larry, adding, "He plays double kicks that sound like machine guns, and Bob's just actin' too crazy lately . . . And this Artimus takes *acid* before he goes on stage!" to which Larry replied, "And you're tellin' me *Bob* is actin' crazy?" Pyle could play the drums, no doubt, but he wouldn't become a part of Skynyrd until he also had proved he was tough. Aside from enduring many learning sessions at the height of that hot, humid summer in Hell House, the biggest test he would face was practically a trial by fire.

In Jacksonville in late August, when the "dog days" of summer were in full, blast-furnace mode on one of the hottest, muggiest days of the year, Skynyrd played for a charity show in a converted grocery store in the Lakewood Shopping Center. Three cans of food and three bucks got you into Sgt. Pepper's nightclub to see the amazing Lynyrd Skynyrd, who were no longer a local band but real-life rock stars with a growing international following. Every square inch of space was crammed with people, the air conditioning wasn't working, and the stifling humidity of a Florida summer hung heavy in the air. Artimus lasted about a song and a half before he gave out, and as Bob took up the slack he said, "You didn't learn how to do this in the Marines!" When Ed left the stage early to escape the oppressive heat, his hands were pickled from perspiration, as if he'd lingered too long in a hot bath. Leon actually passed out and stage manager Joe Barnes had to carry him outside. "It was hotter than a sauna. It was so hot that duct tape wouldn't stick to itself," Barnes said.

Reviewing the event for the Jacksonville *Journal*, Doreen Dube, a friend of the band from high school, wrote that she had noticed a new air of confidence and poise in the boys. "Gone is the precarious cockiness of vocalist Ronnie Van Zant. He now speaks with his audience rather than to them. No longer does Gary Rossington stand insecurely on stage with his eyes fixed to the floor, his face hidden by a cascade of dark hair. Nor does Allen Collins go flailing about the stage, staring at Van Zant as if waiting for a cue to continue. Each man has developed into a self-assured musician, confident of the group's music and aware of his position within the band."

In mid-November, with Pyle on board for some more on-the-job training, Lynyrd Skynyrd launched a month-long tour of Europe that would mark the end of the line for Bob. In early September in New York City, Joe Barnes recalled, during a reception after Skynyrd had played Avery Fisher Hall with the Blues Project, Bob had chugged a fifth of Jack Daniels on a dare, but everyone figured he didn't have any brain cells left to kill at that point, and anyway, nothing awful happened. But a week later in Richmond, Virginia, Bob ripped the sink from a bathroom wall in a movie theater. That was strike one. (That was the sort of thing done in a hotel room, *not* a movie theater.) Strike two came in England, when he killed a hotel owner's cat by throwing it out of a top floor window. Bob claimed he saw the devil in the cat's eyes. The strikeout came shortly afterward, when he saw the same fiendish look in the eyes of a human being, road manager Russ Emerick. "We were trying to get him to go to the show," said Kevin Elson, the sound engineer. But Bob wasn't having any part of it, and then he suddenly went on the offensive. Spotting a likely weapon at a nearby work site, Bob grabbed a pickaxe and chased Russ down the street. No one got hurt, but it was the end of the line for Bob. Whatever his problems were, they seemed to have started after the band had seen the movie, *The Exorcist,* in Los Angeles, while they were recording *Second Helping.* The subject of the film was satanic possession, and whether or not it had triggered something in Bob, it was shortly after seeing the film that his odd references to Lucifer had begun. He'd also begun mixing whisky with a codeine-based cough medicine, which didn't help matters.

Alcohol continued to be a problem for the rest of the band, too,

unfortunately, and no one seemed to take any lessons from the automobile crashes in which Bob and Billy had been involved. In Billy's accident in Jacksonville, a state trooper's wife was critically injured and almost killed. Ronnie had sense enough not to drive when he was home, but he never caught on that the drinking would catch up to him in other ways. Like an alcoholic in denial, Ronnie once told a reporter the band had a serious problem with alcohol, but in the same breath he repeated almost exactly what he'd told me. "We're really not into alcohol, 'cause when I'm home I only get drunk maybe once a week. When we're on the road, it's different."

They were on the road more than three hundred days a year.

CHAPTER 6

HALL
OF FAME

In what may be one of the great ironies of modern music, the song that launched Lynyrd Skynyrd to the heights of popular acclaim may also have kept them, thus far, from taking their rightful place in the Rock and Roll Hall of Fame.

For almost thirty years now, because of the words to a three-minute song and the pattern on a piece of cloth, Ronnie Van Zant and Lynyrd Skynyrd have been branded as racists. It's an absolutely false assertion for anyone to make, but it's understandable nonetheless, as two average music fans, fifteen years apart, clearly illustrate. When "Sweet Home Alabama" was re-leased in 1974, Wayne Minter was a twenty-four-year-old student at Virginia Commonwealth Univer-sity. His reaction was, "Hey,

SKYNYRD FOUND PERFORMING FOR HUNDREDS OF THOUSANDS OF PEOPLE NO MORE OF A CHALLENGE THAN PLAYING FOR THOUSANDS OR TENS OF THOUSANDS: "ONCE YOU GET PAST THE FIRST FEW ROWS, ALL THOSE PEOPLE ARE REALLY JUST A BLUR," RONNIE SAID. (STEELE)

they're knocking my favorite guy, Neil Young," who he felt was correct on the issue of race. Minter thought the band was saying, "Don't tell us how to live," and he never listened to Skynyrd again. In 1989, the song triggered a similar reaction in someone who had been only four years old when it was new. Upon hearing it for the first time, Jennifer Sieck, a nineteen-year-old student at Davidson College, was appalled that a popular cultural figure would boast about being racist. Both Minter and Sieck feel differently about Lynyrd Skynyrd today, because now they know the truth.

Such is the value of clarity and context in lyrical composition. Ronnie said one thing, but people heard something else. A similar thing happened to Bruce Springsteen several years later. His "Born In The U.S.A." was clearly an anti-war, anti-establishment song, but even conservative politicians rallied around it, and still do, because they didn't get the true message.

How many people still have the same negative impression that Minter and Sieck once shared? And how many of them might there be among the rock and roll historians who serve on the Rock and Roll Hall of Fame Foundation nominating committee, and the one thousand rock experts who comprise their international voting body?

With lyrics that began as a lark, in 1974, "Sweet Home Alabama" put Lynyrd Skynyrd in the Top 10 on the pop charts, boosted sales of their first two albums, and sparked a debate that lingers today. Why the controversy? Because some people took the lyrics the wrong way, and because Skynyrd's marketers chose the boldest symbol of the Old South, the Confederate flag, to brand Lynyrd Skynyrd as genuine "Southern Rock." Ronnie thought the label was too limiting—"We're not a 'Southern Rock' band. We're a rock band from the South," he said later, but it had seemed like a good idea at the time.

By responding to two Neil Young tunes that were critical of racism in the South ("Southern Man" from *After the Gold Rush* in 1970 and "Alabama" from *Harvest* in 1972), some of the lyrics to "Sweet Home Alabama" raised eyebrows. But the racist tag really

stuck when the band associated itself with the Confederate flag and accepted honorary titles as lieutenant colonels in the Alabama State Militia from America's foremost champion of racial segregation, Governor George Wallace.

Some of the lyrics to "Sweet Home Alabama" were meant as a tongue-in-cheek response to Neil Young, whose music the band members loved. In "Southern Man," Young had disparaged slave owners of the previous century, but the song's release in the racially charged atmosphere at the end of the 1960s lent weight to the inference that it was directed at narrow-minded Southerners of the present. And to the extent the inference may have been true, Young was right. But regardless of his intentions, in a lighthearted way Ronnie felt that all Southerners shouldn't be painted with the same brush, even by implication. "Sweet Home Alabama" would have been a hit on its musical merits, alone, but with its biting lyrical retort to Young, controversy naturally followed.

For anyone who listens carefully to both Neil Young songs and to "Sweet Home Alabama," it's clear that Ronnie agreed with Young's message: discrimination is wrong. Ronnie's lyrics imply that Alabama Governor George Wallace was wrong, eleven years earlier, to block African-Americans from attending the University of Alabama. Having lost an earlier election because he'd treated blacks fairly as a judge, Wallace pandered to fear and prejudice in his next campaign and won, but at a price his state would pay in the years to come. In the eyes of the world, Alabama was a cauldron of ignorance and hatred. But in June of 1974, that image was softened somewhat by a toe-tappin' song from some good ol' boys from Florida. Released as a single, "Sweet Home Alabama" quickly rose to No. 8 on the Top 40 chart. Three months later, both the single and the band's newly issued second album, *Second Helping*, became gold records, and by the end of the year, largely due to the popularity of "Sweet Home Alabama," their first album, *Pronounced*, also went gold.

Spurred on by Skynyrd's successes, MCA Records made a marketing decision to feature a Confederate flag behind the band at their concerts, and Lynyrd Skynyrd started opening their shows by playing an upbeat instrumental version of "Dixie." It was meant to symbolize both their Southern rock sound and their rebellious nature, but it had the unintended side effect of furthering a negative connotation that, frankly and unfortunately, some people didn't regard as negative. As if to encourage such sentiments, in 1975, Governor Wallace signed individual certificates for every member of the band, making each of them an Honorary Lieutenant Colonel in the Alabama State Militia. If there were any doubt about the band's "true colors" at the time, the governor's office had made them seem official, even though most critics failed to notice that in 1974 Wallace had won a third term as governor with a huge majority of black votes—a poll commissioned by the University of Alabama and the Birmingham News found that seventy-four percent of blacks considered him "the best governor the state ever had." What had happened was simple math and good politics. Once black voters had showed their strength, Wallace stopped playing to the fears of poor whites and started championing the rights of those whom Ronnie Van Zant identified with most: poor people, regardless of color. In later years Wallace criticized President Ronald Reagan for creating a "crippling" tax structure in which "the rich got richer while the poor and the middle class didn't get anything at all," and Ronnie would have agreed with him.

As for their honorary titles in the state militia, however, Ronnie called it a "bullshit gimmick thing." Leon Wilkeson probably best summed up the band members' feelings when he said, "I support Wallace about as much as your average American supported Hitler." Wallace was a skillful politician, and in all likelihood it was his political acumen that motivated him to honor Lynyrd Skynyrd for refining his state's image with a great song. Either he actually heard it and liked it, or, more likely, one of his aides saw an opportunity to capitalize on the band's success. Either way, there were a lot of Lynyrd Skynyrd fans in Alabama at the time, and Wallace figured that some of them might be voters.

As for the rebel flag, except for the racial animosity that it

clearly represents for some people, some folks fly it for other reasons that only Southerners can appreciate, even if they can't articulate it in a way that others would understand. After losing the Civil War, it was only natural for Southerners, the majority of whom had never owned slaves, to want to believe that they had fought not to preserve an ignoble institution, but to further some noble cause, such as states' rights. Today, many people who wave the flag are carrying on that tradition; they're proud to be Americans who live in the South. I mention this historical perspective because of speculation that lingering suspicions of racism may be keeping Lynyrd Skynyrd from being inducted into the Rock and Roll Hall of Fame. If there's any truth to this notion, the selection committee should know how Ronnie really felt. They should also listen to "Curtis Loew," Ronnie Van Zant's heartfelt tribute to an awful lot of talented artists who, in their day, never had an opportunity to be in anyone's hall of fame.

Despite the veracity in Ronnie's anti-racist views, it's also true that he really didn't put much thought into writing "Sweet Home Alabama." In fact, he said he wrote it as "a joke." Song lyrics came quickly and easily for Ronnie, and this song was no exception. He was simply making a record; everyone else had made a big deal of it. Before recording "Sweet Home Alabama," Ronnie asked Ed King how he thought Neil Young might react, and Ed said he thought he'd get a kick out of it, and Ed was right. Wanting to put Lynyrd Skynyrd's rebellious image behind them, Ronnie eventually stopped flying the rebel banner at concerts, and Lynyrd Skynyrd stopped playing "Dixie" to open their shows. He continued to be a Neil Young fan, and he often wore a Neil Young T-shirt on stage. Young, who loved "Sweet Home Alabama" the first time he heard it, actually sang it a couple of times during his own concerts, including a wonderful tribute during a show that followed Lynyrd Skynyrd's airplane crash. He said he was proud to have his name in such a great song. Earlier that year, by way of *Rolling Stone* writer Cameron Crowe, he had sent Ronnie a tape with three of his new songs to see if Skynyrd might use one on *Street Survivors*, but

"Powderfinger," "Captain Kennedy," and "Sedan Delivery" just didn't fit the scheme for the album.

Whatever anyone might think of Lynyrd Skynyrd's image, it was the power of their music that made them popular on three continents. That's why they deserve a place of distinction in the Rock and Roll Hall of Fame. One of the functions of the Rock and Roll Hall of Fame Foundation is to recognize the contributions of those who have had a significant impact on the evolution, development and perpetuation of rock and roll by inducting them into the Hall of Fame. In each of these areas of accomplishment, and particularly with the contribution they've made to perpetuating rock as a form of musical expression, Lynyrd Skynyrd merits induction into the Rock and Roll Hall of Fame.

While "Sweet Home Alabama" spawned record sales and controversy, another song on *Second Helping*, "The Ballad of Curtis Loew," probably generated more fascination than any other Lynyrd Skynyrd tune, even though it was performed only once in concert by the band's original lineup, on stage in a hotel basement. A quiet country blues number about "the greatest picker who ever played the blues," it's a song that continues to evoke strong feelings among devoted Skynyrd fans. One such loyal listener is an earnest young man who, when he overheard plans for this book being discussed in a restaurant, expressed his fervent hope that it would tell the story of "Curtis Loew." A few minutes later, the song came on the radio. So here's the whole story.

Although Ronnie may have had an actual "Curtis" in mind when he wrote this song, he chose "Loew" because its single syllable "o" sound perfectly fit the verse. Loew's Normandy Drive-In Theater on Normandy Blvd. was a familiar spot on Jacksonville's Westside, and when Gary Rossington suggested "Loew" for that spot in the song, Ronnie put it in. For Ronnie, "Curtis Loew" was a man he had known for most of his life, but he was also a composite of several people.

"Curtis Loew" was mostly about Claude H. "Papa" Hamner, who owned a small, neighborhood grocery store where Ronnie and

I played and worked as boys, and who could have been a musical star if he'd ever wanted to try. But the fanciful "Curtis Loew" is also about Rufus "Tee-Tot" Payne, an old black man who inspired country music star Hank Williams; it's about legendary blues guitarist Robert Johnson; and it's about Shorty Medlock, whose son, Rickey, played drums on some of Lynyrd Skynyrd's Muscle Shoals recordings and later joined the band full-time on guitar. In masking his childhood hero in color and verse, along with these other musical idols, Ronnie Van Zant revealed a lot about himself, including his love for the purity of expression he found in country and blues music, his respect for hard working men of every color, and his ardent wish to be like them and be held in the same regard. Foremost among them was Claude Hamner, whose Woodcrest Grocery was just a short walk from Ronnie's boyhood home at the corner of Woodcrest Road and Mull Street.

Raised on a farm in Colquitt County in south central Georgia, Claude Hamner moved to nearby Adel in 1939 and bought two hundred and fifty acres of land for twenty-five cents an acre. Clearing twenty-five acres with a mule, he planted a crop and built a house with timber he cut from the land. In 1952 he and his wife, Ollie Mae, sold the property and moved to Jacksonville, Florida, where he worked for the railroad until he opened a grocery store in the late 1950s. While he was farming, Claude taught himself to play guitar, although he never learned to read music. If you could hum it, he could play it, and Claude loved picking an old steel dobro and singing "The Zoo Went to the Ballgame," "Wildwood Flower," and other songs for his children, Vernon, Gene, Betty, and Glenda, and for all of the neighborhood kids. Glenda remembers evenings when children would hang around the store hoping to see Claude, and fretting if "Papa" was off that night. Mrs. Hamner, who turned eighty-eight in April of 2002, still has a photo of Ronnie that he gave her when he was a boy. She remembers him coming to the store at the age of eight or nine, fresh from playing "tadpole" baseball, and for years afterward, often just to ask Claude to play for him. "My dad taught Ronnie Van Zant and 'Red' Odom (my older brother) how to play guitar," Vernon Hamner said, adding that his father called Ronnie his "bottle boy," as that was his job, sorting empty soda bottles by brand, as well as sweeping the store every day and doing other odd jobs.

"They'd do anything in the world for Claude; they thought the world of him," Mrs. Hamner said, noting that other boys sometimes stole bottles from the store and took them elsewhere for the two-cent deposit. "The Van Zants were really good people who taught their children right from wrong," Glenda said, recalling that Ronnie's mother had a great sense of humor. In 1963, Claude and his son, Vernon, opened a second store, Claude's Midway Grocery, about a quarter of a mile away at the intersection of Lake Shore Boulevard and Plymouth Street, where Ronnie had caught the bus to Lee High School, and where he had staged his amateur boxing matches. ("Midway" was halfway between Normandy Blvd. and San Juan Avenue.) They sold the Woodcrest store about a year later, but Claude kept the Midway grocery open until just about the time Lynyrd Skynyrd's first record album came out. "Ronnie Van Zant thought a helluva lot of my dad," Vernon said, noting that as an adult, Ronnie often visited Claude when he was back in town from touring. When Lynyrd Skynyrd's second album was released, hearing "The Ballad of Curtis Loew" on the radio for the first time, Vernon's son, Jesse, was thrilled to say, "That's about 'Papa'." That same week, Ronnie's friend, Bill Ferris, also heard the song for the first time while he and Ronnie were fishing. "Listen to this!" Ronnie exclaimed, when it came on the radio.

When Ronnie died, Claude and Vernon went to the funeral home to say their good-byes. When Claude Hamner died in 1985, at the age of sixty-seven, he was buried near Ronnie.

To the extent that "Curtis Loew" was any other person Ronnie actually knew, it was also Shorty Medlock, a popular Florida country/bluegrass musician of the 1950s and the father of Rickey Medlocke (Shorty was really Rickey's grandfather; he adopted Rickey, who added the "e"s to his name). The son of a north Georgia sharecropper, Shorty played guitar, dobro, banjo, fiddle, and

harmonica. He was a regular performer on a weekly musical TV program in Jacksonville, *The Toby Dowdy Show*, where Rickey played banjo when he was six years old. During the time that Rickey was recording and performing with Lynyrd Skynyrd in 1971, Shorty sometimes played for Ronnie, Allen, and Gary on his front porch, and his wife, Ruby Juanita, loved to have them visit. Ronnie dedicated Lynyrd Skynyrd's third album, *Nuthin' Fancy*, to Shorty, who inspired the song, "Made in the Shade," having told the boys that if you work hard and believe in yourself, that's how life will turn out. Shorty played banjo and harmonica on every album recorded by Rickey's band, Blackfoot, and he played with them until his death in 1982. Three years earlier, they had made a hit of Shorty's "Train, Train," written in 1970. Ruby Juanita passed away in 1994.

When Ronnie wrote this memorial ballad, "Curtis Loew," he was thinking of every front porch picker he'd ever heard or had even heard of, some of whom had made a name for themselves, like Robert Johnson and Muddy Waters, but most of whom had not. He knew that, although he'd worked hard to become successful, he'd also been very fortunate. He'd been in the right place at the right time with just the thing that someone else valued, which doesn't always happen with music. A country music lover at heart, Ronnie also loved the blues, and he understood where the blues came from. Having grown up in a poor neighborhood with a poor black family living just a couple of blocks away, Ronnie was very much aware that many talented blues artists had never had the opportunities that he had, simply because they were black. And so, to honor them all, along with the men he'd known, Ronnie made "Curtis" an old black man with white curly hair.

Such was the variety to be found in Lynyrd Skynyrd, as first-time listeners would soon discover. In *Second Helping*, after hearing "Sweet Home Alabama" on the radio, Skynyrd neophytes encountered not only a depth of lyrical expression, as confirmed in "Curtis Loew," but a richness of composition. In songs like "Workin' for MCA" and a rousing send-up of J.J. Cale's "Call Me The Breeze," aficionados of traditional rock and roll found the hard charging, back-to-the-basics rock they'd been missing. Once they came up for air after playing the album over and over, their craving for more was quenched for the moment in *Pronounced,* where a song that would catapult the band even further had been lying in wait for several months. It was "Free Bird," which, along with Led Zeppelin's "Stairway To Heaven," would receive more radio play than every other American song from the 1970s.

With two strong albums out, what would they do next? Toward the end of 1973, Skynyrd bought out their contract with Walden and signed with Peter Rudge, who managed the Who and the Rolling Stones, and Kooper sold his interest in Skynyrd to MCA. This set the stage for a new record album, because MCA wanted one before the end of January, when they were scheduled to hit the road again. Skynyrd wanted Kooper to produce their third album, so they returned to Atlanta. But this time they would work in Bang Records Webb IV Studios, where they would have exactly three weeks in which to make a record. "Saturday Night Special" had already been recorded, but only one other song, "On The Hunt," was even under way. The rest would have to come in a flurry of forced collaboration, and it would have to come soon.

Already weary from touring, the band set out on a mission that was almost guaranteed to fail. Working sixteen-hour days, every day, for twenty-one days, was a helluva way to make music. And yet, despite a product that Ronnie considered pallid, it was certified gold within three months of its release on March 24, and *Billboard* called the album Skynyrd's strongest overall effort. A review in *Melody Maker* called Ronnie "a singer of consummate ability with a fine delivery," and praised the band for delivering the "same lunky, tight, controlled aggression, same excellent sense of timing, same drive." But for some it didn't rock hard enough. After praising its "powerhouse rhythms [that] don't let up throughout the album," a reviewer for *Sounds* magazine was disappointed "because, rightly or wrongly, you expect a band like Lynyrd Skynyrd to wipe the floor with you every time." Ronnie said *Nuthin' Fancy* was nothing special, but he was always overly critical of himself. This album was no mean achievement. In fact, it was the biggest challenge yet for Skynyrd, and they had clearly passed the test. Having "Saturday Night Special" already down on tape was a blessing when MCA assigned them to do the album, but composing seven more songs in just three weeks—none of them throwaways—was truly a mark of achievement.

When it comes to the subject of handguns, no one has ever written a song as strongly worded as "Saturday Night Special," which Ronnie conceived while Ed was leading the band in an arrangement he'd put together. It was the kind of strong-arm rocker that fans had come to expect, with a contentious message they hadn't foreseen. Ronnie's serious tone was matched in severity by the vigor of Ed's rhythm and Gary's solo work, while Kooper summoned an eerie glissando sizzle from a Moog synthesizer for a hint of the touch of death. Ronnie liked the effect and said it sounded like an airplane crashing. But some Skynyrd fans drew back when they heard this song, thinking their man Ronnie was advocating gun control. As he told me, he was simply stating a fact: you can't fire a small-caliber weapon with any accuracy, which makes it worthless for hunting and inadequate for self-defense. All it's good for is killing somebody up close, which, all too often, happens in domestic disputes. In any case, it was already a part of a major motion picture, *The Longest Yard,* and it would spend ten weeks on the Top 40 singles list and help *Nuthin' Fancy* reach No. 9 on the album chart.

On the album's second track, "Cheatin' Woman," Ronnie pursued this theme further with a first-person account of a man betrayed, who thinks shooting his lover will end his pain. Helpless to stop him, listeners are helped to carry his burden with a searing slide guitar by Ed, and Allen capped it off with a solo that seems to ask "Why?" Gary and Ronnie wrote this song with Kooper, who played organ and piano.

"Railroad Song" is an upbeat country song that Ronnie came up with while listening to Ed play a piece he'd just composed. "It sounds to me like the song should be about a train," Ed said, and fifteen minutes later, Ronnie had it all figured out. "Ronnie never wrote anything down, *ever*. As long as the band could remember the music, the lyrics would always come back to him," Ed said. At least three times during the course of this whirlwind recording session, while the band was playing too loud for normal conversation, Ronnie thought up lyrics on the spot and sang them into Ed's ear. "I can remember hearing 'Saturday Night Special' this way and my jaw dropping. He was an inspiration," Ed said. Ed played all of the guitar parts on "Railroad Song," except for a solo from Allen; and Jimmy Hall, the lead singer for Wet Willie, stepped in to play harmonica. Kooper played organ, and he and Leon sang the "choo-choo train" chorus. Ronnie's vocals managed to bring both Mick Jagger and Leon Russell to mind in the same song, which borrowed a beat from "Tax Man" by the Beatles and ended with a slowed-down harmonica that recalled "Midnight Rambler" by the Stones.

"I'm A Country Boy" is an unlikely name for a hard-funk rocker that would never be mistaken for the country boy ditty that John Denver had recorded the previous year. This song by Allen highlighted the power of Skynyrd's three-guitar arsenal, with Allen on lead (there's a clear harbinger here of "Cult of Personality," which Living Colour would record twenty years later), Gary on rhythm, and Ed on slide. Kooper played percussion, Leon sang backup, and, as on every song on the album, Artimus's strong, steady drumming is inspired and creative. Allen also wrote the slow rocker, "On the Hunt," an echo of "The Hunter" by Free, on which Ronnie sang like Paul Rodgers and Gary soloed in a continuing nod to his favorite guitarist, Paul Kossoff.

"Am I Losin'?" is an easygoing country song and probably the best overall cut on the album. Although Ronnie was thinking of Bob Burns when he wrote the lyrics, Gary had Elvis Presley in mind when he'd first imagined the music. Elvis had sent each member of the band a dozen roses after they'd broken his attendance record for Memphis Stadium in March and July of 1974, but when they went to Graceland to thank him, Elvis wasn't home.

That's when Gary started working on this song. He and Ed played acoustic guitars on it, which brings to mind some of the Allman Brothers' lighter moments. Ed had a wonderful solo that sounds a little like Dickie Betts, with just a brief echo of "Sweet Home Alabama" thrown in for good measure. Kooper sang backup for Ronnie, whose voice was soft, smooth, and sincere.

"Made In The Shade," which Ronnie dedicated to Shorty Medlock, had a sort of natch'l, Tennessee hill country feel from the turn of the last century. To achieve that rustic, backwoods sound, the band played a number of offbeat instruments. Artimus played a big bass marching drum, a tambourine, and a wooden soft drink crate; Ed produced a powerful tuba sound on a Moog synthesizer; and Kooper played piano. The song needed a mandolin, a dobro, and a harmonica, so Ronnie called on a friend of his in Jacksonville, Barry Harwood, who would join the group a few years later, and Jimmy Hall came from Macon to play harmonica. In tenor voice, Ronnie sang in the Deep South style of Leon Redbone, even giving out a yodel at one point. It was the only Skynyrd song that Kooper would ever cover on any of his own records. Next comes some honky-tonk dance rock in "Whiskey Rock-A-Roller," the only song that was credited to Billy, along with Ronnie, and Ed. When Kooper mixed the album later in California, on this shuffle with a bouncy beat he overdubbed a piano part played by David Foster, a musician, composer, arranger, and holder of fourteen Grammy awards.

Anyone buying a Skynyrd album for the first time, expecting to hear only hard driving rock, would get not just a good rocking on *Nuthin' Fancy*, but an education in the roots of rock as well, with four good songs from country and blues. Once again, there was a rich variety in composition, styles, and vocals, and even though it had come together in just three weeks, to a layman's ear it doesn't sound contrived or hurried. A reviewer in *Rolling Stone* wrote that Skynyrd was "an important group whose populist character, no-frills intelligence, and resolute directness place it closer to

Creedence [Clearwater Revival] than to the superficially more similar Allman Brothers Band. . . . Creedence with firepower—this is a band with a future."

Lynyrd Skynyrd's rise to stardom would continue, but for Leonard Skinner, the future would become a mixed blessing. After leaving the teaching profession in 1970, Leonard Skinner had become a real estate broker and opened an office that he "modestly named 'Leonard Skinner Realty.' " Asked if he was capitalizing on the band's success, he smiled and shook his head. "You'd be surprised at how many high school and college kids weren't buying houses back then," he said. Before *Nuthin' Fancy* was released, MCA Records contacted Skinner to ask if they could use a photo of one of his real estate signs on the record album. That would be just fine, he said, but he may have spoken too soon.

"I got the first call at four o'clock in the morning from a guy in California," Leonard began. When the caller asked, "Who's this?" Leonard answered sleepily, "Leonard Skinner," and the caller responded, "Far out." It was the first of "thousands" of calls he would receive in the months and years that followed the album's release, some from as far away as Sweden, and some from females who "made some outlandish offers," Leonard said, adding, "When I come back next time, I'm going to be a rock star." He and his wife and some friends took a cruise shortly afterward, and on their last night at sea, when the winners of the week's recreational events were announced over the ship's public address system, Leonard's name was called for ping-pong. The next day, more than fifty people lined up to get his autograph, the first of thousands he would sign in the years to come. It was a lot more fun than the phone calls.

After *Nuthin' Fancy* was finished, Kooper and the band would remain friends, but he would cease to be their producer. On the final day of recording he headed for California to mix the album, and they immediately set off on the first leg of their well-named "Torture Tour." More travel, more work, and no rest for the weary after a very taxing time in the studio, and it would all catch up to

them soon, as drinking and fighting began to overshadow the performing. In negative terms, it was a record year for Skynyrd— nine concerts canceled, including five that were scrubbed before the end of May, when Ed finally had enough. Ronnie, who was arrested for drunkenness five times that year, simply became too unpleasant for Ed, who was having problems of his own in the form of cocaine, which he had tried to keep under wraps. On one occasion in April, in Lake Charles, Louisiana, a drunken Ronnie tried to knock down the door of the hotel room in which Ed was quietly feeding his habit, and he wouldn't answer the door. The worst of it came in May, when Ed left in the middle of the night after a concert in Pittsburgh's Syrian Mosque had ended badly. Before they'd finished "Free Bird," every guitar had broken strings, and Ronnie blew his top. "In the middle of tour, I said, 'I've had it' and walked out," Ed recalled. "I've never regretted leaving, but I shouldn't have left the way I did. What a jerk . . . I wish we could've parted on easier terms."

His frustration stemmed from the same controlling factor that burdened everyone equally. Peter Rudge had scheduled the band for too many gigs without any time off. It was as if they were slaves, with no time for anyone to get away from the others for a breath of air and an opportunity to think. At one point, according to Ed, Allen and Gary broke down and wept from the strain of being bone-tired and desperate to go home but knowing they had to stay. For a while, the guys traveled from hotels to concerts by themselves, to avoid the tension that was in the air. The straw that broke the camel's back for Ed was Ronnie, who was drinking way too much and becoming abusive to everyone around him. "Ronnie was two people. When he was straight, he was one of the finest people I'd ever met. When he was drunk, he was a mad man. Unfortunately, towards the end of my tenure with the band, he was drunk the whole time. That's mainly why I left. Working with him just wasn't fun anymore, and he was the only reason I wanted to join the band anyway," Ed said. Allen and Gary called him later, but he never spoke with Ronnie again. If Ronnie had asked, Ed probably would have returned, so it was good for him that he didn't, or Ed would have been on the airplane, instead of the equally gifted artist who would replace him in 1976, Steve Gaines.

And so, the tour kept on going, and Ronnie and company kept on drinking. And fighting. In Louisville, Kentucky, in June, Ronnie punched Billy in the mouth and knocked out two front teeth. Hearing Billy and the road manager arguing outside his hotel room, Ronnie opened his door wearing only a towel and told them to stop. Billy said he should mind his own business, in so many words, and Ronnie put them both on the floor, losing his towel in the process and exposing hotel guests to the sight of a naked rock star. Four days later in Charlotte, Ronnie collapsed back stage after a show, and a week after that, in Jacksonville, on the final night of this terribly exacting tour, the booze and the yelling came to a head for Ronnie, and the result was an actual riot. Ronnie had never learned to sing from his gut; he'd always sung from his throat, which can be done for only so long before it wears out. He'd worn out his throat before, but this was their sold-out, homecoming show with the Charlie Daniels Band, which should have been a fabulous night for all. Skynyrd hadn't gotten very far into their act when Ronnie started coughing up blood and had to leave the stage. This greatly displeased some of the folks in the audience, who tossed bottles onto the stage, forcing a hasty retreat by the band. The police arrested sixteen youths, some of whom had damaged Skynyrd's equipment and broken windows on their way out of the Jacksonville Coliseum. One officer was hurt when he fell to the ground and was kicked, and at least one police dog earned his chow that day by mangling a young man's arm. All in all, it was a pretty ugly sight.

But at long last, they had forty glorious days off. Time for lots of sleeping and fishing, not quite as much drinking and snorting, and no arguing or fighting. Ronnie and Gary could hit the river in their bass boat, "Bad Company," and everyone's transgressions would be forgotten.

Back on the road, life was moderately more pleasant than it

had been before the break, but there were constant reminders that Ed was no longer there. His departure had left a very large hole in the program. Ed had been a real blessing for the band, both musically and in terms of group dynamics. He'd been a key ingredient, and in some cases *the* critical component, in some of the band's most commercially successful songs. And until the quarreling had begun, he'd also been a source of calm. Before Ed had entered the picture, practice sessions under Ronnie's stern direction were often filled with tension. Once Ed was on board, rehearsals were initially much more relaxed, and everyone seemed to have an extra measure of confidence. Ed also asserted himself as a leader, which took some of the pressure off Ronnie, and no one could fail to see the benefits. Now, without him, the three-guitar army was missing not only an entire division, but a top ranking officer and a fountain of creative talent, as would become apparent very soon, when it was time to create a new album.

The loss of Ed King was especially troubling for Ronnie, for whom it was both a personal and a professional failure. You just don't alienate a respected friend who is also a creative spark for your band, but that's what Ronnie had done, and he had only himself to blame. Although he never admitted that he'd made a mistake, the frustration he felt was palpable, as was evident on the night he told Leon to destroy the guitar that Ed had left behind. Ed had taken all of his guitars but his Fender jazz bass, which he'd left for Leon to use. One night on stage, while Allen and Gary were playing the closing bars of "Free Bird," Ronnie walked over to Leon, looked him in the eyes, and told him to smash it to smithereens. Leon hesitated for a moment, and then he grabbed it firmly by the neck and slammed it into the floor. He didn't want to do it, but he didn't want to cross Ronnie, who would've done it himself if Leon hadn't. At least this way, it might appear to be only a part of the act, just a touch of the Who coming out in a band where showmanship was usually subtle, at best—Ronnie paced around in bare feet, often hoisting a microphone stand or a whisky bottle; Allen jumped up and down sometimes; Artimus was always in motion, of course, but seated; and Leon was never without a hat. Other than that, Skynyrd's showmanship was all in their music, and for bands that had to follow them, that was always more than enough.

In September of 1975, Skynyrd was supposed to open for the Kinks in Fresno, California, but the Kinks bowed out. The talk around the band was that the Kinks hadn't wanted to be upstaged by Skynyrd, especially when their final number was always "Free Bird." Whether or not that's why they canceled, Skynyrd was always a tough act to follow. "Their attitude was to play their asses off and be able to say, 'Follow that!' " stage manager Joe Barnes said. Even so, on some nights they failed to hit the mark, usually due to drunkenness, fighting, or some other unprofessional conduct, although most of their audiences probably never even noticed. "On what they would raise hell about as being a bad night, ninety-nine percent of the time it was still better than anybody we played with. Very few bands were as consistently good as they were, and on their great nights it was really exciting. They had half a dozen to a dozen bad shows over the three and a half years I was with them," said Barnes, who was with them from mid-1973 until November of 1976. During concerts, whenever someone was inebriated and making too many mistakes, the instant solution was always available and often employed. "I'd just turn 'em off," said Kevin Elson, who mixed sound for the band. "Ronnie always said, 'Just turn 'em off if they're messin' up.' "

As strict as Ronnie always was about rehearsing, once they were up on a stage performing, it rarely seemed to matter to him how drunk they were, unless they committed the cardinal sin of screwing up noticeably in a crucial part of their set, and then he would explode in a tirade immediately after the show. For the most part, however, Ronnie knew that his boys never set foot on a stage without being so thoroughly well rehearsed that they could go through their repertoire practically in their sleep. His goal had been to get them there, but once they'd arrived, he was often drunk himself.

LYNYRD SKYNYRD

CHAPTER 7

RUNNING ON AUTOPILOT

The approach of fall brought the call for a new album, as Skynyrd owed MCA one more under contract, plus a live album or a compilation of "greatest hits." With Al Kooper gone, Peter Rudge wanted Skynyrd's next producer to be Tom Dowd, whose impressive portfolio of clients included Aretha Franklin, Otis Redding, Wilson Pickett, Rod Stewart, Cream, Eric Clapton's Derek and the Dominoes, and the Allman Brothers Band. Dowd had been an important part of some of the most commercially successful records of the previous decade, but all of his experience and credentials would prove to be less than Skynyrd would need for their fourth album, and more than they could handle. Dowd was twenty years older than Ronnie and a wise old man in the eyes of the band, who were so awed by his reputation that they would mistakenly place themselves almost entirely in his hands, with none of the heated arguments they'd waged with Kooper, who at four years older than Ronnie had been practically a member of the group.

"To understand Lynyrd Skynyrd, you have to understand Ronnie Van Zant, who, at the peak of his success, was still the same person he was when he started out." (Odum)

The process of making a record is typically one of give-and-take, in which ideas converge but often clash, as occurred with great regularity on each of Skynyrd's first three albums. Kooper had made some excellent calls in those very successful efforts, but he also had lost some debates with the band, and the albums were much better because of their confrontations. Their fourth album, *Gimme Back My Bullets,* would have been better if they hadn't surrendered their normally good instincts to the notion that a producer could always be right. It also would've been better if they had been able to take a little more time with it, and if they had been fortunate enough to have a smash-hit single.

Despite what he sang in the title song—that he'd been drinking too much because of the pressure, but now he was on the mend—on this album Ronnie was practically running on autopilot. He was tired, he wasn't up to battling in a studio any more, and he wanted someone else to handle some of the decision-making for a while. His attitude became, "These are good songs, we're still Lynyrd Skynyrd, and I hope people will like it." People did like it, but the quality of the recording simply came up short. Actually, the more the album is heard, the more likable it is. They're all good songs and the musicianship is fine. It just lacked the spark of their earlier work and only approximated the hard-rock romps that fans had come to expect, although "Searching" came very close.

Dowd met the band in September after hearing them perform in Long Beach, California. The opening act was Peter Frampton, whose phenomenally successful live album, *Frampton Comes Alive,* was about to be released. During the next three days, Skynyrd joined Dowd in the Record Plant in Los Angeles to record the initial takes on three new songs, "Cry For The Bad Man," "Double Trouble," and "Every Mother's Son," and a cover of "I Got The Same Old Blues" by J.J. Cale. There was hardly enough time to get acquainted, but Rudge needed another album to sell, and time was in short supply for a band with a long list of scheduled bookings. Aware of their wild reputation, Dowd wisely set some ground rules at the start, declaring that if they wanted to work with him it would

have to be on his terms, with set hours for rehearsing and zero tolerance for drunkenness. The boys were ready to do as he wished, but they weren't fully prepared to record, which would be true for the entire album. Dowd was dismayed to find that they were willing to fiddle with songs in the studio instead of coming to work with thoroughly rehearsed arrangements. Their success with *Nuthin' Fancy* had made them think they could "wing it" in the studio again and score another home run, but they couldn't have been more wrong.

Critiquing *Gimme Back My Bullets*, Kooper observed that it had missed the mark for two reasons: it lacked his insight into how to enhance their sound, and it lacked Ed King, whose creativity and leadership had proved to be the missing link in Skynyrd's evolution. Ed's absence remained a festering wound for Ronnie, whose lingering self-reproach for alienating Ed would reveal itself in acts of senseless aggression when he'd had too much to drink, which was basically every day, although never in the studio with Dowd. But before they could finish the record, there were dates to play in western states, and three weeks to tour through Western Europe. Headlining abroad for the first time, Skynyrd was well received in Rotterdam, Holland; in Belique and Brussels, Belgium; and in Soarbrucken, Mannheim, Frankfurt, and Dusseldorf, Germany, before their return to England, where they'd built up not only a huge base of fans but a rowdy reputation as well. As if to confirm their status as roughnecks, on the eve of a four-night stand in Portsmouth, Ronnie erupted in a fit of drunken rage, injuring himself, Gary, and John Butler from the road crew. Without warning, he cracked John's head with a beer bottle, and in the melee that followed, Gary's left hand and both of his wrists were cut badly. Ronnie wound up with a broken hand and a bruised windpipe—Gary played the next ten shows with just two fingers on the frets, which was really quite a feat. Who knows what the fight was about? It started with an argument about how to pronounce "schnapps."

The next night, the walking wounded delivered what felt like a flop. But the fans and the critics loved it. One reviewer wrote, ". . . if what they think is bad is in reality quite good, think what they'll be like on a good night. Barring any more rounds of schnapps, of course." Another reviewer called them the best band he'd heard in a long time, adding, "If this were a bad performance, I can't wait for a good one." Beneath a magazine photo of the band, a caption read, "When a band starts slashing each other's wrists before gigs you know they're confident." Ever in denial about the full effects of his drinking, Ronnie refused to accept any blame and laid the onus on Billy for having his amp too loud. He could be that way, sometimes.

But there were plenty of good times, too. For Skynyrd, distractions often came in the form of antics and pranks, which usually were meant to try your patience and usually did, but they didn't always lead to fights. Just for sport, someone would instigate trouble and then implicate someone else. Leon, for example, would toss unlit matches or tiny wads of paper into Billy's hair and point to Allen or Gary as the offender, all the while singing a little verse he'd made up, "Little tiny wads hiding in the briar patch." Allen's idea of fun was less benign. Using his middle finger as if he were flicking a bug, he'd surprise his victims by thumping them in the ear or nose or just below the knee. With those long, powerful fingers of his, it felt like getting hit with a rock, and then, to avoid a counterattack, he'd offer a friendly grin. Other ongoing diversions were the swirling currents of sexual intrigue in the ever-present "soap opera," as they called it, the incessant, mindless melodrama of who was doing what with whom. Although spouses and children accompanied the band on some excursions, those were the exceptions to the "No wives on the road" policy for the married men who were miles from home thinking no one would ever know. The only story I'll tell is something that happened to Ronnie one night, because he laughed about it later and explained it away to too much booze. Bursting from his hotel room with a stunned look on his face, he stammered, "She ain't . . . She's a - a - a he! . . . It's a, it's a he! . . . Oh, man!"

One way or another, travel with Lynyrd Skynyrd was never

uneventful, and because it was show business, the show would have to go on. Battered and bruised for their opening night in Portsmouth, they played out their schedule there and went on to electrify crowds in Birmingham, London, Brighton, Liverpool, and Sheffield. Then they filled the first week in November with engagements in Glasgow, Scotland; Oxford, England; Cardiff, Wales; London again and Paris. Then it was home for the holidays and a couple of weeks with their families. But normalcy such as that would be short-lived, because just as their loved ones were feasting on Thanksgiving leftovers, the boys in the band were bound for Capricorn Studios, in Macon, Georgia, where the pressure-filled weeks in Studio One were only a distant memory. Compared with the tense times they'd had recording *Nuthin' Fancy,* the atmosphere with Dowd was like a refreshing soak in a hot tub. And that was part of the problem, although no one realized it at the time.

The song that became the album's title, "Gimme Back My Bullets," has nothing to do with ammunition and everything to do with yearning for recognition. "Bullets" were symbols of success in a magazine for artists whose records were selling like hotcakes. Ronnie wanted his bullets back, but he knew they weren't something you could just ask for; they had to be earned. Skynyrd's first three albums had been certified gold, most recently in June for *Nuthin' Fancy,* but a truly hot single had eluded them since "Sweet Home Alabama." More than anything, Ronnie was hoping for a hit so he could pick up a copy of *Billboard* and see Lynyrd Skynyrd's name with a bullet beside it. [A bullet was a five-pointed star that *Billboard* magazine used for songs on its Hot 100 list that moved up dramatically from the week before, or that entered the list at a very high position. It was commonly called a "bullet" in the entertainment industry, which prompted *Billboard* to adopt a bullet symbol in 1970 for records that sold a million copies. (Since 1958, the Recording Industry Association of America has issued its Gold Award for records that sell five hundred thousand units. In 1976, the RIAA initiated its Platinum Award for one million certified sales.)]

Gary Rossington wrote the music for "Gimme Back My Bullets," which was recorded on November 30, the band's final day in LA. Packed with power, this chugging, hard-stomp bounder begins with a three-stroke scraping sound from Gary, recalling for a moment the start of "Wooden Ships" by Crosby, Stills and Nash. In this throbbing, hard-edged number, Gary demonstrates his mastery of his instrument and an ability to use a variety of tricks and sounds to good effect, without ever overusing them. It's his guitar work, in fact, that redeems this otherwise muddled recording. Amid an explosive, plodding bass from Leon and the clamor of overdone cymbals, Ronnie's voice is drowned out. Billy plays organ and clavinette, a wiry sounding electric clavichord that's similar to a harpsichord, but it's wasted here because you can't quite make it out, and Artimus's drum part is otherwise sharp, but it's also lost in the mix. And yet, despite the lackluster recording, it's still a very good song that begs for more solo work from Gary. As for the lyrics, Ronnie's claim that he had his act together again would prove to be premature.

You wouldn't think that such a sweet sounding song would have been born in the harsh summer heat of Hell House, but that's where Allen came up with "Every Mother's Son," which was recorded on September 9 in LA, with Allen and Gary strumming eloquently on acoustic guitars and Billy providing a beautiful piano accompaniment. With tender lyrics and a crisp, clean sound overall, it offers a striking contrast to the fire in the opening number, and an inkling that Ronnie wasn't entirely out of touch with his problems—the message is, don't take success for granted. Still mining treasures from their trove from Muscle Shoals, on their last day in Macon, the band resurrected "Trust." This was a better overall rendering of this leftover song, although the strength of Leon's excellent bass part is diminished, despite having one less guitar in play. Returning to J.J. Cale for material, Skynyrd covered "I Got The Same Old Blues," on which Gary is featured in a superb slide solo, and a guest artist, Lee Freeman, plays harmonica, stirring bittersweet memories of Ed King. Freeman had been a singer, guitarist, and harmonica man for Strawberry Alarm Clock.

"Double Trouble" brings to mind what was, perhaps, the first time Ronnie's occupation was ever recorded officially as "musician." The record is a jail docket in Jacksonville, where, at the age of nineteen, shortly after midnight on April 29, 1967, he was fingerprinted and booked into the Duval County Jail for fighting and disorderly conduct. One year earlier, he'd been arrested for assault and battery after a fight in an ice cream parlor, but the charges were dropped when every eyewitness said he was only trying to break up the fight. It was the first in a series of arrests, the eleventh of which was for drunkenness in the summer of 1975. Sitting in a cell with Gary, Ronnie counted his previous collars and determined that this was number eleven. Gary said, "You're just double trouble, Ronnie," so, of course, Ronnie wrote a song about it. Although Skynyrd and Dowd were a bit of a mismatch, the band learned a lot from the veteran producer, who made a good decision in adding female backup singers on a couple of songs. "Double Trouble," with music Allen had composed, was well chosen as the album's strongest single, partly because of the thumping, upbeat tempo and a package of clever lyrics, but also because of the girls, The Honnicutts, who for some reason weren't named individually in the album credits. Their hauntingly powerful backing, which got fans "WHOO-ing" and spelling "T-R-O-U-B-L-E" right along with them, added a rich, resounding quality that Ronnie would come to love. Despite the compelling rhythm and a full measure of sound to go with it, this "double" lacked the muscle to become a hit single.

On "Roll Gypsy Roll," Gary and Allen's music provides the perfect accompaniment to Ronnie's story about touring with a band with no clear, ultimate purpose, and yet bound to keep rolling along. It's a medium-tempo number with a well-orchestrated, all-around sound that features Allen on twelve-string, Billy on organ, and Gary playing an appropriately forbearing solo. This moment of mild introspection having passed, they launch vigorously into

"Searching," a toe-tapping boogie with an answer for Ronnie's conjecture, that finding love should be his goal. There's a fine sense of balance to this recording, which offers solos and fills by Gary, until he and Allen combine for a commanding, well-executed duel that was ended much too soon. To close out a driving, hard-charging song that is only three minutes long, just thirty-two seconds with two great guitarists is simply not enough.

Without ever naming the person, Ronnie made it clear that "Cry For The Bad Man," for which Gary wrote the music, was a song about Skynyrd's former manager, Alan Walden. As if Ronnie couldn't wait to unburden himself of the wrath and resentment he felt toward the "money miser," this was the first song recorded for the album. With a heaviness reserved for the truly harsh feelings that Ronnie harbored, the hard-toned, somber sound from the band is made all the more severe by the voices of the Honnicutts. Writing it was a way for Ronnie to get it out of his system, and it provided a powerful song for the album.

The last song on the album, "All I Can Do Is Write About It" is a plaintive country ballad that Dowd considered a "masterpiece," with all of the elements that typically are found in Ronnie's favorite genre, country music. Barry Harwood came in to play dobro and mandolin while Gary and Allen stroked acoustic guitars, and Billy added almost the feel of a symphony on piano and organ. Some people called it smarmy, but for Ronnie the song was a heartfelt expression of disappointment at seeing countryside spoiled and disappearing. Working with Gary's music, Ronnie put strong Southern bend on this song, recalling one of his favorite artists, Hank Williams. In its own way, this was really a brilliant song, and it signaled a direction that Ronnie was hoping to take in the future.

More work went into *Gimme Back My Bullets* during the next couple of months, while the band got back to performing. Released on February 2, 1976, it rose to No. 20 on the *Billboard* chart, which was higher than *Pronounced* had climbed. But it began tapering off in just four months, and wouldn't reach gold for five more years. The first week the album was on the street, Ronnie had

called Dowd from jail to say he'd been arrested for the twelfth time, this time for fighting. As he clearly knew better, by now, than to continue this kind of behavior, it was another sign that Ronnie was still unsure of his future and badly needed a spark that would reinvigorate his band. Back when Leon had rejoined the group after *Pronounced* was released, Ronnie had used a baseball analogy to convey his expectations. He wanted home runs, he said, so every time they played they would have to "swing for the fence." But on *Gimme Back My Bullets*, Ronnie had settled for a double, and the critics generally concurred. As one reviewer wrote, Skynyrd was a good band in limbo.

Ronnie liked it, Leon said it was sterile, Allen felt the material and the mixing were better than ever, and Gary considered it an unfortunate result of their being uninspired and somewhat "lost" at the time. But regardless of how they and the critics felt, their box office draw was never better, on both sides of the Atlantic. Just as *Gimme Back My Bullets* was hitting retail stores back in the states, Skynyrd was booked for a weeklong series of shows in England and Scotland, where they were welcomed as working class heroes. In Glasgow, a couple of magazine reporters spent the day with the band and got a fairly accurate picture of their favorite collective hobby: drinking. After rising late in the morning, Billy started the day with a double screwdriver, the first of four he would down in an hour and a half. Brunch for Ronnie and Gary was double scotches, straight up, with a chaser on the side. But the two of them kept well shy of their normal bottle apiece a day and no one got out of line, because on that night off, they were celebrating the sixty-first birthday of Ronnie's father, Lacy, who was touring with his son for the first time. The party was a quiet affair, oddly enough, and the reporters made note of how polite these Americans were.

Two nights later in a London hotel, someone from a carnival convention teased Billy about his hair, and Billy decked him, breaking his right little finger in the process. What happened next was fit for a movie comedy. Wanting to get in on the fun, Artimus and Gary sought out the carnival crowd, but they burst through the wrong door and wound up disturbing a meeting of the police athletic league, whose well-trained members took an instant and physical dislike to the intruders. Gary was literally thrown from the room, and Artimus held on long enough to be hauled off to jail with knots on his head. And while these very polite boys from the birthday party were nursing their lumps, Leon was having problems of his own, trying to explain how a wooden table had fallen out of the fifth floor window of his hotel room.

On another evening in England, an inebriated Leon found a hotel lounge closed, so he picked a lock, got behind the bar, and poured himself a drink. By the time the bobbies arrived, having been alerted by the hotel manager, Leon had gone to his third floor room. When they knocked on his door, he crawled out the window, made his way along the ledge, eased back inside through the window of the room next door, and hid under a bed. Startled by this odd turn of events, the man who was in the bed called the front desk, and by the time Leon had extricated himself and made it into the hallway, the bobbies were there to arrest him.

Meanwhile, back in the states, sales of *Gimme Back My Bullets* were going great guns. It became their fastest selling album, in fact, but the run was fairly short-lived, as fans were looking for another monster Skynyrd hit that wasn't there. Just as every band discovers after they've scored big hits, the public will always want more than they're sometimes able to give. It's not really fair, but that's showbiz, and you just keep trying to make them happy, as Skynyrd always managed to do in concerts. Returning from Great Britain in early March to kick off a three-month tour, they were stunned in Denver by the way fans responded to the album's title song. In an odd but well-meant gesture, just as Ronnie began singing the words, "Gimme back my bullets," a barrage of actual bullets began landing all over the stage. It was a bizarre case of misunderstood song lyrics that repeated itself in each of their next few shows, as spirited fans tossed rounds of hard, lead ammo

they'd brought to show their love. It happened again in San Jose, and again in San Francisco, where, on March 3, 1976, Skynyrd set a record for the fastest advance ticket sales ever in Bill Graham's 5,500-seat Winterland Arena. There, before a howling, sellout crowd, they recorded for the first time on film. It was the first of four shows they would film during the next two years for *Free Bird: The Movie*, which wouldn't be released for two more decades. Late that night in a Chinese restaurant, Ronnie and the boys saluted Peter Rudge's birthday with a dish breaking, food fight frolic with a shower of wine and soy sauce falling on everyone. Back on the tour, the showers of bullets continued, but the rain of lead stopped after a few more shows when Skynyrd dropped "Bullets" from the play list. This was partly because it didn't fit with the song list they'd revised for the rest of the tour, but also to keep someone from being hurt. And they weren't only concerned for themselves; they were also looking out for their crew.

No rock and roll band could be successful without a good crew of assistants, and Lynyrd Skynyrd was blessed with some of the best. Names like "Torture Tour" speak volumes about the burdens of travel on the band, but most people never consider the fact that the going was always tougher on their team of able associates. Of course, it was much less demanding in the early days, when the longest trips weren't long at all, and the band members helped out with the heavy lifting. Back then, there was just Bill Ferris, who had sneaked Leon Wilkeson into the Forest Inn when Leon was under age and playing with his pre-Skynyrd band. Bill also had taken Gary to get his first driver's license, and he'd accompanied Ronnie to see the Rolling Stones. And there was me, who, like Bill, was a designated driver for out-of-town gigs when everyone else was drunk. Then there was Dean Kilpatrick, who became their career-long personal assistant and a magnet for personal goodwill toward the band. With his warm disposition and charming personality, Dean always put their best foot forward wherever they went. And then came Kevin Elson, a musician whose keen ear for sound would help them throughout their career, although his most noticeable early contribution was urging Ronnie to listen to fellow roadie Billy Powell play the piano.

Kevin and Dean were the only crew for a while, and then came Joe Barnes and Craig Reed, who would become Skynyrd's longest serving crew member—he's their production manager today. Other crew members included Gary Bouchard, John Butler, Ron Eckerman, Russ Emerick, Chuck Flowers, Clayton Johnson, Billy McCartney, and Raymond Watkins. Lighting and sound crew members who traveled with the band included James Bruce, Marc Frank, Mark Howard, Don Kretzschmeier, Steve Lawler, Bob O'Neal, Joe Osborne, Scott Parsons, Kenneth Peden, Larry Sizemore, and Paul Welch. Everyone in the band appreciated everyone on the crew, and Ronnie, who was, of course, their boss, always treated everyone fairly, which is confirmed in a story that Craig tells. In the early part of 1977, Chuck Flowers, who was a close friend of the band since junior high school and a Skynyrd employee since April of 1974, asked for a raise for himself and Raymond Watkins. Chuck wanted his salary tripled, and Ronnie offered to pay him almost that much. But Chuck said he'd quit if he didn't get it all, and so Ronnie let him go. Ronnie made the same generous offer to Raymond, but he opted to leave, too. Then Ronnie made Craig an offer he couldn't refuse. "I just gave Chuck a raise, so I'm giving you a raise, too. Now you do Chuck's job, and since he's not here, you can have his raise. And you do Raymond's job, and you can have his raise, too," Craig recalled. And so, for as long as Craig could stand doing the work of three men, which was about a month, he was paid almost nine times his former salary. Ronnie gave Kevin a big raise, too.

At first, riding in a van with stacks of equipment and the smell of engine exhaust was a mixture of adventure, amusement, and discomfort, and if you weren't busy driving you could sleep. When the band started flying in airplanes, however, the travel became even less enjoyable and more tedious, and sleep was harder to come by. Except for when you were working, it was a hurry-up-and-

wait way of living and a test of endurance that most people would probably fail. Leave the hotel. Load up the limos. A half-hour ride to the airport. A half-hour loading the plane and waiting for stragglers. A half-hour waiting for takeoff. Fly. Land. A half-hour to disembark and get into the airport. Wait for the courtesy vans. Life with a rock and roll circus was a grueling existence for everyone in the troupe, but on top of it all, the crew worked much longer hours than the band. For a nighttime show, for example, crew members had to be at the stage from noon until midnight, getting everything ready for the show and then taking it all down and packing it up afterward. Do that up to three hundred days a year, and you can readily understand why rock stars, whose job was only performing, trash hotel rooms and toss TVs from windows. But only rarely, if ever, will you hear of roadies doing those things, because the guys on the crew could never afford that kind of behavior. They would have to pay for the damage, just like the band, or else they'd be fired. Roadies weren't paid enough to act like idiots, so only the boys in the band would blow off steam by breaking furniture. Only once, as Joe Barnes recalled, was there a time when the crew got into the mix. At a birthday party for Allen in a posh London restaurant, following a sumptuous dinner and lots of wine, a food fight erupted when Chuck Flowers smashed Allen's face with a piece of a custard cream cake that was six-foot-square and delicious. But even then, the damage was minimal.

Roadies initially were paid only a few dollars per diem and slept four to a room. They weren't there for the money, of course, but the pay got better for the skills that were required once Skynyrd had hit the big-time. Making things run smoothly for the band was important at all times, but without a skilled crew on stage, consistently good performances would not have been possible. As was typical for a musical production like Skynyrd's, depending upon the size of the venue, two or three guys handled sound, two or three men worked the lights, and at least three more supported the instruments. Joe became stage manager because of his craftsmanship and technical know-how, and, like Craig Reed, he always ensured that everything was functioning properly. One example of this kind of care came when Craig warned Bob Burns that the head on his bass drum needed replacing. Bob said it didn't, and later that day it broke. Crew members also had to keep people off the stage, although on one occasion, keeping the stage off the people became a concern. At an outdoor show in Birmingham, the show's hosts had built the stage without pads to support the scaffolding, which started sinking as the stage was literally falling apart.

"Our job was to make sure when the band walked on stage nothing would interfere with their performance," Barnes said. "And then our job also became security, and crowd control." This sometimes required grabbing and pushing people, but usually a stern look in the eye would deter a would-be crasher. In England once, during "Free Bird," so many fans rushed the stage that the crew couldn't keep them off. When they were told they couldn't stand in front of the band, instead of leaving, they politely lay down. "By the end of the song the stage was carpeted with guys lying on their backs." On another occasion stage security succumbed to an advance from a novel intruder. In Little Rock, Arkansas, during "Free Bird," a naked man jumped on stage and stood facing the crowd with his arms raised. Ronnie motioned for the spotlight to shine on him, and eventually Mr. Natural withdrew. Skynyrd's grand finale was interrupted on several occasions over the years, including the time that Edgar Winter had played a little longer than scheduled as the opening act. When it was time for the concert to end, an overly time-conscious cop ended the show by shutting off power to the stage during the middle of "Free Bird."

Screwing up or being cut off in the middle of their closing number was just about the worst thing that could happen to Skynyrd. Unlike other bands who might vary the tempo of a song or rearrange the order of their songs, Skynyrd's approach was designed to be formulaic—play every note exactly as rehearsed, run through their repertoire in a carefully selected order with pre-planned peaks and valleys, stir the audience into a frenzy, and leave with fans screaming for more. But, aside from mishaps that

couldn't be helped, there were times when their biggest problems were self-inflicted. On one such occasion, Skynyrd was supposed to open for ZZ Top in the Sugar Bowl in New Orleans, but Ronnie had blown out his throat yelling and screaming at people the night before—this was a bit out of character for him, as his tirades were usually more physical than vocal. As a result, the road crew showed up but the band didn't.

Another "Free Bird" mishap occurred in Boston in early April, when, at a peak moment in the middle of the song's closing sequence, Allen accidentally pulled the whammy bar off his old Gibson Firebird, the one he'd crushed with a car, and Leon's amp blew a fuse. Both of them ended up destroying their guitars, Who-style, and throwing the parts into the audience. Immediately after the show, Allen sent the crew out into the crowd to retrieve his whammy bar and the guitar pickups, leaving the rest for the fan who'd picked it up. The next day in New York, he bought another Firebird, which he took very good care of during that night's concert. But the evening ended differently for Leon. During "Free Bird" in the Beacon Theater, Leon broke up his guitar and tossed it into the audience again, inadvertently slashing the face of a girl who was sitting in the front row. The night was also eventful for the fact that Leslie West of Mountain stood in for Gary, who had broken his hand in a fight. (Skynyrd had opened for Mountain in Jacksonville in 1970, during Billy's first gig as a Skynyrd roadie.) They'd been missing a third guitar for almost a year now, and West was more than able and willing to fill the gap. The next day in the hotel bar, Ronnie interviewed him as if he were hiring a farm hand, but as good as West was, and as much as all the Skynyrd boys liked Mountain, Ronnie felt that he just wouldn't fit into the mix. Skynyrd also considered hiring Wayne Perkins, a studio guitarist who that year had overdubbed parts on "Preacher's Daughter" and "Down South Jukin' " from the 1972 sessions in Muscle Shoals. He says they offered him the job, but that his gut instincts told him not to accept.

It was about this time that Ronnie told a magazine reporter

that he'd begun to settle down and was laying off the booze. But that was only partially true. At the end of April in Lakeland, Florida, headlining for Pure Prairie League and the Outlaws, Ronnie stood alone on stage in the glow of a single spotlight, and he held up a bottle of Jack Daniels whisky to toast the audience. Ronnie never held up a bottle unless he was also drinking from it, and, in fact, everyone was fairly looped when the first song got under way. Leon kept banging into Ronnie during the set, and midway through the performance, Ronnie finally had enough and slugged him, which caused a minor brawl. Skynyrd left the stage for about twenty minutes, and then they returned, arm in arm, to finish out the show. Ronnie was at least aware of the fact that his habits would have to change, but while he was trying to clean up his act, the rest of the band continued their overindulgent ways—Billy had just crashed in a car and escaped with only minor injuries. A wake-up call came during a concert on May 23 in Charlotte, North Carolina, when Ronnie got drunk on whisky and high on cocaine, lost his voice, and walked off the stage halfway through the show. There were rumors that someone had plied him with inebriants in order to sabotage his performance, but Ronnie knew he had only himself to blame, and he vowed he would never let it happen again.

Skynyrd had planned to do a live album in the spring, but they had to postpone it twice because of Artimus. The first time they had planned to rehearse in Jacksonville, Artimus opted to go hang-gliding and didn't show up. The next time they tried, he couldn't play because he'd broken his leg in a car crash. But both of Artimus's missteps proved to be a very good thing for the band, however, because by the time they were all ready to record, they had added a brand-new member, Steve Gaines. The three-guitar army was back, and it had come as a complete surprise.

 For the past four months, fans at Skynyrd concerts had been enjoying a different kind of surprise. During the previous summer,

as Bill Ferris remembers it, Ronnie had told him he was thinking of expanding the Skynyrd sound with female singers. "We were out fishing one day, and Ronnie stood up in the boat and made like he was dancing, the way he imagined the girls would sway when they sang," Bill said. After hearing the Honicutts, Ronnie was convinced it would work, and he let it be known that he was looking for female talent. Leslie Hawkins, who had opened some shows for Skynyrd when she was singing with "Wet Willie," was performing in a club in her hometown of Jacksonville in mid-January, when sound engineer Kevin Elson told her there might be an opening with Skynyrd. Deborah Jo Billingsley, a Tennessee lass whom everyone would know as "Jo Jo," was singing with a group called "Oil Can Harry" when she learned of the opportunity from her friend, Bob O'Neal, who was working lights for the band. Shortly afterward, Kevin called her and invited her to hear them perform in Nashville on January 17. During the show, she sat with Bob and Kevin at the sound console, and afterward, Ronnie asked her if she'd like to join up. Now that he had a soprano and an alto, respectively, Ronnie wanted someone who would handle the middle range between them, and Jo Jo suggested her friend, Cassie Gaines, an Oklahoman who'd sung with the cast of *Hair* at Memphis State University. At the end of the month, the guys met the girls in Jacksonville to see how they sounded together, and two weeks later they were all on a plane to England.

On several occasions during the next three and a half months, Cassie recommended her younger brother, Steve, as a third guitarist. He could play, he could write, he could sing, she would say, and they finally agreed to a tryout. Cassie called Steve, who was playing in a band called Crawdad and living on a farm near West Seneca, Oklahoma, and told him to come to the Lynyrd Skynyrd concert in Kansas City, Missouri, on May 11. Steve jumped at the chance, as Crawdad was idle that week, but when he got to Memorial Hall he was stunned at what he was told. This would not be an ordinary audition; he would join them on stage at the show. This novel idea had sprung from Cassie's confidence in her brother. Gary objected at first, but he went along with the idea, knowing that Kevin would manage the sound if the Okie was flunking the test. "They said, just turn him off if he's bad," Kevin recalled, but the need would never arise. No stranger to the hometown crowd, who gave him a nice round of applause when he ambled out onto the stage, the tall, lanky Steve was primed and ready when they told him to jump in on "Call Me The Breeze" and a new song they'd been playing lately, "T For Texas," an old song written by one of Ronnie's favorite artists, Jimmie Rodgers, the "Father of Country Music." As Allen and Gary swapped leads on this blistering guitar workout, Steve began playing slide, showing a deftness it had taken years to develop, but with a refreshing level of enthusiasm the others hadn't felt for a couple of years.

This was the chance of a lifetime for Steve. A truly polished professional, he had known just what to do. Even so, Gary and Allen were not completely convinced, because, in fact, they really hadn't heard him well enough to know if he was their man or not. Steve had played through his own small amplifier, which couldn't compete with the ear-splitting power of theirs, so they asked Kevin what he thought. "Man, this guy can play," said Kevin, who'd been wearing a headset and had no doubt about it. But just to be sure, Steve jammed with the band again, and the rest, as they say, is history, although he remained in suspense for a couple of weeks until he got a call from Ronnie. He asked Steve to join them in Myrtle Beach, South Carolina, and they would go from there to Jacksonville, where Skynyrd would be on vacation for all but the last day of June. There would be time to get acquainted and learn the ropes. On July 7, Lynyrd Skynyrd set up shop in Atlanta's beautifully restored Fox Theater for a three-night stint to record a live LP, *One More From The Road*. It was Steve's fourth concert appearance as an official member of the group.

CHAPTER 8

"IF YOU RELEASE THIS, YOUR CAREER IS OVER"

"Cassie and Steve are the best thing that ever happened to Ronnie," said Dorman Cogburn, who'd known Ronnie and the band for many years. It was a bit of an overstatement, perhaps, and yet, were it not for Cassie, Steve wouldn't have come along, and because of Steve, Ronnie was free to become his old self again. Steve's vitality had a transforming effect on Ronnie. His spirit was roused, his hope was renewed, and his drive to excel was restored. The rest of the group was energized, too, but this was especially true for Allen and Gary, who suddenly realized they would have to work very hard to keep up with the exuberant new-comer. This was due to his many musical talents, of course, but there was something else about

RONNIE WAS BLESSED WITH NOT
JUST ONE BUT TWO, AND FOR MANY YEARS
THREE, ABSOLUTELY SUPERB GUITAR PLAYERS.
(UPHAM)

Steve that really charged their batteries. Allen and Gary had tasted success already and they were tired. Steve had been playing in motel lounges and he was hungry.

Steve Gaines was exactly what Lynyrd Skynyrd needed, and more. Although comparisons with Ed King were inevitable, except for the fact that Steve could sing and had his own style of play, the biggest difference between them lay in their personalities. Both played a musical director's role much of the time, but while Ed could sometimes be abrasive, Steve was always so agreeable that no one would ever take offense. With his quiet, unassuming manner, he was able to get his point across without seeming to mind if it mattered. With Steve it was always, "How does it sound this way?" instead of "This is the way it has to be," and when his ideas were right, there was never a need to argue.

Born September 14, 1949, in Miami, Oklahoma, Steve Earl Gaines was fourteen years old when he fell in love with the idea of playing a guitar. He'd just seen the Beatles perform in Kansas City, and once he'd pestered his father enough to buy one, Steve immediately went to work figuring it out, playing by ear until he could imitate some of his favorite artists, including Bob Dylan, Lonnie Mack, and Jimmy Reed. The following year, he met the other love of his life, his future bride, Teresa, with whom he would have a daughter, Corrina. Steve's first role in a band was playing rhythm guitar in the Ravens in high school. Next, he joined the Cellar Door, then the Pink Peach Mob, and then Manalive, while enrolled as an art student at Pitt State University in Pittsburgh, Kansas. The band spent the summer in California and then moved to Colorado, where Steve wrote the future Skynyrd song, "I Know A Little." Cassie, who sang with the group for a while, got them a gig in Memphis in 1971, which led to a record deal and a chance to open for ZZ Top. Steve next played briefly with Elmo's Smokehouse in Illinois, and then with a band called Detroit. After that, he moved back home and helped form Crawdad, which recorded in Leon Russell's Church Studio in Tulsa, and in Capricorn Studios in

Macon. Many of Steve's early songs wouldn't be heard until 1988, when they were released on an album called *One In The Sun.*

Despite their potential, Manalive was basically just spinning their wheels, playing so-so gigs while Steve grew weary of doing practically everything. He wrote, arranged, and sang songs, played rhythm and lead guitar, booked engagements and drove the van. He was also a morale builder, at which he was very good, with his buoyant, outgoing personality, just like Cassie's. Steve likened his pre-Skynyrd life to factory work, and just when he was wondering how long he could keep it up, Cassie called, and he was saved. With Skynyrd, all he had to do was play and sing and write, and he absolutely loved it. And because of him, the old-time Skynyrd boys had never felt more positive about themselves. It was interesting to watch, because Steve wasn't at all like any of the others. He enjoyed a good smoke and a beer, but always in moderation. He never had an unkind word to say about anyone and he never got into fights. A story that defines Steve's likable nature has been told by his friend, Skipper Trask, who remembers being with Steve one night, in a bar in Missouri, when two big guys threatened to cut their long hair. Steve struck up a conversation, and before long, the big guys were laughing along with Steve and buying beers for him and his friend.

When Skynyrd arrived in Atlanta to make the live album, Steve, the peacemaker, got a pretty good idea of what travels with his new teammates would be like. After recording four songs on opening night in the Fox Theater, some of the guys and Jo Jo walked across the street to a nightclub, where Gary, who was drunk, more than met his match in a fight with a bouncer. Someone from the Outlaws band, who happened to be there, started the fracas by lobbing ice at the band on stage. Before it was over, one of the bouncers pounded on Gary, and soon it was time to leave. Back at the Fox, Allen and Gary and Jo Jo joined Cassie, Leslie, Ronnie, and Tom Dowd, who had remained in the theater listening to tapes, and they all piled into a rental car to return to their hotel in nearby

Marietta. Being thrown out of a nightclub wasn't at all unusual for Jo Jo, whose excessive drinking and barroom belligerence rivaled anything the guys had ever achieved. On this occasion, she kept up her ranting and raving in the car, which infuriated Ronnie, who was practically sober. When she didn't shut up when he told her to, he redirected his fire at Allen, who, oddly enough for the sake of everyone's safety, was driving. "Shut her up, Allen!" he said, and when Allen replied with a smart remark, Ronnie punched him in the head, even though they were racing up Interstate 75 at eighty miles an hour. Allen pulled over and she finally shut up, said Leslie, who saw Ronnie pummel every member of the band but Steve during the time she spent with the group.

The rest of their stay in Atlanta went reasonably well. *Second Helping* had just gone platinum, and there was a ceremony on stage to mark the occasion. But alas, once again, after three straight nights of singing his best on songs such as "Whisky Rock-A-Roller," "Saturday Night Special," and "I Ain't The One," which carried him beyond his natural vocal range, Ronnie ravished his vocal cords. This was especially unfortunate for Skynyrd's home-town fans, because after the shows at the Fox the band was bound for Jacksonville to help raise money for the presidential campaign of Georgia Governor Jimmy Carter. It was the "Sunshine Jam" in the Gator Bowl, where the Outlaws, the Charlie Daniels Band, .38 Special, and the Marshall Tucker Band had also come to support their fellow Southerner. Before the show, watching Ronnie cough up blood in a trailer behind the stage, Dorman Cogburn asked him, "What are you even doing here, man? You can't sing. Hell, you can't even talk! Why don't you just go home?" Ronnie stayed to hear his brother, Donnie, perform with .38 Special, but when Skynyrd walked on stage that day, their special guest singer was Charlie Daniels, who graciously took Ronnie's place.

On August 1, Lynyrd Skynyrd broke the Allman Brothers' attendance record in the Macon Coliseum. On the 15th, they shared the bill with Ted Nugent before a thundering crowd of one hundred thousand fans in Chicago's Soldier Field. It was a very

good warm-up for the "Woodstock of the 1970s," the Knebworth Fair, which followed a few days later in Hertfordshire, England. Attendance estimates ranged from two hundred and fifty thousand to half a million, many of whom had come to see the headline act, the Rolling Stones, who, it was rumored, would be performing for the last time. The show began about eleven o'clock in the morning, beginning with the Don Harrison Band, and followed by Hot Tuna, Todd Rundgren, and Utopia. Arriving by helicopter in the glow of a warm, bright blue sky, Skynyrd took the stage at five o'clock for a ninety-minute set that would have brought down the house had there been one there to topple.

From the opening number, "Workin' For MCA," all the way through "Free Bird," the show was a smashing success. Skynyrd won the crowd over with their "confidence and professionalism" and their "hellfire boogie played at a quickfire pace," one reviewer wrote, adding, "Their main ace lies in their ability to give a hungry crowd exactly what they want. A lot of searing guitar work but not too much." Complimenting every band member by name, the reviewer concluded, "Tasting Lynyrd Skynyrd live feels like having a bottle of Jack Daniels shoved down your throat."

Skynyrd found performing for hundreds of thousands of people no more of a challenge than playing for thousands or tens of thousands—"Once you get past the first few rows, all those people are really just a blur," Ronnie said, recalling the biggest show of their lives. The only thing that didn't go well was a technical glitch that couldn't have been foreseen. Out from the main stage, a sixty-foot tongue had been built to accommodate Mick Jagger's wont for wandering, and as soon as Skynyrd saw it, they had to make it their own. But there wasn't enough extra guitar cord to go around, so when Allen, Gary, and Steve ran out on the stage tongue, framming their frets and basking in rock and roll glory, like a dog that suddenly runs out of rope, Leon ran out of cord almost halfway out on the tongue, tripping microphone stands over in the process. It was the only blemish in an otherwise flawless performance. Afterward, some of the band and crew shared a joint backstage with

Jack Nicholson, who was there to see the Rolling Stones. Paul McCartney and Linda McCartney arrived a little later to see 10cc, who were running two hours late. Delayed by four hours, the Stones ended the festival shortly after two in the morning, trying their professional best to please by playing an unbelievable twenty-eight songs. But even so, coming on at such a late hour, in comparison with Skynyrd the Stones were almost anticlimactic, as ensuing reviews implied. For example, commenting on the festival's line-up of bands, a *Sounds* reviewer wrote of Skynyrd, "They are THE Festival band." And for anyone who might doubt the power and magic of Skynyrd, seeing their performance at Knebworth on *Free Bird: The Movie* will surely change some minds. (The final two filmings would come the following year, in the Oakland-Alameda County Coliseum on July 3, and in Asbury Park, New Jersey on July 13.)

On a side note, one of the celebrities who gathered backstage that evening was John Paul Getty III, a scion of the billionaire oilman. Aware of Ronnie's reputation as a connoisseur of Jack Daniels whisky, Getty challenged the barefoot boy from Mull Street to a spirited duel to the finish. Ronnie accepted, of course, and as dawn drew near after a very long night of drinking, the clear-cut winner was the barefoot boy from Jacksonville, Florida. This wasn't at all surprising for Ronnie, but interestingly enough, it came on the eve of a conscious decision he made that sobriety shouldn't be just for breakfast anymore.

Two weeks after Knebworth, in what might have been only a coincidence were it not for the drivers who were involved, Allen and Gary were drunk and caused two separate accidents, although Gary's was much the worse. It was Labor Day weekend in Jacksonville, near the entrance to the Hyde Park Country Club, when Gary, who was drunk on whisky and sedated on Quaaludes, passed out at the wheel and drove his car into a large oak tree, knocked down a telephone pole, then continued across the road and slammed into a nearby home. Gary, whose self-proclaimed motto when drinking was, "If you ain't pukin', you ain't high," was hospi-

talized briefly and too sore to move for a week. By all rights, both
of them should have been killed, but if it wasn't a wake-up call for
Gary, it sent a very strong signal to Ronnie. This was the mishap
that inspired him to write "That Smell," a warning for wayward
souls who won't change their ways. It was directed at Gary—he's
the "Prince Charming" in the song—but it was also meant for the
rest of the group. Earlier that year, Billy had banged himself up
pretty badly on a motorcycle, Allen had fractured his skull when he
drove a jeep over an embankment, and Artimus had broken his leg
in a crash. In every instance, these "accidents" could have been
avoided.

Ronnie had more foresight than to drive under the influence of
liquids, powders, or pills, and now that he'd cut down on his own
drinking, he was much more aware of the consequences. So, when
he visited Gary in the hospital, Ronnie let him know exactly what
he thought. "I told him he was stupid, 'cause what he was doing
was only gonna hurt the band and everything we've worked for,"
Ronnie told me, and he resolved then and there to bring his band
back from the brink of disaster. That's when he asked me for help.

As a joke, Ronnie used to call me "the last rebel" because I was
the only person he'd ever known who had never consumed alcohol,
smoked pot, snorted cocaine, or ingested anything other than food.
But after Gary's latest flirtation with death, Ronnie suddenly and
unexpectedly put great value on this most unusual quality of mine.
"Gene, you're the only one I can trust," he said. "I need your help
if we're ever gonna get this drinking under control. These boys are
still boys, and they're never gonna stop on their own. We're just
getting back in a real good way now, and if this keeps up, somebody's gonna get killed." He also told me I wouldn't have to keep
my eye on him because he had an extra incentive to stay on the
straight and narrow. His wife, Judy, would soon have a baby, and it
was time for him to settle down. (The child would be born on
September 19, and named Melody.) And so, without saying
anything to anyone else, I set out to try to help. Partly because of
my nature, and partly because everyone else was usually drunk or

high on something, I had become sort of a mother hen around the band, trying to keep them out of trouble and picking up the pieces when they strayed off course, in addition to keeping them safe on stage. Now that I had a new mission, I did what I thought would have the best chance of succeeding. I began by taking the first limo to every concert, and when I got to the "green room" that every hall or arena has for performers, I'd take one of the two bottles of whisky and one of the three bottles of champagne that had been *de rigueur* for Skynyrd, and I would give them away or pour them out, leaving only the balance to anoint them before the show. Believe it or not, for a bunch of heavy drinkers like them, this seemingly mild deprivation made a difference in their demeanor and also helped their performance.

I'm not saying there weren't serious lapses. In fact, once they realized what I'd been doing, Allen and Billy, especially, would get around the roadblock by getting in their usual share of licks at the hotel bar before they arrived at the show. And this kind of behavior continued, although, toward the end of our final tour, Gary and Leon, and even Allen and Billy (Artimus's excesses had never been alcohol, and Steve was never excessive) expressed their appreciation. "We never thought we could play in front of fifteen thousand people sober. We appreciate what you've done for us," said Allen, whose fingers had actually grown numb from so much liquor, and had begun to affect his guitar playing. By then, I had done away with all of the whisky and champagne before the shows, leaving only a six-pack of beer to ease any pre-show jitters there might still be in a band of seasoned veterans.

Coming as it did between two week-long periods of rest, Gary's crash caused five concerts to be canceled. But when touring resumed in the third week of September, it was back to business as usual, and time to sell their new album. Released on September 13, *One More From The Road* sold three hundred and fifty thousand copies in its first month and quickly rose to No. 9 on the chart, striking gold in just six weeks and turning platinum a week before Christmas. Some people say it captured the excitement of a live

performance, while others contend that Dowd's studio refinements sapped it of its strength—still on autopilot, Ronnie never listened to the album before it was released. But while bona fide audiophiles might disagree, most folks felt like the *Billboard* reviewer who called the fourteen-song, two-disc package "one of the most white-hot sets imaginable" from "a consistent gold record act." On it were "Gimme Three Steps," "Free Bird," "I Ain't The One," and the only non-rocker of the bunch, "Tuesday's Gone," from *Pronounced*; "Workin' For MCA," "Sweet Home Alabama," "Call Me The Breeze," and "The Needle And The Spoon" from *Second Helping*; "Saturday Night Special" and "Whisky Rock-A-Roller" from *Nuthin' Fancy*; and "Searching" from *Gimme Back My Bullets*. Three other songs were new recordings for Skynyrd: "T For Texas"; "Travelin' Man," (the only Skynyrd song written by Leon) which Ronnie had dedicated to his father; and "Crossroads," the song the Skynyrd boys had always used for an encore before they had "Free Bird." Theirs was the familiar Cream version of the Robert Johnson classic, recalling their original, pre-Skynyrd sound: Southern blues-rock with a British accent.

As if to confirm the reverse maxim that no good deed will go unpunished, two weeks after the "less booze is better" policy went into effect, at a show in Salt Lake City, Utah, a man crawled onto the stage and sliced my arm with a knife. I kicked him as hard as I could and sent him reeling backward down to the ground, where security guards grabbed him. "I don't like what you did to that guy," Billy yelled out. He hadn't seen the knife, but he apologized when he noticed the blood running down my arm from a two-inch cut. Ronnie joked that I was only earning my pay. And then, while working the stage at another show, someone threw a bottle that hit me in the face, leaving my nose and lips red and swollen like a clown's. Once again, Ronnie followed up with a laugh. "Damn, they want an encore bad, don't they?"

But nobody was laughing in November, when Ronnie pounced on Joe Barnes, the band's highly valued stage manager, during a flight to Houston. The only explanation for this unprovoked attack—he'd never gotten violent with him during Joe's four years with the band—was the fact that Ronnie was drunk once again. It had begun with a broken wardrobe case that Dean Kilpatrick had used as a bar, and Joe had thrown it away before someone got hurt handling it. Dean complained to Ronnie, who punched Joe in the face and then held him down and bit his stomach until somebody pulled him off. When the plane landed, Joe left and never returned. Unlike the boss's other victims, he had more self-respect than to tolerate that kind of treatment. Allen apologized later, but not Ronnie.

This was just the sort of behavior Ronnie had been trying to put behind him, although at times it was like trying to escape his own shadow. But one thing he could control was their schedule, which he managed much better in the second half of 1976. Having survived those torturous tours of the past, the group needed to take it easy. The change would cost them some money, Ronnie said, but there was plenty of that already, and no need to run themselves ragged again. So they would play a few shows and then rest for a few days, and then repeat it in a fairly regular pattern. Considering that they were traveling all over the country, it was the closest they'd come to leading normal lives since the Skynyrd train had first rolled out of Jacksonville more than three years before. Except for a stretch of fourteen consecutive shows and a nine-day series in September and October, the balance of the year was filled with one-, two-, three-, and four-night stands, with plenty of days free in between. By year's end, "Free Bird" had replaced "Stairway To Heaven" as the most requested FM radio song in America, which only added to the feeling that they'd fully earned the right to relax. The most enjoyable respite of all, perhaps, was in January 1977, when they spent a week lying on the beach and sightseeing in Hawaii, and then flew west for a working vacation in Japan.

Skynyrd had developed a large following of devoted Japanese supporters, who greeted them at the Tokyo airport the way New Yorkers had welcomed the kings of the British invasion in 1964. "It was just like the Beatles," said Leslie Hawkins, recalling the

welcome they received from thousands of exuberant fans who were bearing flowers and cheering. This level of enthusiasm continued in all of their concerts in Tokyo and Osaka, where, despite differences in culture and language, the fans sang along on every song. On the eve of their final performance in Tokyo, the whole group went to a nightclub to celebrate Ronnie's twenty-ninth birthday, and what better way to mark the occasion than to end up in a fight? A group of German tourists had taken an instant dislike to the long-haired Americans, and one of them focused his ire on Ronnie, who was sitting at a table, conversing with a local girl. The guy went out of his way to flick Ronnie's hat a few times, but Ronnie, who was sober, was sticking with his new, self-imposed code of behavior, which included a no-fighting clause. When the German escalated his goading by touching the girl in a most inappropriate manner, however, Ronnie calmly stood up, took off his hat, and knocked him down with a solid right to the jaw. This sparked a free-for-all that ended with two of the Germans and one of the crew being deported. Looking on the bright side, a lady's honor had been defended, and with little time left in the land of the rising sun, Lynyrd Skynyrd had lived up to their rowdy reputation, albeit reluctantly.

Next came a three-week tour of England and a triumphant return to the states, where, from April through August, during breaks from a much fuller concert schedule, Lynyrd Skynyrd would record their final album, *Street Survivors*. The work would be considered their finest, but the way it had started out, it might have become their worst. In fact, the original version was tossed in the trash. Tom Dowd initially had been the producer but would not be named on the album cover due to several factors: a poor original production, his inability to continue with the band because he was committed to do a Rod Stewart album, and Ronnie's feeling that Tom had let them down. Compared with their rehearsals on Riverside Avenue in Jacksonville, in an eight-track studio they'd built to replace Hell House, the initial recordings in Miami's Criteria Studios seemed lifeless. The first person to notice was Kevin Elson, their sound manager, who'd driven down from Jacksonville to hear the finished product. "I told them if they released it their career was over, and Steve Gaines was the only one who agreed with me," he said. That got everyone's attention, and after several twists and turns and further reflection, in Doraville's Studio One they decided to re-record every song but "What's Your Name?" and to replace the vocals on that one. Representing Dowd, Barry Rudolph spent a week helping to engineer the sound on four songs with Kevin, and after Barry left, Kevin and Rodney Mills continued enhancing the sound for almost a month. (Kevin would later continue his career with Journey, Aerosmith, and more recently, Bush.)

While a studio recording can never capture the excitement of a live performance, it's also true that no live show can ever provide the perfection that's possible on a crisp, clean, carefully crafted recording, with all of its strengths and subtleties. All of the songs on *Street Survivors* had been thoroughly audience-tested before the studio sessions began, and when they were finally ready for release on vinyl, Steve was confident in paraphrasing one of its songs. "Yeah, we sure got that right," he said. And they had. Released on October 17, 1977, three days before Lynyrd Skynyrd's airplane crashed, *Street Survivors* was an instant hit. On its race to No. 5 on the album chart, it earned gold-record status within ten days, and two weeks before Christmas it was certified platinum. As Ronnie had always wanted, Skynyrd had stepped up to the plate and knocked the ball over the fence. Like baseball, it was simply great.

If there had been any doubts about Skynyrd's staying power, they were amply squelched with *Street Survivors*. From the opening downbeat on drums and the stabbing guitar work on "What's Your Name?" it was clear that Skynyrd was back, and this time with all top-drawer songs, exceptional virtuosity, and a superb studio production. With Billy's hammering honky-tonk piano, a bold blast of brass, and a strong Skynyrd statement from all four guitarists (Leon's bass was more than just bottom), this was full-tilt boogie at its best. The subject matter has been stretched just a bit in the telling. One night in a lounge, Ronnie was sitting at a table having

CASSIE GAINES, SENIOR YEAR AT
MIAMI HIGH SCHOOL, MIAMI,
OKLAHOMA, 1966.

STEVE GAINES, JUNIOR YEAR
AT MIAMI HIGH SCHOOL,
MIAMI, OKLAHOMA, 1966.

STEVE GAINES'S
FIRST ROLE IN A BAND
WAS PLAYING RHYTHM
GUITAR FOR THE
RAVENS IN HIGH
SCHOOL.

STEVE GAINES (ON RIGHT) LOOKING HIS 1950S ROCK AND ROLL BEST FOR THIS 1966 HIGH SCHOOL PHOTOGRAPH.

STEVE GAINES WITH BABY DAUGHTER, CORRINA, MARCH 1975. STEVE AND TERESA PURCHASED THEIR FIRST HOUSE JUST ONE MONTH BEFORE SKYNYRD'S FINAL TOUR BEGAN. (GAINES)

STEVE AND TERESA GAINES WITH DAUGHTER, CORRINA, IN NEW ORLEANS, OCTOBER 1976. (GAINES)

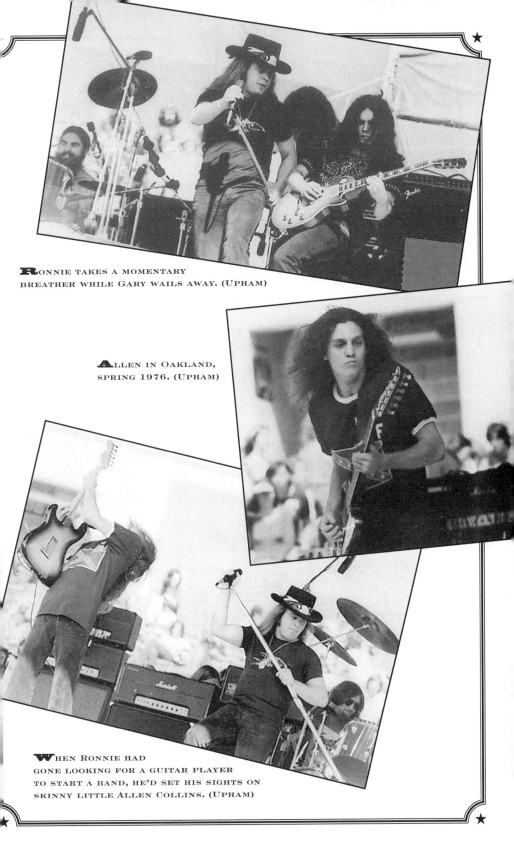

RONNIE TAKES A MOMENTARY
BREATHER WHILE GARY WAILS AWAY. (UPHAM)

ALLEN IN OAKLAND,
SPRING 1976. (UPHAM)

WHEN RONNIE HAD
GONE LOOKING FOR A GUITAR PLAYER
TO START A BAND, HE'D SET HIS SIGHTS ON
SKINNY LITTLE ALLEN COLLINS. (UPHAM)

A FIERY DISPLAY OF GUITAR WORK FROM THE MAN WHO CREATED "FREE BIRD." (ROSS)

RONNIE WITH THE GAINES, COLLINS, ROSSINGTON VERSION OF LYNYRD SKYNYRD'S "THREE-GUITAR ARMY," AS GARY LIKED TO CALL IT. (BULLARD)

ALLEN COLLINS WAS ESPECIALLY HAPPY TO HAVE STEVE GAINES, WHO SAID OF STREET SURVIVORS, "YEAH, WE SURE GOT THAT RIGHT." (UPHAM)

ALLEN'S JUMPING AROUND
ONSTAGE WAS PRACTICALLY
ALL THE THEATRICS
SKYNYRD EVER PROVIDED.
THEIR MUSIC SPOKE FOR
ITSELF. (UPHAM)

"YOU GOTTA
HEAR THIS GUY!"
ALLEN COLLINS
SAID. "HE PLAYS
DOUBLE KICKS
THAT SOUND LIKE
MACHINE GUNS."
(UPHAM)

WITH THE ADDITION OF STEVE GAINES, THE
"THREE-GUITAR ARMY" WAS BACK IN BUSINESS,
HAVING MISSED THE PRESENCE OF ED KING FOR A
VERY LONG YEAR. (UPHAM)

ALLEN PLAYS WINTERLAND IN MARCH 1976. (UPHAM)

STEVE GAINES BACKSTAGE IN JAPAN. A TRULY POLISHED PROFESSIONAL, STEVE HAD KNOWN JUST WHAT TO DO WHEN HE GOT THE CHANCE OF A LIFETIME IN JUNE 1976. (GAINES)

SOFT-SPOKEN BUT ENERGETIC, DRUMMER ARTIMUS PYLE OVERCAME HIS CHERUBIC FACE THE SAME WAY LEON WILKESON COVERED UP HIS, BY GROWING A DENSE, OLD-GROWTH FOREST OF A BEARD. (ODUM)

ALLEN COLLINS AND
GARY ROSSINGTON
WERE VIRTUALLY
INSEPARABLE IN
JUNIOR HIGH SCHOOL,
SPENDING COUNTLESS
HOURS PRACTICING.
YEARS LATER, THEY
WERE SIGNING AUTO-
GRAPHS AND INSPIRING
YOUNGER GUITARISTS.
(ODUM)

ALWAYS QUIET AND
SHY, GARY DEVELOPED
A NATURAL STYLE OF
PLAYING THAT WAS
MUCH IN THE MANNER
OF RY COODER AND OF
PAUL KOSSOFF OF
FREE. IN FACT, IT'S
BEEN SAID OF GARY
THAT HE WAS THE ONLY
GUITARIST BESIDES
CLAPTON WHO COULD
PLAY LIKE KOSSOFF.
(ODUM)

LEON WILKESON AND BILLY
POWELL AWAIT FANS ON AUTOGRAPH DAY
IN ALTAMONTE SPRINGS. (ODUM)

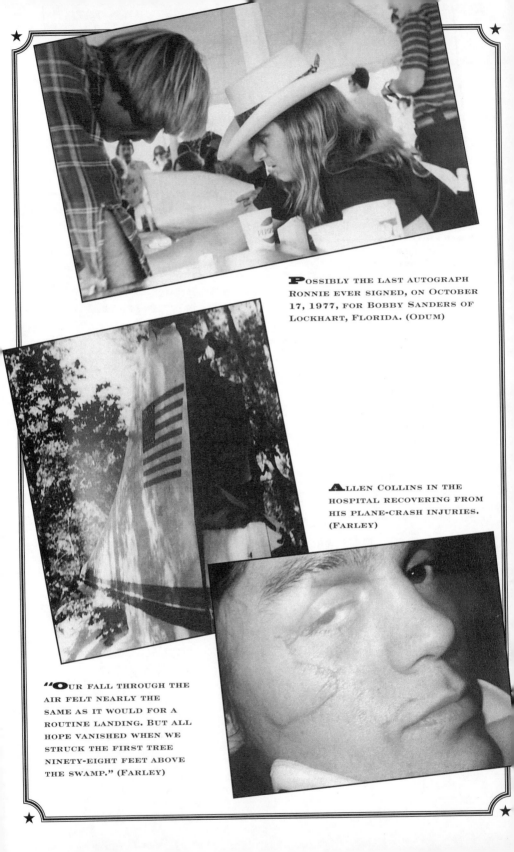

POSSIBLY THE LAST AUTOGRAPH
RONNIE EVER SIGNED, ON OCTOBER
17, 1977, FOR BOBBY SANDERS OF
LOCKHART, FLORIDA. (ODUM)

ALLEN COLLINS IN THE
HOSPITAL RECOVERING FROM
HIS PLANE-CRASH INJURIES.
(FARLEY)

"OUR FALL THROUGH THE
AIR FELT NEARLY THE
SAME AS IT WOULD FOR A
ROUTINE LANDING. BUT ALL
HOPE VANISHED WHEN WE
STRUCK THE FIRST TREE
NINETY-EIGHT FEET ABOVE
THE SWAMP." (FARLEY)

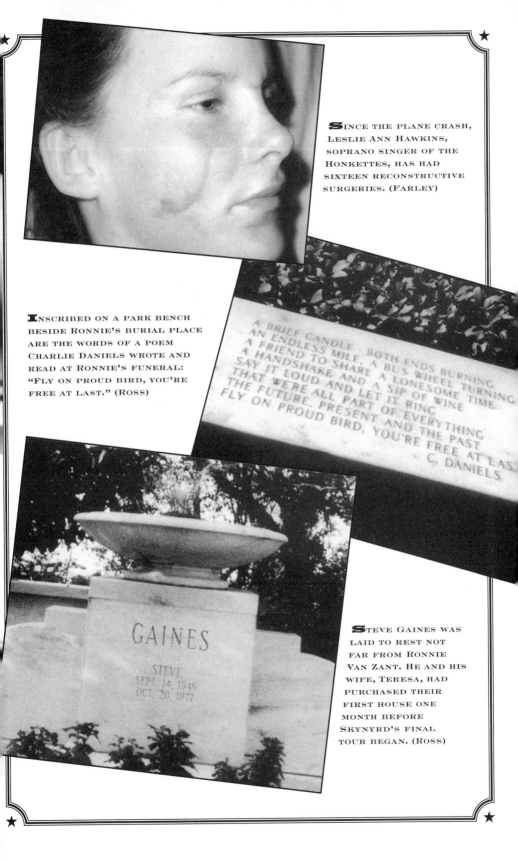

Since the plane crash, Leslie Ann Hawkins, soprano singer of the Honkettes, has had sixteen reconstructive surgeries. (Farley)

Inscribed on a park bench beside Ronnie's burial place are the words of a poem Charlie Daniels wrote and read at Ronnie's funeral: "Fly on proud bird, you're free at last." (Ross)

A BRIEF CANDLE, BOTH ENDS BURNING.
AN ENDLESS MILE, A BUS WHEEL TURNING.
A FRIEND TO SHARE A LONESOME TIME.
A HANDSHAKE AND A SIP OF WINE.
SAY IT LOUD AND LET IT RING.
THAT WE'RE ALL PART OF EVERYTHING,
THE FUTURE, PRESENT, AND THE PAST.
FLY ON PROUD BIRD, YOU'RE FREE AT LAST.
— C. DANIELS

Steve Gaines was laid to rest not far from Ronnie Van Zant. He and his wife, Teresa, had purchased their first house one month before Skynyrd's final tour began. (Ross)

ARROW EDELSTEIN GROSS & MARGOLIS, P. C.
1370 AVENUE OF THE AMERICAS
NEW YORK, N.Y. 10019

(212) 586-1451

ALLEN H. ARROW•
GERALD F. EDELSTEIN•
JOHN M. GROSS
GERALD A. MARGOLIS•
___
CLAIR G. BURRILL••
PAUL TRUSS
DOUGLAS V. BROWNE

• ADMITTED IN NEW YORK AND CALIFORNIA
•• ADMITTED IN CALIFORNIA ONLY

TELEX
224600
___
CALIFORNIA OFFICE
9200 SUNSET BLVD.
LOS ANGELES, CAL. 90069
(213) 274-6184
___
CABLE ADDRESSES
SUMMALEX NEW YORK
SUMMACAL LOS ANGELES

October 30, 1978

Mr. Leonard Skinner
Leonard Skinner Productions
1702 Osceola Street
Jacksonville, Florida

Dear Sir:

Re: Lynyrd Skynyrd v.
Leonard Skinner

Please be advised that we represent the individuals who created
a group called Lynyrd Skynyrd and companies established in the State
of Florida under the names of Lynyrd Skynyrd Productions, Inc. and
Lynard Skynard, Inc.

Our clients for the past several years have publicized or caused
to be publicized, promoted and otherwise established the name Lynyrd
Skynyrd as being identified with a particular group of people, a
particular segment of the entertainment industry and in addition have
established a relationship with the name Lynyrd Skynyrd as being
symbolic of the quality of their performances, recordings and
identification with the general public. In short, a secondary meaning
and identification attaches to the name Lynyrd Skynyrd.

We are advised that you, your company or persons deriving
authority from you have begun to engage in the entertainment industry
and in particular in the field of concert programming. We understand
further that you have advertised concert performances of popular music
and rock music performers using the name either Lynyrd Skynyrd or
Leonard Skinner by means of radio, television and other verbal communications knowing fully well that the average member of the public
would regard the two names as interchangeable and identify the name
as belonging to our clients attaching to it the secondary meaning
which has been established through our clients' efforts over the past
several years.

to deceive the
ith your organ-
attempting to
comes even more
d musical com-
of the above
related to our
and harm.

Our clie...
substantial co...
tainment industry an...
to multitudiness telephone ...
our clients' names have been used ...
project and tarnished. We are therefore ...
should be responsible for damages which have been suffered by yo...
actions.

nsing the name
ther name or style
ve the public.
has already caused
c and in the enter-
annoyance of respon
other communication
on with a commercial
nding that your comp

Should you not give me a satisfactory undertaking that your
objectionable conduct will cease forthwith, I shall immediately
advise our clients to pursue other remedies. Pending the recei
of your response, all of our clients' rights are reserved.

Sincerely yours,

Allen H. Arrow

AHA:ch
cc: Allen Collins
    Joe Rascoff
    Gary Rossington
    Judy Van Zant

IN 1978,
AN ATTORNEY
REPRESENTING
LYNYRD SKYNYRD
PRODUCTIONS
WARNED LEONARD
SKINNER OF LEONARD
SKINNER PRODUCTIONS
TO STOP USING HIS
NAME TO PROMOTE
HIS BUSINESS.

Leonard Skinner Productions
1702 Osceola Street, Suite 1, Jacksonville, Florida 32204 Telephone (904) 389-1395

November 6, 1978

Mr. Allen H. Arrow
Arrow Edelstein Gross & Margolis, P.C.
1370 Avenue of the Americas
New York, New York 10019

Dear Sir:

In response to your letter of October 30, 1978, please be advised of the following:

1. My name is Leonard Skinner. I was given this name at birth and have used it personally and in business for my entire life (which is 45 years and eleven months.)

2. At no time have I ever used the spelling "Lynyrd Skynyrd" nor do I have any desire to do so.

3. At no time have I ever attempted to deceive the public.

4. At no time have I encouraged, authorized or suggested that anyone use your clients' recordings and musical compositions in connection with my advertising.

5. If anyone over the years has had to respond to multidiness telephone calls, letters and other communications and had his name tarnished; it is I and not your clients.

6. If anyone has suffered damages over the years, it is I and not your clients because they used my name, not because I used their name.

In closing, let me say that I must insist upon my right to use my name in any business venture in which I choose to engage. For several years, I have resisted suggestions from attorneys that I seek remedy from your clients' use of my name; however, because of your clients' position in this matter, I now feel I must re-evaluate my resistance.

Sincerely yours,

LS/rs

Leonard Skinner

"MY NAME IS LEONARD SKINNER. I WAS GIVEN THIS NAME AT BIRTH AND HAVE USED IT PERSONALLY AND IN BUSINESS FOR MY ENTIRE LIFE . . . FOR SEVERAL YEARS, I HAVE RESISTED SUGGESTIONS FROM ATTORNEYS THAT I SEEK REMEDY FROM YOUR CLIENTS' USE OF MY NAME; HOWEVER, BECAUSE OF YOUR CLIENTS' POSITION IN THIS MATTER, I NOW FEEL I MUST RE-EVALUATE MY RESISTANCE."

A FEW YEARS AFTER THE PLANE CRASH, A SHIRTLESS ALLEN SHOWED HE COULD STILL BE BRASH AND DEFIANT. (BULLARD)

IN 1980, ALLEN AND GARY FORMED THE ROSSINGTON COLLINS BAND AND HIT NO. 13 WITH THEIR ALBUM ANYTIME, ANYPLACE, ANYWHERE. ONE YEAR AND A LACKLUSTER SECOND ALBUM LATER, THE LONGTIME FRIENDS FEUDED AND DISBANDED. (ROSS)

ALLEN COLLINS BECAME A MUSICAL HERO FOR MANY A YOUNGER GUITARIST, INCLUDING TONY BULLARD OF VIRGINIA BEACH. THEY EVENTUALLY MET AND BECAME CLOSE FRIENDS. (BULLARD)

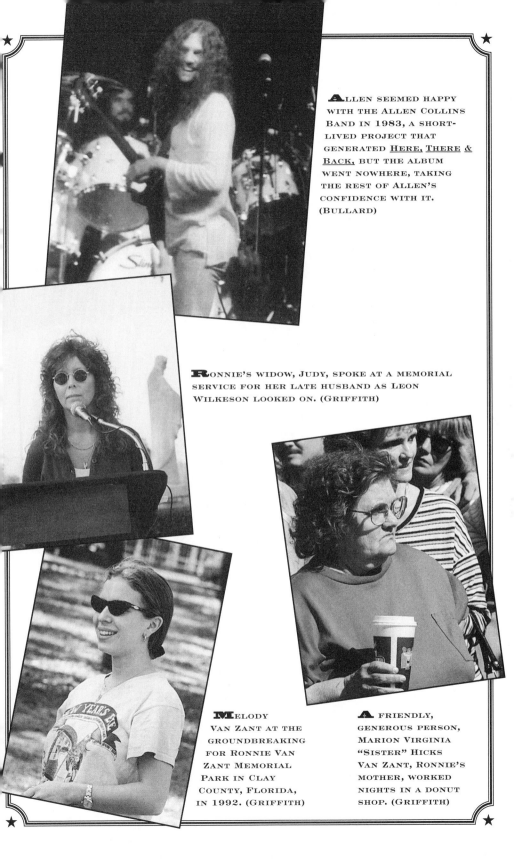

ALLEN SEEMED HAPPY WITH THE ALLEN COLLINS BAND IN 1983, A SHORT-LIVED PROJECT THAT GENERATED <u>HERE, THERE & BACK,</u> BUT THE ALBUM WENT NOWHERE, TAKING THE REST OF ALLEN'S CONFIDENCE WITH IT. (BULLARD)

RONNIE'S WIDOW, JUDY, SPOKE AT A MEMORIAL SERVICE FOR HER LATE HUSBAND AS LEON WILKESON LOOKED ON. (GRIFFITH)

MELODY VAN ZANT AT THE GROUNDBREAKING FOR RONNIE VAN ZANT MEMORIAL PARK IN CLAY COUNTY, FLORIDA, IN 1992. (GRIFFITH)

A FRIENDLY, GENEROUS PERSON, MARION VIRGINIA "SISTER" HICKS VAN ZANT, RONNIE'S MOTHER, WORKED NIGHTS IN A DONUT SHOP. (GRIFFITH)

LACY "PAPA V" VAN ZANT, THE SELF-STYLED "FATHER OF SOUTHERN ROCK," IS A FORMER TRUCK DRIVER. ON ONE MORE FROM THE ROAD, RONNIE DEDICATED "TRAVELIN' MAN," WRITTEN BY LEON, TO HIS DAD. (GRIFFITH)

AUTHOR VISITS HIS OLD FRIEND RONNIE AT HIS GRAVESITE IN JACKSONVILLE MEMORY GARDENS. (BEAZLEY)

"YOU DON'T REALIZE HOW MUCH HE ADDS TO THE BACKBONE OF THAT BAND. IF YOU TAKE LEON OUT OF THE EQUATION, IT JUST AIN'T LYNYRD SKYNYRD." PHOTOGRAPH TAKEN ABOUT ONE MONTH BEFORE HE DIED IN JULY 2001.

NOT VERY LONG BEFORE
HIS OWN DEATH IN 2001, LEON
WILKESON RAISED A TOAST AT
THE GRAVE OF HIS LATE
FRIEND, RONNIE.

LEONARD SKINNER BECAME
PRACTICALLY A CELEBRITY IN HIS
OWN RIGHT. TODAY, HE STILL MAKES
APPEARANCES AT ROCK AND ROLL SHOWS
AROUND THE COUNTRY.

LEON WILKESON AT THE
HELM OF THE AIRCRAFT
USS <u>ENTERPRISE</u> IN
NORFOLK, VIRGINIA.

LEON AND GARY PLAYING
TO BEAT THE BAND AT A LYNYRD SKYNYRD
SHOW IN 2001.

WITH FACIAL HAIR AND A FEW MORE POUNDS, GARY ROSSINGTON CONTINUES TO BE ONE OF AMERICA'S FINEST ROCK GUITARISTS. (ROSS)

KID ROCK DOWNS A COLD ONE WHILE A PATRIOTICALLY HATTED LEON TAKES A MOMENTARY BREAK BACKSTAGE.

IN LATER YEARS, LEON PLAYED WITH POST-CRASH VERSION OF THE "THREE-GUITAR ARMY." LEFT TO RIGHT: HUGHIE THOMASSON, RICKEY MEDLOCKE, AND GARY. (ROSS)

a quiet drink. He didn't want to be interrupted but a drunk at the bar kept prodding him with smart remarks. Ronnie handed Craig some cash and told him to take care of the problem, so Craig walked up to the bar, and when the guy made a hostile move toward him, Craig lent him an elbow that dropped him to the floor. That's all there was to it. The Skynyrd crowd was asked to leave, and Ronnie wrote a pretty good song about it.

If '70s rock had gone to Broadway, it would've had to include "That Smell"; it was just that good. Transforming a near-tragedy into practical advice that anyone could grasp, Ronnie reached into the bottom of his throat to summon the stark, eerie voice of the devil, invoking a frightful specter of death with lyrics he considered morbid. Allen came up with the tune and Steve crafted a very sophisticated arrangement, with the angelic voices of Cassie, Leslie, and Jo Jo, alternating solos and fiery duets among Allen, Gary, and Steve, and a classic Leon Wilkeson bass part that was so well conceived and executed that veteran bassists are still awed by it. The song was another upbeat hit that Skynyrd followed with "One More Time," a slower-tempo song about loving a lying woman. If it sounds a little out of place, it's because the song was the original Muscle Shoals recording, with only some minor tweaking for the new album. Still a good song after six years in the can, it gave fans a sound they hadn't heard from Skynyrd, with Ronnie singing from an echo chamber to a beat from one of their early influences, Jethro Tull.

A masterwork for the band, *Street Survivors* was a *tour de force* for Steve Gaines, who not only arranged "That Smell," but composed and sang on four other songs, including two for which he wrote the lyrics. And while "One More Time" was a novel sound from out of the past, Steve's "I Know A Little" had a new jazzy style with the air of a classic oldie. Starting with the familiar, rat-tat-tat cymbal splashes heard by every drive-in movie-goer in the sixties, this was lickety-split, country-jazz boogie, played by a guitarist who may have been as fast and as clean as Alvin Lee of Ten Years After. "Man, that boy can play!" Ronnie would say, thinking how great it was, once again, to have not just two great guitarists in his band, but three! And Steve wrote the lyrics, to boot! Billy was equally thrilled to have this new shot of fire in their bellies, and his bouncing keyboard play was nothing less than inspired.

Right off the bat on this first song from Steve, Skynyrd fans knew they were in for a treat, and then came his next one, "You Got That Right," a fast-paced, up-on-your-feet boogie that begins like something from Delaney and Bonnie and Friends, but with Ronnie and Steve sharing the singing. And they sounded *good* together, like they'd been doing it for years. This was another outstanding display of individual shapes and styles from the three-guitar army, who launched into a bridge that's as lively and thrilling as anything Skynyrd had ever done. The train was rolling again.

The second of the two Gaines-Van Zant collaborations, a medium-paced song about longing for a woman's return, may be the most original offering on the album. "I Never Dreamed" demonstrates a welcome new sound and a new level of arranging that Steve had brought to the band, ranging from soft, sweet slide work with light organ backing, a high-pitched, off-beat staccato accent, and some very fast, very clean picking. Then it's off to the country and "Honky Tonk Night Time Man," a classic country blues rambler by Merle Haggard, on which Steve's black Les Paul was featured again. "Sounds like Roy," Ronnie said on the record, referring to Steve's rapid-fire picking, which brought to mind no less a guitar virtuoso than the great Roy Clark. (Ronnie also saw in Steve something of another guitarist named Roy, the great blues guitarist Roy Buchanan.) Merle Haggard had become Ronnie's favorite singer, topping off a list that included Ray Charles, Muddy Waters, Paul Rodgers, Jimi Hendrix, Hank Williams, and Jimmy Rogers. Ronnie had always been a country singer at heart, fronting for a rock and roll band because that's where the money was. "This is where it's at right now," he'd said in the early days, referring to rock, but he had embraced country music on every album and he wanted to take it further. "Country music is the kind of music you

never get tired of," he'd say. "I can listen to it every morning, like biscuits and gravy."

The last track on *Street Survivors* offered another new attraction for Skynyrd fans, in the form of a blues guitar. While Allen and Gary could sound like Eric Clapton, some of their peers suggested that Steve Gaines might have become as good as the master himself. Because Steve captured not just the sound but the feel of the blues, and his country blues number, "Ain't No Good Life," was a prime example, a slowed-down honky-tonk funk that he sang by himself—it was the only Skynyrd song that didn't have Ronnie's voice. But Steve's soulful blues guitar, wailing as Stevie Ray Vaughn might have played it, set this number apart from every other song that Skynyrd ever recorded. And Billy's soft, sweet touch on the ivories produced a sound as much like an antique upright as he had ever coaxed from a keyboard. Like so many other Skynyrd songs, the last one on the final album left their listeners yearning for more.

Street Survivors drew universal praise from music critics, who called it a mature, sophisticated recording with "exemplary performances," "tasteful arrangements," and "intricate melodies." If Skynyrd had wanted to stop writing and coast through the rest of their lives playing oldies, they now had a repertoire that would carry them as far into the future as they might ever have cared to go. But the way they all felt, this band was just getting started. As Leon remarked, "We didn't have a single worry right then. We really had our act together; we were really gonna fly."

Having performed for huge crowds all summer long and anticipating the release of an album that just might bust the charts, Ronnie and the rest of the veterans were poised to turn a corner in their career, and Steve was excited to be there. Rescued from the dreary prospect of playing motel lounges, he'd been to the top of the mountain at Knebworth, and one year later they were still a huge draw in the states, introduced to crowds with the theme from the movie *The Magnificent Seven* playing over the public address system. In July, almost ninety-one thousand people had filled Philadelphia's JFK Stadium for a music festival where Peter Frampton was the headline act. But concert reviewers agreed that Lynyrd Skynyrd stole the show. The following night, in the Civic Center in Charleston, West Virginia, everyone was charged and confident, so much so, in fact, that Ronnie produced a joint and shot-gunned all four guitarists during "T For Texas," and then asked the crowd, "And you don't think they ain't messed up?" With the kind of responses the group was getting, night after night, every show was a party, and it just kept getting better. Two weeks later in Oakland Stadium, Frampton was the headliner again, joined by Santana and the Outlaws, but many of the ninety thousand fans left after Skynyrd was done, and by the time Frampton was finished, the stadium was less than half-filled.

Skynyrd was clearly on top of the world, and yet, for Ronnie, the world seemed a little too big sometimes and he longed to get back home, "where people are real, and nobody bothers you," he said. Late that summer, returning from a fishing trip south of Jacksonville, Ronnie, a friend, Tom Vickery, and I stopped at a fast food restaurant in Palatka, Florida, and as we sat there eating, some teenagers walked in playing a boom box. "Sweet Home Alabama" came on the radio, and they all started singing along, unaware that Ronnie was sitting just a couple of tables away. I motioned for him to let them in on our little secret, but Ronnie put his finger to his lips to be sure I wouldn't say anything.

What a thrill that would have been for those kids, but Ronnie just couldn't do it. He really didn't like the limelight, and he never made a show of himself when he wasn't performing on stage. Another example of this side of Ronnie came just two days before his final concert appearance, on a day between shows in St. Petersburg and Lakeland in Florida. Skynyrd had come to the Altamonte Mall, where hundreds of fans had gathered in the parking lot,

hoping to see the stars and collect their autographs. Ronnie had always shied away from that sort of thing, preferring, that day, the quiet of the band's motor home. Although he was relaxed on stage telling stories, he never felt he deserved the adulation he received, and he was always uncomfortable signing autographs. "You have to go out there. Those people came here just to see you," I told him, so he reluctantly walked out to the tent where the rest of the guys were already greeting the crowd. One of the last fans he spoke to there was Bobby Sanders of Lockhart, Florida, who asked him if he knew the song "Little Black Egg" by the Night Crawlers from the early '60s. Ronnie graciously said it was his favorite song, and then he signed a Skynyrd promotion poster for Sanders, never realizing how much those simple gestures had meant to a devoted fan. "The next night, Skynyrd opened a sellout show in Lakeland with 'What's Your Name?' and two days later, Ronnie Van Zant was dead," Sanders recalled, noting that he framed the poster and still has it.

Ronnie could never accept the fact that he was anyone's idol. He would've been stunned that a poster he signed would be displayed in someone's home twenty-four years later. But that was the effect he had on people through his music. Sanders, who attended the invitation-only, premier showing of *Free Bird: The Movie* in Atlanta's Fox Theater in 1995, told me how much it meant for him to be there, to feel the presence of his hero. "I was so proud to share that experience with my family, of seeing Ronnie Van Zant, because their spirit that night made it seem as if Ronnie was really there." Before the film was shown, surviving band members had performed with several guest artists, including Charlie Daniels, the Atlanta Rhythm Section, and Al Kooper, who sang and played mandolin on "Made In The Shade." Bob Burns was also there on the night before the movie was shown to the public.

Sanders's sentiments are similar to those of Skynyrd fans all over the country, and in Europe and Japan, as shown by how many people have traveled to Jacksonville over the years just to be where Ronnie had lived. "This area is our version of Graceland," said thirty-five-year-old Randall T. Carter, who came from Chicago on the twenty-second anniversary of Ronnie's death. "Ronnie Van Zant wrote music that was about our lives. He wrote about real people," he added. That same year, thirty-six-year-old Keinchi Sakita traveled to Ronnie's grave from his home in Osaka, Japan, as he does every year, expressing his feelings as tears filled his eyes. "We have the same soul," he said. "We have the same heart."

What can explain the effect that Ronnie Van Zant still has on so many people of different origins and cultures, so many years after his death? John Lennon wrote that a workingman's hero is something to be, and that's what Ronnie was. He thought of himself as a simple man, his songs were about regular people, and the message hit home no matter where home might happen to be.

For Ronnie, home had become a new house on Brickyard Road near Orange Park, Florida, where reality was fishing for bass, cooking steaks on the grill, and playing with Melody, his baby girl. It was his first time in a house of his own, having lived in apartments for years, while traveling almost constantly. Not far from Ronnie's place, Steve and Teresa Gaines bought their first house, too, just one month before the final Skynyrd tour began. Ronnie's property on Doctor's Lake, which is really a tranquil inlet off the St. Johns River, was a peaceful wooded area most notable, perhaps, for being near Whitey's Fish Camp, a dockside restaurant and unofficial bass fishing headquarters for the greater Jacksonville area, and a symbol of what Ronnie would usually rather be doing. He could have chosen a larger house in a high-end neighborhood, but if "Lifestyles of the Rich and Famous" had ever come to Brickyard Road, instead of showing off his home, Ronnie probably would've taken the audience to Whitey's, where the people are as real as the hush puppies.

Much has been made of the fact that Ronnie was withdrawing from whisky, getting some exercise, and generally getting his act together at the end of his life, but old habits die hard, and Ronnie still had a way to go. One indication is a magazine interview that quoted an obviously inebriated Ronnie ranting and cursing, which he had never allowed himself to do in previous interviews. It sounded as if he was angry, but if you knew him, it simply reflected

the fact that Ronnie never should have been around alcohol. He was a good person but often a mean drunk, and woe be to anyone who crossed him when he'd had a little too much. He was also generous, and the best friend anyone could ever hope to have.

The week before Skynyrd's final journey began, Ronnie invited his old friend, Bill Ferris, to dinner, and urged him to help manage the tour. It was an offer he'd made several times over the years, but for Bill, college and family had always come first. "That night at Doctor's Lake, if I had accepted his offer, I would have been on that plane," Bill recalled, although his training as an Army aircraft mechanic just might have made a difference. "I wonder if I could've convinced him not to fly [from Greenville] . . . This was a case where his strong will worked against him."

"I lost one of the finest men I've ever known," Bill said, expressing sentiments shared by so many others who knew Ronnie well. "He knew who he was, he knew where he came from, and he never forgot who his friends were before he made it big. He had a certain amount of backbone, a certain amount of stature, a certain amount of character. He cared about one thing: Who are you?" Another old friend, Harley Lamoureaux, happened to be in Greenville, South Carolina, for Skynyrd's final concert. He remembered their stellar performance and the spirited response from the crowd, but he also recalled something about Ronnie that few people ever knew. "Ronnie had a fear of being booed off the stage. He told me about it one night. He said, 'I don't know what they see in me, and one day they're gonna wake up.' He didn't see himself as something special." Ronnie had other fears, too, and he was superstitious. After a black cat crossed the road in front of us one night, he wet his index finger and made three Xs on the car windshield. If you stepped over his fishing pole in a boat, he'd make you stop in mid-stride and step back, and then he'd throw you in the water. He hated snakes, and he always hated to fly.

CHAPTER 9

DEATH ON THE WING

I couldn't imagine our plane coming apart like it did, as if only our hopes had held it together. Originally designed with a single passenger area holding ten rows of seats, four abreast, the plane had been modified to carry twenty-four persons in three seating areas without partitions. In other words, if you stood in the back facing forward you could see all of the interior except for the cockpit and the galley behind it, which were separated from the passenger area by two wall panels with a doorway in between.

Everyone but me was wearing a seat belt when we crashed, yet every seat but one was ripped from the floor, and almost everyone was hurled forward into the wall panels in a pile of broken bodies that smothered the people on the bottom. Ronnie, the heart and soul of the band and its distinctive Southern voice, lay at the bottom of the heap, a knot on his forehead his only apparent injury. He'd also suffered broken bones in his lower legs, as had Steve Gaines and Dean Kilpatrick, the band's personal assistant, both of whom apparently were killed instantly from head injuries. The forward

RONNIE VAN ZANT'S FINAL RESTING PLACE. (ROSS)

passenger section where they'd sat had flipped over and split open, both armed swivel seats were torn loose, and a wraparound couch in the forward right corner was ripped apart. Allen Collins had a cervical spine injury and a bad cut over his right eye, and his right arm was slashed so deeply he almost lost the use of it. Gary Rossington had broken both of his arms, his right leg, and his pelvis. Kevin Elson, the sound engineer, suffered a collapsed lung, and both of his legs, his right arm, and his right ankle were broken.

In the center section, where only one of six double-unit seats remained bolted to the floor, only one person was killed, Cassie Gaines, Steve's sister, from head and neck injuries. Leon Wilkeson suffered a chest wound and a badly broken left arm and leg, plus internal injuries that caused his heart to fail twice until doctors revived him. Billy Powell was cut severely on his face and right knee. Leslie Hawkins, who had been sitting across the aisle from Cassie above the wings, had cervical spine injuries and severe lacerations on her face. Artimus Pyle suffered multiple contusions and abrasions. Others in the center section were Skynyrd road crew members Kenneth Peden, Clayton Johnson, James Bruce, Joe Osborne, Don Kretzschmeier, Paul Welch (who remained unconscious for more than four days after the crash), and Bill Sykes (who had joined the group in Greenville to film the band's next concert). Everyone on board received lacerations and abrasions, and most had broken bones, but all of the passengers in the rear compartment survived the impact, including Mark Howard, Ron Eckerman, Marc Frank, Steve Lawler, and Craig Reed, the longest serving member of the Skynyrd team, who has been with the group for more than twenty-eight years.

I was thrown from the plane through a hole in the fuselage. My neck was broken, and my face and head were cut deeply. I was the only person burned in the accident. The doctors thought it must have been caused by oil, battery acid, or hydraulic fluid, but I was told later that the plane had carried de-icing flares, and that phosphorus from a flare had melted the side of my head and liquefied

my left eye. Billy later told me I had crawled from beneath a piece of the wreckage and tried to reach out to him, but he pushed me away. His nose was almost torn from his face, and he was afraid he might lose it in the mud in the dark if I happened to touch it. I fell back, unconscious, as were most of the others who were still alive. Both of the pilots were killed instantly.

Ronnie, Steve, Cassie, and Dean must have expired within minutes after the crash, if not upon impact. For the rest of us, help was on the way, but we didn't know it. Shortly before 7 p.m. the U.S. Coast Guard Station in New Orleans, about seventy-five miles away, had learned of the accident from the air traffic control center in Houston, Texas, which had been in touch with the flight crew for several minutes before the crash. Already airborne, a Coast Guard HH3F helicopter immediately headed north to find us, and at 7:23 the chopper crew picked up a signal from the plane's emergency locator transmitter, the only thing still functioning on the aircraft. In thirteen more minutes they found us.

Hovering one hundred and fifty feet over the trees, the helicopter illuminated the wreckage with a searchlight until rescuers arrived on the ground a half hour later. About 9 o'clock six more Coast Guard helicopters arrived with medical supplies and a portable VHF-FM radio for state and local agencies to use, with communications coordinated from a Coast Guard HC-131 Convair "Samaritan" helicopter as it circled overhead. A light chopper owned by Southwest Mississippi Air Ambulance Service also brought supplies from Southwest Regional Medical Center. At least six medical doctors, including one who came from Mobile, Alabama, on a Coast Guard chopper, and twenty medical corpsmen and emergency medical technicians, mostly from Pike County, diagnosed, treated, and stabilized us as we were evacuated and taken to hospitals. Nineteen persons were taken to Southwest

Regional Medical Center about seventeen miles away. One person was taken to Beachman Memorial Hospital in Magnolia, Mississippi. Dr. Verner Holmes, who was on the scene with the first rescue personnel and remained until all of the survivors were evacuated, later remarked that if not for the timely, on-scene efforts of the U.S. Coast Guard, the Pike County Civil Defense Council (twelve radio-equipped, privately owned pickup trucks and more than twenty volunteers), and EMTs, most of the twenty survivors probably would have died.

I returned to the crash site some time later, just to see it and to talk with people who had been there. We had crashed in southern Mississippi just above the Louisiana border. It was about five miles northeast of the town of Gillsburg in Amite County, whose mostly flat landscape is otherwise distinguished only by an abundance of wild timber, pines mostly, with small farms scattered among the trees.

The place where six people died is in a tree-filled swamp about a quarter of a mile from the nearest hard road—"Slaughterhouse Road," as folks in the area later called it. Close by, crossed by an old, worn logging trail, lay two freshly plowed fields that had just been planted with soft rye grass. If only we could have landed there. I met the man who tended the property, and he told me what he remembered of the accident and why he had fired his shotgun toward some of the survivors that night.

With night setting in, Johnny Mote was tossing hay for his cattle when suddenly a loud scratching noise came from somewhere out in the woods. "It was like a car skidding in gravel, and right after that I heard a deep rumble, like it was underground," he said. An odd stillness fell upon the area, muzzling every frog and cricket for what seemed an unnaturally long time. And then the silence was gone, replaced by a low, dull drumbeat of a sound that

was barely audible at first, a persistent staccato pulse that grew increasingly louder as it approached through the eerie darkness.

Once it reached the woods near Mote, the chopper halted its progress and started circling, shining its searchlight downward to reveal the trees, the field, and the ghostly presence of three strange men walking toward him from the direction of the swamp. Aware that some escaped prison inmates might be in the area, Mote got into his pickup truck and drove past the men twice, looking them over without stopping. Then he drove to his mobile home, hurried inside to get his shotgun, and told his wife to lock the doors. "I was watching *The Waltons*. He said there were escaped prisoners behind the trailer and for me to lock the doors," Brenda Mote said. Weapon in hand, Mote rushed back outside, turned off the truck engine, and grabbed the keys as the "inmates" approached. They were Artimus Pyle, Marc Frank, and Kenneth Peden, Jr., who were all covered with blood.

Peden, a Mississippi native, could recall hitting the trees but not the final impact. "I remember the plane clipping the trees. I must have gotten knocked out. I came to outside the plane and walked around in circles for about five minutes." In total darkness, the only survivors who could get to their feet without falling somehow found each other and made their way through the swamp toward a light they could barely see.

"Once we got through the woods," Peden continued, "we walked through a cow pasture and came to a dirt road. A pickup truck came by and we tried to stop it, but it didn't stop. It came back by, and we tried to stop it again, but it kept going. We walked up to the trailer, and the man fired a shotgun over his head and told us to stop. I just yelled to him, 'Our plane just crashed; it's bad; they need help.' "

"I don't know how they got up here," Brenda Mote said. "It's so dark down there, just a swamp. They had blood all over them, and mud, and their hair was all down in their faces." Her husband remembered one of the men "hugging me around the neck and telling me, 'We've got to get them out.' " Peden and Frank went into the house while Pyle waited outside until rescuers arrived and took them to the hospital.

The first of many ambulances soon arrived and took the men twenty miles to the hospital in McComb. About that time people began arriving in large numbers, emergency workers and others, and helicopters were plunging into the pasture with medical supplies. "By the end of the evening the National Guard wouldn't let us in our own pasture," Brenda Mote said.

One of the survivors was Steve Lawler of Houston, a member of the band's road crew who had been playing poker in the back of the plane. "I crawled out of the plane," Lawler said. "I don't know exactly how I did it. I remember getting down on my stomach and crawling. I grabbed hold of a tree and just sat there, trying to collect my thoughts. I remember having glass all over my face. It was very, very black. Then everything got real quiet. Our concern was to get ready for a hard landing on a runway. I don't think it was in anyone's mind that we were headed for the trees." Hearing desperate moans and cries from people who were trapped inside the plane, he wanted to help but couldn't. "I wanted to, but I just couldn't physically get up," he said.

Some time later, after the first helicopter had been hovering for a while, a crowd started gathering. "There were just thousands of people there, it seemed. They were really nice for just a bunch of people who had come from their farmhouses to try to help." Lawler was taken to the hospital in the bed of a pickup truck. "It wasn't really that bad. It could have been a lot worse," he told a newspaper reporter.

Leslie Hawkins and Bill Sykes, who had been seated together, found themselves sitting in a section of the plane that was suspended ten feet above the ground, with a piece of the roof hanging precariously over their heads. Fearing the roof might collapse when rescuers walked on it, Leslie screamed for them to get off. Sykes remembers hearing people "yelling and screaming and moaning, and I started to move from my seat to help them, but

my right arm was broken, and the bone was sticking out. I couldn't move." When the helicopter landed, he said, "I got up on top of the wreckage and started yelling for people to find us. When help arrived, they took me down and propped me up against a tree."

Among the first rescuers to reach the scene was Gerald Wall, a constable with the Amite County Sheriff's Department. Speaking of Pyle, Peden, and Frank, whom he'd seen at Mote's home, he said, "They were in pretty bad shape. One of them had some ribs sticking out." At the wreckage he found dead bodies and injured persons, some still unconscious, lying together in the front of the crumpled fuselage. "Some people were crying and some were moaning. Some didn't know what was going on," he said. "They were all in the front of the plane, and they were all shouting, 'Get me out. Get me out.' We were actually standing on top of some people to get the others out."

One by one, rescuers lifted them out through a hole in the fuselage at the top of the wreckage, covering them with blankets that people had brought from their homes as more helicopters arrived and directed their lights toward the scene. The rescue operation was difficult. Curiosity seekers sometimes interfered with medical treatment. At times, no one was directing newly arrived ambulances to the most desirable point to pick up the injured. Some of the ambulances, pickup trucks, and vans that were used got stuck in mud two hundred yards away, before they could reach the swamp. Once on foot, rescuers had to cross an open field, slog twenty-five feet through a waist-deep creek, and wade through a wet timber marsh as eerie shadows shifted about constantly under a helicopter searchlight. Carrying four bodies and seventeen injured persons on stretchers—the pilots' bodies couldn't be removed that night—made the trek back from the swamp exhausting.

Donald Chase, who lived a few miles from the crash site, was another of the first people to reach the wreckage. One of the first things he saw was the bodies of the pilot and co-pilot, still strapped into their seats in the inverted cockpit, which was suspended above the ground and too badly mangled against a tree to permit their removal that night. Chase recalled the struggle to climb the steep bank of the creek while carrying a victim. Looking for a helping hand from the onlookers gathered above him, he saw that they were content just to watch. Disgusted, he grabbed one of them by the shirt and pulled her into the water.

Chase left his teenage son at the crash site and rode in an ambulance with three victims to McComb's Southwest Regional Medical Center, which had initiated its disaster response plan thirty minutes before the first patients arrived. Twenty-nine doctors were called in to treat the accident victims that night. I vaguely remember lying in the back of a pickup truck, and then in an ambulance on the way to McComb, falling in and out of consciousness and trying to sit up. Helicopters later transferred me, along with Allen, Gary, and five others, to Jackson Memorial Hospital, one hundred and three miles away, in Jackson, Mississippi.

When Chase rejoined his son, it was after midnight. A television crew from Baton Rouge was interviewing the administrator of Amite County while several hundred people lingered quietly in small groups, embracing the depth of the tragedy and not wanting to leave.

"That was a night to remember," Chase said.

As many as three thousand people eventually gathered at the edge of the swamp and along the roadway leading into the area, slowing the movement of rescue vehicles as they arrived, and again as they left with victims. They were drawn by the news on television and radio that a plane had gone down with the nation's top touring rock and roll band aboard.

Scores of people waded out to the wreckage that night, and some of them left with souvenirs. By the time the National Guard arrived to secure the accident scene and keep bystanders from hindering the rescue effort, it was too late to keep the "bone pickers" away. In the darkness and confusion they took wallets,

purses, jewelry, and cash, as well as airplane seats, seat belts, pillows, and anything else they could carry. They took my watch, my wallet, my ring, and my money as I lay bleeding on the ground. I would like to think that only one "grave robber" was involved, but so many items were missing that I have to believe otherwise.

Why did six people have to die like that? What had gone wrong?

In his preflight report, McCreary, the pilot, had estimated that it would take two hours and forty-five minutes to fly from Greenville, South Carolina, to Baton Rouge, Louisiana. But two hours and forty minutes into the flight, at 6:42 p.m., he called the air traffic control center in Houston, Texas, with an unexpected request.

"We need to get to an airport, the closest airport you've got." Less than two minutes earlier he had left twelve thousand feet, having been cleared to descend to six thousand feet.

Houston asked if he was in an emergency status. "Yes, sir, we're low on fuel and we're just about out of it. We want vectors to McComb, posthaste, please, sir." Gray, the co-pilot, may have quickly plotted our position on a navigation chart and advised McCreary, correctly, that the nearest airport was in McComb, Mississippi, which they had already passed. At 6:43 p.m., Houston gave McCreary the flight vectors to McComb and advised him to turn around. A full minute passed before he confirmed that he had made the turn, but twenty-two seconds later he called out, "We are not declaring an emergency, but we do need to get as close to McComb as straight and good as we can get, sir."

Thirty-eight seconds passed, and he was on the radio again. "Five Victor Mike. We're out of fuel." The plane's license number was N55VM, which McCreary abbreviated in aviation lingo.

"Roger, understand you're out of fuel?"

"I am sorry, it's just an indication of it," McCreary said, without explaining what he meant. Asked for the plane's altitude at 6:46 p.m., he answered, "We're at four point five (4,500 feet)." That was the last recorded communication between our plane and the ground.

After several unsuccessful attempts to contact the plane, Houston asked McComb to try, but Everett Farley, an air traffic controller at McComb, got no response. When we disappeared from Houston's radar screen Farley asked the pilot of an approaching jet to look for us. At four minutes before 7 p.m. the pilot said it was too dark to see anything, but he had picked up a strong signal from the Convair's emergency locator transmitter, which McCreary or Gray must have activated as they tried to land.

The signal came from a heavily wooded area fourteen miles southwest of McComb, just fifty-two miles from the airport in Baton Rouge.

If gliding were normal for a twenty-one-ton aircraft, our long, hushed descent would have seemed peaceful. All we heard was a muffled whoosh of air and the empty sound of slowly spinning propellers as we fell from the sky like a bird that dies on the wing. I had once seen a bird die that way, in the quiet of mid-flight, its life systems still as it fell toward an end it couldn't feel. How fortunate that bird was.

The accident report stated that we descended at an angle of five degrees, which would have made for a tolerable landing if the pilot had been able to reach an open area. But even if he had been able to see a clearing in the twilight, he couldn't steer the plane because it lost hydraulic power when the engines stopped.

If only the plane had run out of gas sooner, because by the time McCreary called for directions to the nearest airport, we were seventeen miles past it. He could have been looking for the airport earlier, knowing that we needed fuel. When McCreary asked for

the nearest airfield, he seemed to know already that it was McComb. He requested the closest airport, and moments later, without waiting for Houston to respond, he specified McComb. If the flight crew had been looking for McComb earlier, either we were too far away to see its lights, or the lights weren't operating.

The McComb-Pike County Airport's 5,000-foot runway was equipped with medium-intensity runway lights, a medium-intensity approach light system, sequence flashers, and abbreviated approach slope indicators. The runway lights and an outer, rotating beacon were controlled by a light-sensitive photocell. The beacon was out of service at the time of the accident, but investigators couldn't determine if the runway lights had been operating the night we crashed. Monitored two days later, they came on at 6:22 p.m. A notice had been issued to advise pilots that the airport's localizer, a radio signal that identifies the airport, had been impaired for several months and was transmitting without identification. There was no indication that McCreary had tried to contact the airport at any time before he turned around. A flight data recorder and a cockpit voice recorder weren't required on the Convair, and neither "black box" was aboard.

Donald Chase, whose home is about three miles southwest of the crash site, was standing in his yard when the plane passed overhead, moving in a southwesterly direction. "I could tell it was having trouble because it was sputtering. I remember saying, 'I hope he makes it.' I went in the house and came back out and the plane was coming back at a considerably lower altitude, still sputtering," Chase said. He estimated that the plane couldn't have traveled more than a mile before it turned around.

To achieve the correct heading of twenty-five degrees toward McComb, as Houston had instructed, the shortest maneuver for McCreary was a left-hand turn through one hundred and forty-three degrees, which is eighty percent of a complete U-turn. Moments later the hydraulics went out, making steering impossible. At that point McCreary stopped communicating with

Houston, possibly because the radio had lost power, but more likely because he was too busy looking for a clear space to land and fighting to hold the wings level at a safe angle of descent.

At this he was quite successful, because our fall through the air felt nearly the same as it would for a routine landing. But all hope vanished when we struck the first tree ninety-eight feet above the swamp. Despite its all-metal construction, the CV-240 couldn't hold up to the pounding it took as it plowed through the dense hardwood forest, losing both wings and most of the tail section as it fell. At the gruesome end of a trail of debris almost five hundred feet long, suspended above the ground in the overturned cockpit, the lifeless bodies of McCreary and Gray remained until the next morning, when a bulldozer freed their mangled, metal coffin from a tree that is decades older today and appears no worse for the wear.

It was several weeks before anyone told me that Ronnie had died. I was so badly injured, they thought it might hurt my recovery to know he was gone. But I went to his grave as soon as I could, and I spent a lot of time there, just sitting and thinking. I thought about how we had played together as four-year-old boys, and how we had ridden our bikes and shot squirrels as adolescents. I thought about how we had fished together as adults, and I thought about how much he had meant to me as a friend. I thought about the remarkable quality that time has, to be able to make life seem as if it could last forever, or to erase an entire lifetime in a fraction of a second. And I thought about the music.

With eyes closed, I could hear Lynyrd Skynyrd as clearly as I had from the side of the stage at their last performance. The band was playing, Ronnie was singing, and the fans were up on their feet, rocking and clapping and singing along with the words they knew by heart. Ronnie's words. Hearing his voice, I felt Ronnie's presence so strongly I knew he was there beside me. Sobbing like a

child, I told him I was sorry. More than once, I heard him say it wasn't my fault, but I just couldn't accept that, not for a long time.

People are surprised when I tell them there was no fire and no explosion when Lynyrd Skynyrd's plane went down. I guess that's an expectation created by movies and television. I'm thankful there wasn't a fire, but that was never even a possibility. With the exception of one quart of fuel that investigators found in both engines and all of the fuel lines, combined, there was no evidence of any other fuel in the gas tanks, the carburetors, or anywhere else on the plane, or around the crash site.

Why had we run out of fuel? With a maximum fuel capacity of one thousand, five hundred and fifty gallons in the Convair 240, McCreary and Gray had purchased one thousand, three hundred gallons of fuel before they left Addison, near Dallas. When they picked us up in Jacksonville, Florida, to start the tour, they bought two hundred gallons, and they diligently added fuel at each of the stops we made—two hundred gallons in Statesboro, Georgia, four hundred gallons in Miami, Florida, two hundred and fifty gallons in St. Petersburg, two hundred gallons in Lakeland, and four hundred gallons in Greenville.

In his preflight report, filed by telephone in Greenville, McCreary said that after fuel was added there, the aircraft had five hours' worth of fuel on board, which would have been nine hundred gallons. This couldn't have been correct. In its investigation following the accident, the National Transportation Safety Board (NTSB) calculated that the plane consumed five hundred and twelve gallons from Greenville to the crash site, and that two hundred and seven gallons of fuel should have been on board when it crashed, based upon normal cruising conditions with both engines operating in their normal mode.

But the starboard engine hadn't been operating in its normal mode. Bill Sykes, who happened to be a licensed pilot, had noticed the starboard engine smoking during takeoff, and as the airplane gained altitude the flight crew let him sit in the jump seat behind them to observe. Shortly after reaching twelve thousand feet, he later told investigators, the pilot "leaned" the right engine ("auto-lean" mode was the normal position for the fuel mixture control lever, rather than the "auto-rich" position) and it backfired and began to run rough, so he returned the mixture control to full rich, and the problem cleared up. The pilot, who was working the engines at the time while the co-pilot flew the aircraft, told Sykes that the right engine had a bad magneto. Sykes returned to his seat, and not quite three hours later the right engine started acting up. When someone shouted, "Oil!" Sykes looked out a right-side window and noticed a streak of oil three or four inches wide and ten inches long on the inside of the engine cowling. Almost immediately afterward the left engine started acting up, too, and soon came the first of the two messages from the cockpit that the plane was going down.

The Safety Board couldn't determine why the pilot's preflight plan reflected five hours' worth of fuel on board when we took off from Greenville. But without knowing how long the starboard engine had been operating in the auto-rich position on the final flight and on earlier flights, there was no way to calculate exactly how much fuel was on board after four hundred gallons were added in Greenville. The investigators—twelve from the NTSB and ten from the Federal Aviation Administration (FAA)—found no evidence of any malfunction of the aircraft or its control system. The only problem worth noting was the unidentified problem with the right engine, which was not considered a major mechanical failure.

Post-mortem examinations of the flight crew reported no evidence of drugs, alcohol, or elevated levels of carbon monoxide in the blood. To determine the fuel discrepancy, the NTSB analyzed three possible explanations:

First, there could have been a fuel leak. Although this possi-

bility couldn't be eliminated completely because of the remote chance that the impact could have obliterated any evidence of leakage, a fuel leak wasn't considered a likely explanation.

Second, the amounts of fuel recorded on purchase slips might have been incorrect. The Safety Board considered this only a remote possibility because the fuel meters on refueling trucks could not have been reset, and if they were functioning properly, they would reflect the exact amount of fuel that was dispensed to the aircraft.

And third, one or both engines were burning more fuel than normal, and more than the flight crew expected to be burned. Torching from the right engine would indicate a rich fuel mixture or some other discrepancy associated with inadequate fuel combustion. But even with the right engine burning more fuel than normal, nine hundred gallons of fuel, which the flight crew thought they had on board, would have been enough to reach Baton Rouge.

The accident report stated that the crew was either negligent or ignorant of the increased fuel consumption because they failed to adequately monitor the plane's instruments for fuel flow and quantity. Had they realized the actual fuel consumption early in the flight, they could have planned an alternate refueling stop. But I was struck by something else the investigators concluded, something it doesn't take a trained pilot to figure out: "The pilot was not prudent when he continued the flight with a known engine discrepancy and did not have it corrected before he left Greenville." In a synopsis of its investigation, the NTSB stated, "The probable cause of this accident was fuel exhaustion and total loss of power from both engines due to crew inattention to fuel supply. Contributing to the fuel exhaustion were inadequate flight planning and an engine malfunction of undetermined nature in the right engine, which resulted in higher-than-normal fuel consumption."

Like most people, I've run out of gas in my car at least once, and I've come close on many occasions. So I asked a former pilot if it's as easy to overlook the fuel gauge in an airplane as it is to do in a car, and his answer was short but poignant. "You can afford to be complacent in a car," he said.

Unanswered questions have haunted my life. What if our original pilot had been flying the plane on that tour? What if we had chosen some way to get to Baton Rouge, other than flying? What if we had refused to fly that day? After all, we left Greenville on Thursday, and the concert in Baton Rouge wasn't until Friday. What was the hurry? Why didn't we wait and insist that the mechanic fly from Texas to Greenville rather than meet the plane in Baton Rouge?

What if at least some of us had been able to find an alternative? Cassie had wanted to take a commercial flight, but apparently no suitable flights were available. Had the equipment truck not left town right after the concert, she would have gone in the truck. Equally concerned, Leslie had sent her ten-year-old son, Matt, home the day before—everyone with kids had brought them along for portions of summer tours. There had been complaints about the plane since the day we got it, and as this discussion continued the night before the crash, Ronnie had made his wishes clear. "If you're not at the show, you're fired."

What if the limo drivers had arrived at our motel on time in Greenville? By not showing up they delayed our flight, which caused another costly error, inadvertent though it was. Expecting us to arrive at any moment, the flight crew prepared for takeoff the way they normally did, by warming the engines while the air-conditioning system cooled the interior. They kept the engines running for at least a half an hour, unaware that we were still at the motel waiting for the limos. That might have been enough time to burn the few gallons of fuel we would need to reach Baton Rouge, especially since the engines had been running earlier that day, for who knows how long, while McCreary and Gray worked on the starboard engine.

What if the flight crew had been looking for the McComb airport before we passed it, knowing we were burning too much fuel? If so, what if they had been able to see the airport? What if we had lost hydraulic power sooner and the pilot couldn't have turned the plane around? We might have landed in a clear area.

All we needed was enough fuel to take us forty-eight more miles. Based upon the observations of Donald Chase, who'd seen us flying south and then north, that's how close we were to Baton Rouge when we turned around. After touring constantly for four years, playing to sellout crowds in forty-three states and seven countries, the Lynyrd Skynyrd band had flown hundreds of thousands of miles only to fall forty-eight miles short on a tour called the "Tour of the Survivors." Their final album, *Street Survivors*, had been issued just three days earlier. Forty-eight miles.

And, finally, what if the co-pilot had been drunk, and stoned, and high on cocaine until the wee hours of the morning of the fatal flight? Could any of those factors have affected his ability to do his job? This possibility has never been discussed publicly until the present volume.

Sometimes we learn from tragedies and sometimes they can serve to help people. Lynyrd Skynyrd's plane crash yielded both of these results, although neither was worth the loss. In the lawsuit we filed against the L&J Company, we discovered that our lease agreement had relieved L&J of any liability in case of an accident. In fact, the contract that L&J had drafted gave operational responsibility of the aircraft to Lynyrd Skynyrd Productions, which meant that the band had control over the flight crew and everything they did. In other words, we could have ordered them to turn around in Lakeland or we could have grounded the plane in Greenville. According to the contract, Lynyrd Skynyrd Productions had assumed responsibility for the pilots' negligence.

That didn't seem right to us or to the FAA, which sued L&J for violating standard lease requirements and to determine who was the legal operator of the flight. As the National Transportation Safety Board stated in its accident report, "There may have been sufficient information in the lease for the lessee to understand his (Lynyrd Skynyrd Productions) status, if he read it, . . . However, the lessee did not understand what his role was on the basis of the lease, nor would he have had any better understanding if the provision had been drafted as intended by the regulations." As a result of the issue of responsibility that arose because of the tricky lease agreement, the FAA amended its rules one month after the crash so that the agency would have an opportunity to conduct future pre-flight reviews of all aircraft leases. Since then, the FAA has been able to ensure that people who lease airplanes have a clear understanding of who the operator is under their agreement, and what obligations they are assuming.

At some point I came to accept the accident. I stopped blaming myself for what happened, and, for the most part, I've been able to put the tragedy behind me, comforted knowing that Ronnie's legacy will last for as long as people enjoy good music. It's more than a fulfillment of his dreams, I believe, and I know he'd be overwhelmed and humbly grateful, to realize how much joy his music has brought to so many listeners. As for the rest of the band, their future was foretold in a letter to *Rolling Stone* magazine not long after the accident, when a fan wrote, "Last flight, my eye."

At the time that Skynyrd's airplane went down, an MCA Record Company executive rated Lynyrd Skynyrd and Boston as the two most popular rock groups in the country, with retail sales of Skynyrd records valued at $45 million. In Baton Rouge, where the band was booked for the following night, concert promoters had expected ten thousand fans to fill the Assembly Center at Louisiana State University. They issued refunds, but some folks preferred to keep the tickets as mementos. Fourteen years later, one hundred stalwart Skynyrd fans responded to a concert promoter's offer and exchanged those tickets for free admission to hear the 1991 version of the band in Baton Rouge, along with nine thousand others.

Charlie Daniels, who was probably Ronnie's closest friend among recording artists, remembered the night of the crash. "About a half hour before going on stage in St. Louis, when we heard the plane went down and there were fatalities, I went downstairs and asked a friend who worked for a radio station there if he could find out more information. He left to do that, and we went out on stage that night without knowing. It was a tough night, and very upsetting. You know you've lost a friend, but you don't know who they are. About 2 a.m. I found out who had been killed," he said, noting that although he was closest with Ronnie, he counted many of the band and crew members among his friends. "I do a dedication to Ronnie every night on my show," Daniels said. "He is one of the best remembered and best thought of musicians who ever came down the pike.

"It wasn't long before people started calling me for comments, and it seemed like I could never turn loose of it. Sitting in a hotel room, possibly in Phoenix, I wrote [a poem]. That was my response to radio stations that called. At the funeral I read it and sang 'Peace In The Valley' and gave it to Judy." And this is what he wrote:

A brief candle, both ends burning
An endless mile, a bus wheel turning
A friend to share the lonesome times
A handshake and sip of wine
So say it loud and let it ring
That we're all part of everything
The present, future, and the past
Fly on proud bird, you're free at last.

Not far from his home on an overcast day, October 25, 1977, Ronnie Van Zant was laid to rest in Jacksonville Memory Gardens, with a recording of Merle Haggard's "I Take a Lot of Pride in What I Am" in the background. In a simple, private ceremony in a funeral home chapel beforehand, a recording of David Allen Coe's "Another Pretty Country Song" was played, and Charlie Daniels and members of .38 Special sang "Amazing Grace." Among the other mourners present were Dickey Betts, Al Kooper, Tom Dowd, and members of Grinderswitch and the Atlanta Rhythm Section. The pastor for the service was the Rev. David Evans, who'd helped engineer *Nuthin' Fancy.* Billy Powell was the only band member present, as the others were still in hospitals in Mississippi. Another ceremony was held for Steve and Cassie, who were laid to rest near Ronnie. Dean Kilpatrick was buried in Arlington Park Cemetery in Jacksonville.

CHAPTER 10

REFLECTIONS AND RENEWAL

A number of things have happened since the plane crash, some tragedies, some triumphs, some squabbles over money. Things never seem to end up in neat little packages, so that what follows are snapshots from the years that have passed, beginning with another look at the accident investigation.

The "why" behind Lynyrd Skynyrd's plane crash may never be fully understood, but at least one observer believes that the sobriety of a member of the flight crew was never fully investigated. How the pilot and co-pilot spent their time leading up to the fatal flight merits review.

On the morning the band arrived in Greenville, the co-pilot, William Gray, broke his eyeglasses while unloading luggage. Gray was nearsighted, and his commercial pilot's license required him to have his glasses whenever he flew, so, accompanied by Walter McCreary, the pilot, he went to an ophthalmologist's office that afternoon to be fitted for a new pair. While there, they

FRIENDS SINCE THE SEVENTH GRADE, ALLEN AND
GARY HELPED EACH OTHER RECUPERATE AFTER THE
ACCIDENT. (FARLEY)

told Dr. Eddie Holcomb that their passengers were scared, and that they'd just called the airplane leasing company and had been advised that, due to the cost involved, the company would fly a mechanic to Baton Rouge. The next day after lunch, Gray picked up his new glasses, and that night, the flight crew went to the concert. Afterward, McCreary and Joy Ellis, a desk clerk at the band's hotel, the Sheraton Palmetto, went to a nearby Holiday Inn lounge, where McCreary ordered drinks for Ellis and two of her girlfriends and water for himself, explaining that he had to fly the next day. She and a friend and McCreary left the bar about 1 a.m. and parted company. The next day, McCreary seemed well and rested, and the sinus headache he'd had the night before was gone, Ellis told investigators. Gray walked up, but she didn't notice how he looked. She hadn't seen him since before the concert.

From the plane wreckage, crash investigators looked in McCreary's luggage and found an unlabeled bottle with nineteen capsules of five-milligram Librax, which doctors prescribe mainly to prevent painful intestinal spasms that sometimes result from stress. Librax contains a sedative, and users are cautioned not to operate heavy machinery, drive, or engage in other hazardous tasks that require mental alertness. Could McCreary's faculties have been impaired enough to affect his ability to notice that the fuel was being consumed much faster than normal? The accident report didn't explore this possibility, but, of course, Gray was also in the cockpit and could have made that observation. But were Gray's faculties also impaired, possibly from being hungover and getting too little sleep the night before? Skynyrd road crew member Clayton Johnson told investigators that Gray was awake and drunk at 4 a.m. But was he also high on cocaine?

The answer would require a full-scale investigation that had nothing to do with the plane crash and everything to do with cocaine, and the catalyst for the start of the drug bust that followed was the funeral of Ronnie Van Zant.

If not for the plane crash, there's a strong likelihood that some band members might have been caught in a law enforcement

dragnet that snared a movie star and a prominent musician, a Florida state senator's two grown children, and a lot of other folks who enjoyed putting money up their nose. Shortly after the funerals for Ronnie and Steve and Cassie, federal and state police arrested thirty people, initially, and as many more later, for their involvement in a cocaine operation worth an estimated $30 million. Among the defendants were actress Linda Blair, who had starred in the movie *The Exorcist* and had befriended the band in California; jazz trumpeter Phil Driscoll; band friends John and Lynn Scarborough, whose father was then a state senator; and Eddie Mangum, a twenty-five-year-old Jacksonville man who had been selling cocaine to Lynyrd Skynyrd through Leon Wilkeson. After the funeral, Linda Blair had accompanied Lynn Scarborough to get cocaine from Mangum, whom state police arrested on November 28, 1977. At the time, there was speculation that police had been after Skynyrd to make a high-profile bust, but after the crash they'd decided to settle for Linda Blair and Phil Driscoll, who also had a national following but no connection to the band. Two of the criminal investigators who worked the case insist that Lynyrd Skynyrd was never the goal, yet band members might have been arrested if their link with Mangum had been strong enough. Former investigator Jerry Casey said police had wiretapped Mangum for several months before any celebrity drug buyers came into the picture, and that a judge extended the wiretap "after we saw more celebrities and more dealing. We terminated the investigation not long after the crash."

"I don't think Ronnie was involved in getting drugs," Casey said. John Farmer, who was chief investigator for the Florida Department of Law Enforcement, said, "We may have encountered a band member or two, but we never targeted them. We never targeted Linda Blair." If band members had been dealing with Mangum in large quantities, however, they would have been nabbed, too, he said. But Mangum disagrees. "If it wasn't for the plane crash, they'd have busted most of the band. The police said they were looking for my source, but they had my source the first week," said Mangum, whose role as drug "kingpin" had begun eleven months earlier when he was lured with the promise of easy money. Turning a $300 profit in his first week, Mangum quit his low-wage job as a steelworker, and it was all downhill from there, as one of his first customers turned out to be a cop. "The police find out your limit and your publicity value before they bust you," Mangum said.

"I can't tell you how many times Leon called me at 3 a.m., and said, 'We need you over here, man.' He came to my house once at 3 a.m. wearing a buffalo headdress with one horn up and one horn down and said, 'Let's party.' We'd just snort coke all night. Leon liked to snort. Allen liked drinking alcohol and doing Quaaludes. Ronnie liked to drink whisky and smoke a little pot. He was like a good ol' country boy, a regular Joe. Band members usually bought one to two ounces per week, maybe three. They might hit it hard one or two nights a week," Mangum said. "They treated me like I was a real person, not just a drug dealer."

Casey, the former investigator, still believes that cocaine may have played a role in Lynyrd Skynyrd's plane crash. He says that William Gray, the co-pilot, bought an ounce of cocaine the night before the plane crash, although the audiotape that police made of the conversation was destroyed long ago. Whether their wiretap overheard Gray placing an order for cocaine or confirming its delivery, there was no evidence that he snorted cocaine before the crash, and the autopsy found none in his system. Mangum recalls that Leon had invited him to join them for their last show in Miami, just five days before the crash, but that Mangum couldn't make the trip.

Two tragedies followed in the wake of the plane crash, neither of which would have happened if not for the accident. The first claimed Ronnie's friend since childhood, Chuck Flowers, who had worked for the band for about three years. A wonderful guy with a

great sense of humor, he was inconsolable after Ronnie's death. Chuck deeply regretted leaving the band's road crew, and he couldn't help feeling that he should have been on the airplane. Not long after the funeral, Chuck took his own life. The other misfortune befell the mother of Steve and Cassie Gaines. Two months after the crash, Bud and Cassie Gaines moved from Oklahoma to Jacksonville to be near their granddaughter, Corrina. Their son, Bob, also moved there and started a band. One night in February 1979, after hearing Bob's band play in a place called The Still (formerly the Leonard Skinner Lounge), Mrs. Gaines was driving home with Bud beside her, when she nudged the bumper of a car that she passed. Both cars stopped beside the road, and Bud Gaines got out and walked between them. A third vehicle struck the rear car, crushing Bud's legs, and then it struck and killed his wife, who also had gotten out of the car. By coincidence, I drove past the scene just as Bud was being lifted into an ambulance. Mrs. Gaines was buried near Cassie and Steve.

One post-crash story with a happier ending started out sadly over money. Bob Burns, who recovered from the problems that had led him to leave Skynyrd in 1974, had not been fully compensated for the work he'd done with the band, and getting it took some effort. Shortly before the plane crash, Bob spoke with Ronnie to ask for his share of royalties from *Pronounced* and *Second Helping*. Ronnie said Bob should be paid, and he told him to get in touch with an attorney in New York to make the arrangements. As they stood talking outside Skynyrd's rehearsal studio on Riverside Avenue in Jacksonville, Judy drove up with their new baby girl, Melody, and Ronnie picked up the baby and hugged her. It was the last time Bob ever saw Ronnie. But six months after the accident, Bob still had not been paid. He and his Jacksonville attorney felt that the problem lay with the band's management, not with the band, and during the next several months the management office mailed a few small checks to Bob, indicating that this was done only as a favor to help him out. Bob's lawyer flew to New York, where he was shown records indicating that Bob was owed about $10,000, at the most. Bob's lawyer was fresh out of law school and had no experience with entertainment law. Both he and Bob were naive enough to think that what they'd been told might be true, but they decided to visit the home of Allen Collins, whom both of them had known since childhood, thinking he might be able to help the situation.

They found Allen in good spirits and recovering well from his injuries. Other people dropped by, and a party developed that lasted through the night. Complimenting Bob, Allen had him tap out the drumbeat for "Workin' for MCA," which he said had been difficult for Artimus to learn after Bob had left the band. But Allen said he was in no position to help Bob financially, although he was sympathetic. Bob and his lawyer returned to Allen's house a short time later, when they could talk more seriously. This time Gary Rossington was there, and Bob was told that he wasn't owed any money, but that he could have $10,000 if he agreed to relinquish any further interest in the band's earnings. Related legal documents arrived in the mail soon afterward, but Bob and his lawyer rejected the offer. They decided a lawyer with experience in entertainment law was needed, so Bob hired one. In very short order, MCA sent $500,000 to Bob, who later engaged in litigation with the band and received additional compensation in the form of a significant settlement.

One year after the plane crash, Leonard Skinner was drawn into a dispute with the band because of his name. In a two-page letter dated October 30, 1978, attorney Allen H. Arrow of Arrow, Edelstein, Gross & Margolis in New York, demanded that Leonard Skinner "stop using the name Lynyrd Skynyrd, the name Leonard

Skinner or other name or style which is calculated to create confusion and deceive the public. Our clients believe that your use of their name has already caused substantial confusion in the minds of the public and in the entertainment industry and that in addition to the annoyance of responding to multitudinous telephone calls, letters and other communications, our clients' names have been used in connection with a commercial project and tarnished. We are therefore demanding that your company (Leonard Skinner Productions) should be responsible for damages which have been suffered by your actions."

Multitudinous? Arrow's letter continued, "Should you not give me a satisfactory undertaking that your objectionable conduct will cease forthwith, I shall immediately advise our clients (Lynyrd Skynyrd Productions) to pursue other remedies." What had prompted this effusive but empty challenge was the fact that Leonard Skinner had hosted a concert in Jacksonville, and without his knowledge, Lynyrd Skynyrd music was played in the background during radio promotions that were aired on WAPE radio.

Leonard replied by letter on November 6, stating, in part, "My name is Leonard Skinner. I was given this name at birth and have used it personally and in business for my entire life (which is 45 years and eleven months). At no time have I ever used the spelling 'Lynyrd Skynyrd' nor do I have any desire to do so. At no time have I ever attempted to deceive the public. At no time have I encouraged, authorized or suggested that anyone use your clients' recordings and musical compositions in connection with my advertising. If anyone over the years has had to respond to multidiness [sic] telephone calls, letters and other communications and had his name tarnished, it is I and not your clients. If anyone has suffered damages over the years, it is I and not your clients because they used *my* name, not because I used their name.

"In closing, let me say that I must insist upon my right to use my name in any business venture in which I choose to engage. For several years, I have resisted suggestions from attorneys that I seek remedy from your clients' use of my name; however, because of your clients' position in this matter, I now feel I must re-evaluate my resistance."

"My attorney suggested I add a P.S. that would say, 'Gotcha,' but I didn't," Leonard said, and he never heard from the lawyer again. In fact, Leonard had kept a copy of a letter dated January 30, 1975, which he had received from attorney Frank W. Molloy of the legal department of MCA Records, seeking his approval for MCA to use a photograph of his "Leonard Skinner Realty" sign on the *Nuthin' Fancy* album, which he had granted. Today, Leonard Skinner explains, "I'd made enough money in the real estate business that about 1975 I went into the lounge business, and I modestly named the first of my three bars the Leonard Skinner Lounge," on San Juan Avenue at Roosevelt Blvd., which became The Still, and today is the S.O.S. Lounge. When Lynyrd Skynyrd was back in Jacksonville from touring, the boys often paid him a visit there, where his son, Leonard Skinner, Jr., booked bands to play.

The first time that surviving members of the Lynyrd Skynyrd band performed together again was in January 1979, when they walked onto the stage in Nashville's Municipal Auditorium for a special guest appearance at Charlie Daniels's fifth annual Volunteer Jam. In honor of their fallen friend, Ronnie, they chose to play their much-celebrated encore, which they had once dedicated to the late Duane Allman, then to Berry Oakley, following their deaths. Just being together again in front of a crowd was an emotionally moving experience for the band, but playing "Free Bird" under circumstances they never could have imagined fourteen months earlier made the moment especially touching for all of the people who were present. It may also have been the most humbled the band members had ever felt, and it motivated them to

restart their careers with an all-new music format and a name that would carry just enough of the Skynyrd identity to let fans know who they were.

Aside from their obvious talents as musicians, it can fairly be said that neither Allen nor Gary was blessed with all of the qualities that typically are found in a band leader, but there really was no alternative for the Rossington-Collins Band when they formed it in 1980. Perhaps their best executive decision was to choose a singer who would make it impossible for anyone to even suggest they were trying to reprise their former band. Neither Southern nor male (she's from Indiana) Dale Krantz had proved her vocal abilities, having sung backup for Leon and Mary Russell, and then for .38 Special, with whom she had toured with Skynyrd in the early part of 1977. Krantz seemed like a very good choice. She'd been captivated by Skynyrd the first time she saw them perform, and she had a bold presence on stage to go with the musical powerhouse she would front. But problems sometimes develop when a female enters a formerly all-male realm, and the Rossington-Collins Band would prove no exception. Allen and Gary had hoped Artimus would join them on drums, but Pyle didn't care for their choice of Krantz to hold the microphone. This disagreement generated more friction than any team could stand for long and still remain together, but a timely traffic accident made the problem go away. With Pyle suffering from a badly broken leg—he'd crashed a car when he swerved to avoid a motorcyclist who'd pulled in front of him—Derek Hess of Running Easy was offered the job, and his partner, Barry Harwood, was asked to take Steve Gaines's spot on guitar. Harwood, who had done session work with Joe South and Melanie, had played on three Skynyrd albums. Gary played lead and slide guitar, Allen played lead and rhythm, and Barry played lead, rhythm and slide, and helped write songs, as Krantz did.

With their new lineup in place, the band played its first official concert on February 8, 1980, in the Great Southern Music Hall in Orlando, even though Leon was still enduring a five-day-a-week regimen of physical therapy as a result of his plane crash injuries. In June, they played Atlanta, where they were introduced on stage by then-Lt. Governor Zell Miller. That month marked the release of their first album, which they'd self-produced and recorded during a two-week period in El Paso, Texas, of all places. *Anytime, Anyplace, Anywhere* would reach No. 13 on the Billboard chart, earn gold record status, and later enter the Top 10. The previous November, MCA had released a "golden oldies" album of Skynyrd hits, *Gold & Platinum,* which had been certified gold in March, 1980, and platinum in April. (It would go multi-platinum in 1987, along with *Pronounced, Second Helping, One More For the Road,* and *Street Survivors,* while *Nuthin' Fancy* was certified platinum.)

The Rossington-Collins Band performed in their hometown on January 3, 1981, in the Jacksonville Coliseum, where they hosted a "Welcome Home Party" to help build a clubhouse for the Fraternal Order of Police. Advance tickets cost $7.50; the opening act was a band called Stillwater. In July, they finished a second album, *This Is The Way,* which they'd written and recorded during a seven-week period, but Allen and Gary had begun to get at each other's throats, with singer Dale Krantz drawing much of the blame, whether deserved or not. On September 16, a gig in Lubbock, Texas, marked a major blowup. There were loud arguments before they went on stage, and at one point during the show, Allen knocked Dale's mic stand to the floor with his guitar. Then he threw her microphone down onto the floor and stormed off the stage, and they finished the show without him. Neither Allen nor Dale appeared for the encore, and they continued their dispute outside after the show. Dale said she'd quit, Allen said she was fired, and the next night's show in El Paso was canceled. But three nights later they were all back together for a scheduled show in Norman, Oklahoma. And then the roof fell in, but for a totally unexpected reason. Back in Jacksonville, Allen's wife, Kathy, who was pregnant with their third child, died unexpectedly as a result of a miscarriage.

Allen's downward spiral had begun slowly after the plane crash,

but his emotional decline accelerated after Kathy's death in 1981. In a tally that's probably incomplete, Allen was arrested eighteen times from 1974 through 1985, including several stops for drunken and reckless driving, and driving with his license revoked. Allen proved you could have your license revoked permanently more than a few times and still keep driving. Even back then, this kind of reckless behavior usually brought jail time for offenders like Allen, but unlike most people, he could afford the kind of justice where money talked and dangerous drivers walked. In 1983, he formed the Allen Collins Band with Billy, Leon, Barry Harwood, Derek Hess, and Jimmy Dougherty. It was a short-lived project that generated *Here, There And Back,* but the album went nowhere, taking the rest of Allen's confidence with it. He was arrested twice that year for driving with a revoked license—during the previous sixteen months he'd been arrested three times for drunk and reckless driving. Allen was arrested for DUI in September of 1983, and for reckless driving in December. After all that, Allen Collins finally spent some time in the Duval County jail.

I remember an occasion during this period in Allen's life, when I was driving a car with Allen sitting beside me, and without any warning, he grabbed the wheel and jerked it over, and it was all I could do to keep the car from flipping. Allen had done this kind of thing many times, long before then, such as stepping on the accelerator when someone else was driving. He'd always been reckless in cars, regardless of who was driving, but after Kathy died, I believe he had a death wish. In fact, Allen had made it clear to his younger friend, Kent Griffith, that he had no more desire to live, and from what Kent witnessed on January 29, 1986, there was surely no reason to doubt it. It would be Allen's final feat of carelessness behind the wheel.

Late on a Wednesday afternoon, after smoking a couple of joints in his home on Julington Creek Road in Jacksonville, a restless, thirty-three-year-old Allen, who had little to do and was basically dulled from boredom, drove to a liquor store for a little pick-me-up, with Kent along for the ride. It was only a few miles to the store, but even a short drive could be a long and frightening trip when Allen was in the car. When they got to the drive-through window of the package store, Allen ordered a half-pint of whisky (unless it was really a pint, which Kent doesn't remember clearly) and a can of soda. Not being a person who would always drink while actually driving, on this particular occasion, with the package store clerk looking on in amazement, Allen chugged the entire bottle and chased it with the soda, and then he headed for home. Much to Kent's relief, they arrived with life and limb intact, but very soon afterward Allen and his live-in friend, Debra Jean Watts, were embroiled in a heated squabble that prompted Kent to leave. One can only wonder where Allen and Debra were headed when they left his home later in Allen's 1986 Ford Thunderbird, but they didn't get far. At approximately 7 p.m. in front of a house at 12200 Plummer Grant Road, Allen's shiny black automobile left the road, skidded sideways, and slammed into a driveway culvert, violently ejecting its occupants in the process. Debra died in an ambulance on the way to the hospital, and Allen, whose enthusiasm and spirit had enlivened hundreds of exciting performances by one of the finest bands in the world, was paralyzed from the chest down, his six-foot-tall, one-hundred-and-fifty-pound body left to waste in a wheelchair.

There were no witnesses to say who was driving the car, but Allen, who said he had no memory of the accident, pleaded no contest to DUI manslaughter, reckless driving, and driving with a revoked license. Because alcohol was a factor in an inordinate number of Duval County's traffic fatalities at the time, which happened to be an election year, then-State Attorney Ed Austin made investigation of traffic homicides a major effort, and Allen's crash was custom-made for publicity. To prove that Allen was driving, and not his passenger, accident reconstruction experts conducted some rather elaborate tests, and they concluded that his DUI manslaughter charge should stand. It seemed a major waste of resources, given that Allen, who should have been serving time behind bars for endangering people's lives on so many previous occasions, was no longer a threat to society. Allen's attorney, who had helped him get out of so many similar scrapes before, told the judge that prison for Allen would serve no purpose, since the prospect of him ever driving a car again was no longer physically possible. Allen was placed on two years' probation, banned from ever driving or owning a car, and directed to make public service videos against drinking and driving.

With no one content with the way things had gone since the plane crash, in September of 1987, the band appeared informally as Lynyrd Skynyrd during Charlie Daniels's Thirteenth Annual Volunteer Jam near Nashville, with Ed King back in the lineup. Promoted in advance, their presence on the bill helped attract the first sellout for the two-year-old Starwood Amphitheater. Following Charlie Daniels onto the stage to an awesome roar of applause from sixteen thousand, five hundred adoring fans, they were filled with a range of emotions. Holding back tears, Allen briefly addressed the crowd from his wheelchair, saying, "I'm so choked up I don't know what to say. God bless us all." There were nine acts on the seven-hour bill that day, but even a remarkable performance by Stevie Ray Vaughn and his Double Trouble band was eclipsed by the presence of Skynyrd. With Ronnie's younger brother, Johnny, who had rehearsed with the band for only eight days before the show, and with backup vocals from Carol Bristow and Gary's new wife, Dale Krantz-Rossington, the new Skynyrd sound proved more of a crowd pleaser than anyone could have expected.

As it turned out, the Jam was only a warm-up for a run that would pass through the turn of the century. The new band would include Gary, Leon, Billy, and Artimus; Randall Hall, whom Allen had picked to succeed him; Ed King, who returned to the job he'd left in 1975; and Johnny Van Zant, who sang in place of his older brother, Ronnie. But the original plan had called for only a limited-engagement "Tribute Tour" that was scheduled to end in December of 1987. They had wanted to start on October 20, the tenth anniversary of the plane crash, but their chosen venue, Atlanta's Omni, was booked, so they opted for October 14 and 15 instead. The second show, which sold out within two hours, was recorded, as were subsequent shows in the Starwood Amphitheater and the Reunion Arena in Dallas. The result was a two-disc set, *Southern By The Grace Of God*, which was issued the following year.

Starting with a spoken introduction by Ronnie Van Zant's father, Lacy Van Zant, the self-styled "Father of Southern Rock" (his two other sons also were rock singers, Donnie in .38 Special, and Johnny, who had been in the Austin Nichols Band before he joined Skynyrd), the album opens with "Workin' For MCA" and closes with "Free Bird," with a cross-section of favorites in between: "Sweet Home Alabama," "Swamp Music," "Call Me The Breeze," "I Know A Little," "That Smell," "You Got That Right," "What's Your Name?" and "Gimme Back My Bullets," featuring an outstanding solo from former Dixie Dregs guitarist Steve Morse, who appears on the album with another special guest, Donnie Van Zant of .38 Special. The only surprise in the package is a song from the *First and . . . Last* album, "Comin' Home," which Allen had written with Ronnie for the last of their Muscle Shoals sessions in 1971. Now, sixteen years later, Allen was listed on the album only as "arrangement consultant." He was no longer writing music, he could no longer play his guitar, and he would never walk on a stage again. During a show in Wheeling, West Virginia, that year, watching the band from the side of the stage, Allen turned his wheelchair around and cried. As he later explained to his friend, Kent Griffith, he'd wept for a variety of reasons, but mainly because he ached to perform with the band again, and he was sorry he'd ruined his life.

An awkward moment for others in the band came during a comedy show in Atlanta, Georgia, in May of 1988. During a break between Skynyrd concerts, Ed, Leon, Artimus, and Carol Bristow had gone to see comedian Bob "Bobcat" Goldthwait perform at Atlanta's Chastain Park. Making the amusing observation that

there's always someone in a rock and roll audience who'll call out for "Free Bird," no matter who the band is, the Bobcat cracked that the "Free Bird" band was dead, which immediately brought boos from some of the four thousand people in the amphitheater. As living, breathing Skynyrd members rose from their seats and approached the stage, the comic lost his poise, but Artimus helped him recover by hopping up beside him and putting his arm around his shoulders. Artimus gave Goldthwait a backstage pass for their shows and invited him to their June 5 concert in Atlanta-Fulton County Stadium, where more than twenty thousand fans would hear the new Lynyrd Skynyrd perform.

The Skynyrd ship was sailing again, but their sails would soon be trimmed in a federal courtroom in New York City. The crux of the matter was the use of the Lynyrd Skynyrd name. The band had negotiated with Ronnie's widow, Judy, to use the name only for the 1987 Tribute Tour, but tickets sold so well that they decided to keep on touring. The bedrock at the bottom of this weighty legal wrangle was a discussion that was held in Judy's home a few months after the plane crash, when Judy, Allen, Gary, and Teresa Gaines, wife of the late Steve Gaines, had agreed orally that the Lynyrd Skynyrd name would never be used again, to avoid capitalizing on the tragedy. Representing the estate of her late husband, Judy testified that this "blood oath" agreement was restated on several occasions, that it was written in the minutes of a band shareholders' meeting on March 14, 1978, and that a written compact to that effect was signed. This agreement, she said, had modified a three-page document that Ronnie, Allen, Gary, Billy, and Leon had signed on September 15, 1975, forming a corporation, Lynyrd Skynyrd Productions, Inc., to hold rights to their trade name, and agreeing as shareholders to restrict use of the name to material that would be produced before Ronnie's death. Until this dispute began, the shareholders had met only one other time, on June 25, 1982, when they signed an agreement to share the proceeds from the sale of Skynyrd merchandise.

Whether and how to conduct a 1987 Tribute Tour had been the subject of hot debate within the Skynyrd "family," but on September 1, 1987, Judy and the band had reached an agreement. As a result, Lynyrd Skynyrd Productions, Inc. formed a corporation, The Tribute, Inc., allowing it to complete a tour by December 31, produce related videos, sell merchandise, and sell a live album that MCA would produce. Judy and Teresa signed the Tribute agreement but not a licensing agreement regarding use of the Skynyrd name, and neither agreement waived any rights regarding the name. On October 1, 1987, The Tribute, Inc. contracted with MCA Records, authorizing them to produce an album. Judy and Teresa were to receive 28.57 percent of the net proceeds from merchandising.

The 1987 tour was scheduled to run through November 1, with bookings in twenty-nine cities. But once those engagements were completed, without telling Judy, the band had arranged for a 1988 tour to promote the album, with stops in thirty-six cities initially, and with more bookings to be added later. When Judy learned about plans for the 1988 tour, she immediately told Allen their agreement would soon be breached, and he called Gary to complain. By April, she said, she had heard from Allen's father, Larkin Collins, the business manager for Lynyrd Skynyrd Productions, Inc., who told her that the 1988 tour had been canceled at Allen's request.

From Ronnie's death through April of 1988, Judy had been both a director and a twenty-percent shareholder in Lynyrd Skynyrd Productions, Inc. That month, she received notice of a special shareholders meeting that included the statement, "Following the special meeting, persons elected to the board of directors will discuss plans to continue tour." That was the first she had heard of the tour since Larkin had said it was canceled. On April 21, 1988, after failing to reach an agreement on the album and the tour, the corporation removed Judy as a director and took her stock. At this point, Judy went to court.

What's in a name? In this case, money. During court proceedings in July, earnings from the 1987–88 tours were estimated at almost $8 million, and everyone wanted as big a cut as possible. For Artimus and Billy, especially, every penny counted for a lot. Artimus was bankrupt, and Billy had acknowledged to Judy's attorney that the Internal Revenue Service had impressed a lien on his house for $179,000, and a separate lien against him. And so, the band fought back, contending that under Florida law the oath that Allen and Gary had taken after the plane crash had been enforceable for only a year, and that Judy was not a party to their March 14, 1978, agreement, so that she was not a beneficiary. But the judge ruled otherwise.

In order to show that Judy had given up her right to enforce the terms of the non-use agreement, the band also contended that my first book, *Lynyrd Skynyrd: I'll Never Forget You*, was a commercial exploitation of the Lynyrd Skynyrd name, and that Judy hadn't sued me in order to protect the name. But they had forgotten something that would work in Judy's favor. On April 13, 1983, Allen, Gary, Leon, and Billy, as well as Artimus and Teresa, who were not band shareholders, had signed a statement authorizing me to write a book and publish it under the name *Lynyrd Skynyrd: I'll Never Forget You*. (This agreement hadn't been necessary, but I wasn't sure of that at the time, and I had wanted to protect myself in case it was ever contested.) And so, caught in the middle of this muddle, I testified for Judy in order to help Ronnie's and Steve's families. I had worked as road manager for the Rossington-Collins Band for about six months, had worked for the Allen Collins Band for a brief time during its short-lived existence, and had traveled with the band on the "Tribute Tour," selling my book and T-shirts. I had wanted the band to be able to continue earning a living doing what they loved to do, but felt I had to do what Ronnie would have wanted. This I would readily do again, but I hope I never again have to choose sides among friends. As a result of the lawsuit, the tour continued, but the proceeds were shared with Judy and

Teresa, and subsequent versions of the band have continued in the same general manner.

In 1990, there was another death in the family. Depressed and despairing in a wheelchair, at 3:48 p.m. on January 23, after a four-and-a-half-month stay in Jacksonville's Memorial Medical Center, Allen Collins died from respiratory failure due to pneumonia at the age of thirty-seven. His long years of suffering were finally over. Among the many posthumous tributes that were expressed, the best, perhaps, was a piece in *Music* magazine, which stated that Ronnie had been the soul of Lynyrd Skynyrd, and Allen had been the heart. One year later, Kent Griffith and Allen's father were looking at Allen's guitars when they noticed a message he'd stuck on the back of a Gibson Explorer he'd bought in 1974. It was a wish that had come true, but it hadn't lasted long. The message read, "My dream is to see all my people happy. That would mean everyone is living well and that is all that matters."

Musicians who have performed as part of Lynyrd Skynyrd since they re-formed include guitarists Rickey Medlocke, Mike Estes, and Hughie Thomasson, drummers Owen Hale, Jeff McCallister, and Custer; bassists Michael Cartellone and Ean Evans; and backup singers Carol Bristow, Debbie Bailey, Debbie Davis, and Carol Chase. As of this printing, the only members of pre-crash Skynyrd lineups are Gary Rossington and Billy Powell.

A couple of years later, there was more bad news for a member of the band. In the fall of 1992, forty-four-year-old Artimus Pyle was arrested on charges of sexual abuse of a minor. In December, the court allowed him to change his initial plea of not guilty to a plea of guilty for lesser charges: attempted capital sexual battery, and lewd and lascivious assault in the presence of a child. Pyle was pronounced guilty of the capital offense, determination of guilt for the second offense was withheld, and he was ordered to serve a total of eight years' probation. Not the Artimus I know, but that's what happened in court.

In apparent good health at the age of seventy, Ronnie's mother died suddenly on April 9, 2000, from a cardiac arrest. As if she had known the end was near, only days beforehand she'd bought a new dress and said she wanted to be buried in it.

A shameful thing happened on June 29, 2000, in Jacksonville Memory Gardens in Orange Park, Florida. Shortly before 3 a.m. on a Thursday, someone violated the gravesites of Ronnie and Steve. Using a heavy object, they cracked the two-inch-thick stone wall on the front of the marble mausoleum that held Ronnie's casket. They also broke into an ash vault containing Steve's remains. It was fortunate that someone heard the noise and called police, who responded right away. This may have frightened the grave robbers, who had not yet managed to open Ronnie's casket, but who had removed a plastic bag containing Steve's ashes, some of which appeared to have passed through a hole in the bag. This wasn't the first time Ronnie's grave had been disturbed. In February of 1982, someone had gone to Ronnie's tomb and taken a stone memorial bearing an inscription that Charlie Daniels had composed for Ronnie's funeral. As a result of the second encounter, family members decided to relocate their lost loved ones to a private burial site, although memorials to the deceased band members were kept at their original place of rest. "We are saddened that we had to do this, but we have been left no choice. We were lucky that they were not able to pry open the casket," Ronnie's widow said, adding, "Next time, we may not have been so lucky." The two families created a $5,000 reward fund for information that would lead to the arrest and conviction of whoever perpetrated the crime. In less than a week, Lynyrd Skynyrd fans chipped in more money, enough for a $22,000 reward. But no one was ever caught.

Another death for Lynyrd Skynyrd came in 2001. At the age of forty-nine, after years of smoking and heavy drinking, Leon Wilkeson died of chronic liver and lung disease. Good ol' Leon, whose creative bass playing had been compared with Paul McCartney, and whose heart was as big as the hats he liked to wear, was gone.

Seemingly in great spirits, Leon had checked into the Marriott Sawgrass Resort in Ponte Vedra Beach, Florida, near Jacksonville, for a week's rest from touring with the band. About 10 a.m. on July 27, he told his bodyguard, Myron Cecil Gray, Jr., who was staying in the next room, that he didn't feel well and he wanted to go back to sleep instead of eating breakfast. Gray returned to Leon's room, No. 632, about 2 p.m. and found him lying on the bed face down, with his feet off the bed and resting on a chair. His back felt cold, so Gray turned him over and felt for a pulse, then immediately called the front desk clerk, who called rescue. EMTs found Leon lying on his back, shirtless in blue jeans, with blood from his nose on the bed sheets. The autopsy report called his death accidental. Leon had died of complications from emphysema, with drug intoxication and cirrhosis of the liver as contributing causes. There were no signs of illegal drugs in his bloodstream, but there were indications that Leon had been living with pain. Leon had maintained long-term prescription drug coverage for chronic pain, anxiety, and insomnia. The autopsy had found high levels of oxycodone, a pain-relieving narcotic, and lower levels of Valium, a tranquilizer. The

high levels of oxycodone and its mixing with Valium may have contributed to his inability to breathe properly, one pharmacist said, noting that Valium is safe unless you mix it with alcohol or narcotics, which can slow a person's breathing.

Leon was buried beside his friend, Allen Collins, in the St. Mary's section of Jacksonville's Evergreen Cemetery, as "Free Bird" played in the background. Speakers at the graveside service included Rickey Medlocke, Mike Cartellone, Leonard Skinner, and Leon's sister, Mary, who said that Leon had been a rock star, but that he had never seemed to know it. That's why so many people liked him. He was always a regular guy.

The band postponed eight concerts and dedicated the rest of their tour to Leon's memory. Ean Evans, who had substituted for Leon on previous occasions, as had Tim Lindsey and Rick Wills, assumed the job full-time. On August 23, 2001, while performing before a packed house in Jacksonville's Metropolitan Park, the Lynyrd Skynyrd band was awarded a gold record for their 1998 album, *Lyve From Steel Town.* But then came an even bigger honor, an award for having sold more than twenty-three million records during the past twenty-eight years. Lynyrd Skynyrd was still in flight.

And they haven't stopped flying yet.

DISCOGRAPHY

1973   PRONOUNCED LEH-NERD SKIN-NERD (MCA RECORDS)

1974   SECOND HELPING (MCA RECORDS)

1975   NUTHIN' FANCY (MCA RECORDS)

1976   GIMME BACK MY BULLETS (MCA RECORDS)

1976   ONE MORE FROM THE ROAD (MCA RECORDS)

1977   STREET SURVIVORS (MCA RECORDS)

1978   SKYNYRD'S FIRST . . . AND LAST (MCA RECORDS)

1979   GOLD & PLATINUM (MCA RECORDS)

1982   BEST OF THE REST (MCA RECORDS)

1987   LEGEND (MCA RECORDS)

1988   SOUTHERN BY THE GRACE OF GOD—TRIBUTE TOUR 1987 (MCA RECORDS)

1989   SKYNYRD'S INNYRDS—THEIR GREATEST HITS (MCA RECORDS)

1991   LYNYRD SKYNYRD BOX SET (MCA RECORDS)

1991   LYNYRD SKYNYRD 1991 (ATLANTIC)

1993   THE LAST REBEL (ATLANTIC)

1993   LYNYRD SKYNYRD: A RETROSPECTIVE (MCA RECORDS)

1994   ENDANGERED SPECIES (CAPRICORN)

1996	FREE BIRD: THE MOVIE—OFFICIAL SOUNDTRACK (MCA RECORDS)
1996	FREE BIRD: THE VERY BEST OF LYNYRD SKYNYRD (NECTAR)
1996	SOUTHERN KNIGHTS (CBH/SPV RECORDS)
1997	TWENTY (CMC INTERNATIONAL)
1997	OLD TIME GREATS
1997	WHAT'S YOUR NAME? (UNIVERSAL SPECIAL MARKETS)
1998	THE ESSENTIAL LYNYRD SKYNYRD (MCA RECORDS)
1998	SOUTHERN ROCK (UNIVERSAL SPECIAL MARKETS)
1998	SKYNYRD'S FIRST: THE COMPLETE MUSCLE SHOALS ALBUM (MCA RECORDS)
1998	LYVE FROM STEEL TOWN (CMC INTERNATIONAL)
1998	CLASSIC SKYNYRD (UNIVERSAL SPECIAL MARKETS)
1999	SOLO FLYTES (MCA RECORDS)
1999	EDGE OF FOREVER (CMC INTERNATIONAL)
1999	20TH CENTURY MASTERS: THE MILLENNIUM COLLECTION (MCA RECORDS)
2000	ALL TIME GREATEST HITS (MCA RECORDS)
2000	THEN AND NOW (CMC INTERNATIONAL)
2000	DOUBLE TROUBLE (UNIVERSAL SPECIAL MARKETS)
2000	THE COMPLETE LYNYRD SKYNYRD LIVE (CALAMARI RECORDS)
2000	CHRISTMAS TIME AGAIN (BMG/SANCTUARY RECORDS GROUP)
2000	SKYNYRD COLLECTYBLES (MCA RECORDS)

LYNYRD SKYNYRD

Concert Tour Schedule

After the release of their first record album, *Pronounced,* in August 1973, Lynyrd Skynyrd's first live performance was on September 16, 1973, in Jonesboro, Georgia, where they began a twenty-concert tour as an opening act for artists who included Dr. John, B. B. King, the James Gang, John Mayall, and Muddy Waters.

1973 ★★★★

SEPTEMBER	16	JONESBORO, GEORGIA
	21	MACON, GEORGIA
	29	PENSACOLA, FLORIDA
OCTOBER	9	RUSTON, LOUISIANA
	12–13	SPRINGFIELD, MISSOURI
	17	WILMINGTON, NORTH CAROLINA
	18	GREENVILLE, SOUTH CAROLINA
	19	CHARLOTTE, NORTH CAROLINA
	20	BURLINGTON, NORTH CAROLINA
	23	ATHENS, GEORGIA
	24	WINGATE, NORTH CAROLINA

	26	PASSAIC, NEW JERSEY
	27	SALEM, VIRGINIA
	28	CANCELED
	29	CANCELED
	31	NEW YORK, NEW YORK
NOVEMBER	3	CLEMSON, SOUTH CAROLINA
	4	CHARLESTON, SOUTH CAROLINA
	7	HICKORY, NORTH CAROLINA
	10	PRINCETON, NEW JERSEY
	11	GREENVILLE, SOUTH CAROLINA
	18	ATLANTA, GEORGIA
	20	SAN FRANCISCO, CALIFORNIA
	22–23	LOS ANGELES, CALIFORNIA
	25	DALLAS, TEXAS
	27	ATLANTA, GEORGIA
	28	ST. LOUIS, MISSOURI
	29	CHICAGO, ILLINOIS
	30	DETROIT, MICHIGAN
DECEMBER	2	MONTREAL, CANADA
	3	BOSTON, MASSACHUSETTS
	4	PHILADELPHIA, PENNSYLVANIA
	6	LARGO, MARYLAND
	9	KENT, OHIO
	10	CLEVELAND, OHIO
	26	CHATTANOOGA, TENNESSEE
	27	BIRMINGHAM, ALABAMA
	30	CHARLOTTE, NORTH CAROLINA
	31	ATLANTA, GEORGIA

1974 ★★★★

JANUARY	12	SAN DIEGO, CALIFORNIA
	23–27	LOS ANGELES, CALIFORNIA
FEBRUARY	8	ANTIOCH, CALIFORNIA
	9	SAN JOSE, CALIFORNIA
	11	SALT LAKE CITY, UTAH

LYNYRD SKYNYRD

	13–17	DENVER, COLORADO
	21	WARREN, OHIO
	22	CLEVELAND, OHIO
	23	TOLEDO, OHIO
	24	BUFFALO, NEW YORK
	25	UNIONDALE, NEW YORK
	28	BOWLING GREEN, KENTUCKY
MARCH	1–2	NASHVILLE, TENNESSEE
	3	MEMPHIS, TENNESSEE
	5	JONESBORO, ARKANSAS
	6	CONWAY, ARKANSAS
	7	CLEVELAND, MISSISSIPPI
	9	LAFAYETTE, LOUISIANA
	10	NEW ORLEANS, LOUISIANA
	12	FORT WORTH, TEXAS
	15	MOBILE, ALABAMA
	17	TAMPA, FLORIDA
	19	LITTLE ROCK, ARKANSAS
	20	JACKSONVILLE, ALABAMA
	23	BIRMINGHAM, ALABAMA
	24	FRANKFORT, KENTUCKY
APRIL	11	HOLLYWOOD, FLORIDA
	13	WEST PALM BEACH, FLORIDA
	18	COOKVILLE, TENNESSEE
	19	KANSAS CITY, MISSOURI
	20	ST. LOUIS, MISSOURI
	21	MURRAY, KENTUCKY
	22	FLORENCE, ALABAMA
	25	CANCELED
	26	CINCINNATI, OHIO
	27	LINCOLN, NEBRASKA
MAY	3–4	SAN FRANCISCO, CALIFORNIA
	5	BEN LOMOND, CALIFORNIA
	8	DENVER, COLORADO
	11	FRESNO, CALIFORNIA

	12	SACRAMENTO, CALIFORNIA
	16	CHICO, CALIFORNIA
	17–18	CANCELED
	19	SAN DIEGO, CALIFORNIA
	20	SANTA MONICA, CALIFORNIA
	21	ALBUQUERQUE, NEW MEXICO
	22	SALT LAKE CITY, UTAH
	24	PHOENIX, ARIZONA
JUNE	1	ATLANTA, GEORGIA
	7	NEW ORLEANS, LOUISIANA
	8	MOBILE, ALABAMA
	9	NASHVILLE, TENNESSEE
	11	LAKE CHARLES, LOUISIANA
	13	OKLAHOMA CITY, OKLAHOMA
	14	SAN ANTONIO, TEXAS
	16	HOUSTON, TEXAS
	17	AUSTIN, TEXAS
	19	DAVENPORT, IOWA
	20	CANCELED
	21	CHICAGO, ILLINOIS
JULY	10	COLUMBIA, SOUTH CAROLINA
	11	SAVANNAH, GEORGIA
	12	BIRMINGHAM, ALABAMA
	13	CHARLOTTE, NORTH CAROLINA
	14	CHARLESTON, SOUTH CAROLINA
	16	COLUMBUS, GEORGIA
	17	DOTHAN, ALABAMA
	18	JACKSON, MISSISSIPPI
	19	DALLAS, TEXAS
	20	SEDALIA, MISSOURI
	21	INDIANAPOLIS, INDIANA
	24	EVANSVILLE, INDIANA
	26	BUFFALO, NEW YORK
	28	MEMPHIS, TENNESSEE
AUGUST		RECORDING AND REHEARSING

LYNYRD SKYNYRD

SEPTEMBER	5	BANGOR, MAINE
	6	NEW YORK, NEW YORK
	7	WATERBURY, CONNECTICUT
	9	SYRACUSE, NEW YORK
	11	PARSIPPANY, NEW JERSEY
	13	PHILADELPHIA, PENNSYLVANIA
	14	RICHMOND, VIRGINIA
	15	CHARLOTTE, NORTH CAROLINA
	17	BATON ROUGE, LOUISIANA
	18	RUSTON, LOUISIANA
	19	THIBODAUX, LOUISIANA
	20	ATLANTA, GEORGIA
	21	NASHVILLE, TENNESSEE
	22	CHARLESTON, WEST VIRGINIA
	23	HIGHLAND HEIGHTS, KENTUCKY
	24	DAYTON, OHIO
	25	MILWAUKEE, WISCONSIN
	26	ST. PAUL, MINNESOTA
	27	KANSAS CITY, MISSOURI
	28	ST. LOUIS, MISSOURI
	30	LOUISVILLE, KENTUCKY
OCTOBER	1	SOUTH BEND, INDIANA
	2	SPRINGFIELD, MISSOURI
	3	LINCOLN, NEBRASKA
	4	DENVER, COLORADO
	7–31	RECORDING
NOVEMBER	14–30	EUROPEAN TOUR
DECEMBER	1–13	EUROPEAN TOUR
	31	GREENVILLE, SOUTH CAROLINA

1975 ★★★★

JANUARY	1	MACON, GEORGIA
	4	MONROE, LOUISIANA
	5	LITTLE ROCK, ARKANSAS
	6–28	RECORDING

FEBRUARY	1	BUFFALO, NEW YORK
	2	TORONTO, CANADA
	4	ROCHESTER, NEW YORK
	6	RALEIGH, NORTH CAROLINA
	7	RICHMOND, VIRGINIA
	8	CLEMSON, SOUTH CAROLINA
	9	CANCELED
	11	CHATTANOOGA, TENNESSEE
	12	KNOXVILLE, TENNESSEE
	14	PASSAIC, NEW JERSEY
	15	CANCELED
	16	CANCELED
	7–28	MIXING ALBUM
MARCH	1–16	MIXING ALBUM
	17	STARKVILLE, MISSISSIPPI
	18	HATTIESBURG, TENNESSEE
	19	CHATTANOOGA, TENNESSEE
	21	TUSCALOOSA, ALABAMA
	22	JOHNSON CITY, TENNESSEE
	23	SALEM, VIRGINIA
	26	MIAMI, FLORIDA
	27	ST. PETERSBURG, FLORIDA
	29	PENSACOLA, FLORIDA
	30	NEW ORLEANS, LOUISIANA
APRIL	1	LAKE CHARLES, LOUISIANA
	2	SHREVEPORT, LOUISIANA
	3	DALLAS, TEXAS
	5	OKLAHOMA CITY, OKLAHOMA
	6	HOUSTON, TEXAS
	7	AUSTIN, TEXAS
	9	FAYETTEVILLE, ARKANSAS
	11	KANSAS CITY, MISSOURI
	12	MEMPHIS, TENNESSEE
	15	WICHITA, KANSAS
	16	ST. LOUIS, MISSOURI

LYNYRD SKYNYRD

	17	LINCOLN, NEBRASKA
	21–22	LOS ANGELES, CALIFORNIA
	23	PHOENIX, ARIZONA
	24	SAN DIEGO, CALIFORNIA
	26–27	SAN FRANCISCO, CALIFORNIA
	28	SACRAMENTO, CALIFORNIA
MAY	1–2	PORTLAND, OREGON
	3	SEATTLE, WASHINGTON
	4	CANCELED
	14	TUCSON, ARIZONA
	16	DENVER, COLORADO
	17	SIOUX CITY, IOWA
	18	CANCELED
	20	MILWAUKEE, WISCONSIN
	21	ST. PAUL, MINNESOTA
	23	CHICAGO, ILLINOIS
	24	CLEVELAND, OHIO
	25	ANN ARBOR, MICHIGAN
	27	PITTSBURGH, PENNSYLVANIA
	29	CANCELED
	30–31	BUFFALO, NEW YORK
JUNE	1	ROCHESTER, NEW YORK
	3	GREENVALE, NEW YORK
	4	HARTFORD, CONNECTICUT
	6	NEW YORK, NEW YORK
	8	BOSTON, MASSACHUSETTS
	13	FORT WAYNE, INDIANA
	14	EVANSVILLE, INDIANA
	15	DAYTON, OHIO
	17	SARATOGA SPRINGS, NEW YORK
	19	PHILADELPHIA, PENNSYLVANIA
	20	WASHINGTON, D.C.
	21	CANCELED
	23	INDIANAPOLIS, INDIANA
	24	LOUISVILLE, KENTUCKY

	27	CANCELED
	28	CHARLOTTE, NORTH CAROLINA
	29	COLUMBIA, SOUTH CAROLINA
JULY	1	JACKSON, MISSISSIPPI
	2	MOBILE, ALABAMA
	4	BIRMINGHAM, ALABAMA
	5	ATLANTA, GEORGIA
	6	JACKSONVILLE, FLORIDA
AUGUST	16	TAMPA, FLORIDA
	19	CHARLESTON, WEST VIRGINIA
	21	BOSTON, MASSACHUSETTS
	22	JERSEY CITY, NEW JERSEY
	31	SAN DIEGO, CALIFORNIA
SEPTEMBER	1	FRESNO, CALIFORNIA
	5	SAN BERNARDINO, CALIFORNIA
	6	LONG BEACH, CALIFORNIA
	14	TUCSON, ARIZONA
	16	PORTLAND, OREGON
	17	SEATTLE, WASHINGTON
	20	OAKLAND, CALIFORNIA
	22	SALT LAKE CITY, UTAH
	24	TULSA, OKLAHOMA
OCTOBER	16	ROTTERDAM, HOLLAND
	17	ROERMOND, HOLLAND
	18	BELIQUE, BELGIUM
	19	BRUSSELS, BELGIUM
	20	SOARBRUCKEN, GERMANY
	21	MANNHEIM, GERMANY
	22	FRANKFURT, GERMANY
	23	DUSSELDORF, GERMANY
	25	PORTSMOUTH, ENGLAND
	26	BIRMINGHAM, ENGLAND
	27	LONDON, ENGLAND
	28	BRIGHTON, ENGLAND
	30	LIVERPOOL, ENGLAND

LYNYRD SKYNYRD

	31	SHEFFIELD, ENGLAND
NOVEMBER	1	GLASGOW, SCOTLAND
	3	OXFORD, ENGLAND
	4	CARDIFF, WALES
	5	LONDON, ENGLAND
	7	PARIS, FRANCE
DECEMBER	10	SUDBERRY, CANADA
	11	MONTREAL, CANADA
	13	DETROIT, MICHIGAN
	15	TOLEDO, OHIO
	16	ERIE, PENNSYLVANIA
	19	HAMPTON ROADS, VIRGINIA
	20	PASSAIC, NEW JERSEY
	21	BALTIMORE, MARYLAND

1976 ★★★★

JANUARY	9	SAVANNAH, GEORGIA
	10	ASHEVILLE, NORTH CAROLINA
	11	MACON, GEORGIA
	16	KNOXVILLE, TENNESSEE
	17	NASHVILLE, TENNESSEE
	19	MONROE, LOUISIANA
	20	AUSTIN, TEXAS
	21	CORPUS CHRISTI, TEXAS
	23	AMARILLO, TEXAS
	24	SAN ANTONIO, TEXAS
FEBRUARY	10	BRISTOL, ENGLAND
	11	MANCHESTER, ENGLAND
	13	GLASGOW, SCOTLAND
	14	LEEDS, ENGLAND
	15	LONDON, ENGLAND
MARCH	1	DENVER, COLORADO
	4	SAN JOSE, CALIFORNIA
	5–7	SAN FRANCISCO, CALIFORNIA
	9	SACRAMENTO, CALIFORNIA

	12	SAN BERNARDINO, CALIFORNIA
	13	LOS ANGELES, CALIFORNIA
	14	SAN DIEGO, CALIFORNIA
	16	SEATTLE, WASHINGTON
	17	SPOKANE, WASHINGTON
	18	PORTLAND, OREGON
	24	ALBUQUERQUE, NEW MEXICO
	25	HOUSTON, TEXAS
	26	NORMAN, OKLAHOMA
	30	ST. PAUL, MINNESOTA
	31	DES MOINES, IOWA
APRIL	2	CHICAGO, ILLINOIS
	3	ST. LOUIS, MISSOURI
	7	BOSTON, MASSACHUSETTS
	10–11	NEW YORK, NEW YORK
	13	TERRE HAUTE, INDIANA
	16	PHILADELPHIA, PENNSYLVANIA
	17	PITTSBURGH, PENNSYLVANIA
	18	CLEVELAND, OHIO
	21	DALLAS, TEXAS
	30	LAKELAND, FLORIDA
MAY	1	JACKSONVILLE, FLORIDA
	2	MIAMI, FLORIDA
	11	KANSAS CITY, MISSOURI
	14	INDIANAPOLIS, INDIANA
	15	CINCINNATI, OHIO
	16	EVANSVILLE, INDIANA
	18	COLUMBUS, OHIO
	21	GREENVILLE, SOUTH CAROLINA
	22	COLUMBIA, SOUTH CAROLINA
	23	CHARLOTTE, NORTH CAROLINA
	25	MOBILE, ALABAMA
	26	LITTLE ROCK, ARKANSAS
	29	WINSTON-SALEM, NORTH CAROLINA
	30	WASHINGTON, D.C.

LYNYRD SKYNYRD

	31	MYRTLE BEACH, SOUTH CAROLINA
JUNE	1–29	VACATION
	30	DETROIT, MICHIGAN
JULY	2	DAYTON, OHIO
	4	MEMPHIS, TENNESSEE
	7	ATLANTA, GEORGIA
	10	CANCELED
	11–15	RECORDING
	16	BIRMINGHAM, ALABAMA
	17	CANCELED
	24	MIAMI, FLORIDA
	25	TAMPA, FLORIDA
	28	PENSACOLA, FLORIDA
	30	NASHVILLE, TENNESSEE
AUGUST	1	MACON, GEORGIA
	2–9	MIXING ALBUM
	10	CALLAHAN, FLORIDA
	15	CHICAGO, ILLINOIS
	19	HEMEL HEMPSTEAD, ENGLAND
	21	KNEBWORTH, ENGLAND
	24	SPRINGFIELD, MASSACHUSETTS
	25	LEWISTON, MAINE
	27	SOUTH YARMOUTH, MASSACHUSETTS
	28	ASBURY PARK, NEW JERSEY
SEPTEMBER	8–12	CANCELED
	21	WICHITA, KANSAS
	22	OMAHA, NEBRASKA
	24	LAWRENCE, KANSAS
	25	AMES, IOWA
	26	LA CROSSE, WISCONSIN
	28	MINOT, NORTH DAKOTA
	29	BILLINGS, MONTANA
OCTOBER	1	LOS ANGELES, CALIFORNIA
	2	SANTA BARBARA, CALIFORNIA
	3	CONCORD, CALIFORNIA

	5	SALT LAKE CITY, UTAH
	7	SPOKANE, WASHINGTON
	8	SEATTLE, WASHINGTON
	9	PORTLAND, OREGON
	12	DENVER, COLORADO
	14	NEW ORLEANS, LOUISIANA
	20	LANDOVER, MARYLAND
	22	BOSTON, MASSACHUSETTS
	23–24	NEW YORK, NEW YORK
	26	PAWTUCKET, RHODE ISLAND
	27	WATERBURY, CONNECTICUT
	29	BUFFALO, NEW YORK
	30	PASSAIC, NEW JERSEY
	31	UTICA, NEW YORK
NOVEMBER	5	FLINT, MICHIGAN
	6	KENT, OHIO
	7	LONG ISLAND, NEW YORK
	15	TORONTO, CANADA
	19	CANCELED
	20	BINGHAMTON, NEW YORK
	21	HAMPTON, VIRGINIA
	24	HOUSTON, TEXAS
	25	FORT WORTH, TEXAS
	26	MEMPHIS, TENNESSEE
	28	AUSTIN, TEXAS
DECEMBER	2	ST. PAUL, MINNESOTA
	3	ST. LOUIS, MISSOURI
	5	MILWAUKEE, WISCONSIN
	6–7	DETROIT, MICHIGAN
	26	CINCINNATI, OHIO
	27	PITTSBURGH, PENNSYLVANIA
	31	SAN FRANCISCO, CALIFORNIA

LYNYRD SKYNYRD

1977 ★★★★

JANUARY	1	SAN DIEGO, CALIFORNIA
	2	LOS ANGELES, CALIFORNIA
	5	HONOLULU, HAWAII
	14–16	TOKYO, JAPAN
	18	OSAKA, JAPAN
	21	TOKYO, JAPAN
	27–29	LONDON, ENGLAND
	31	BRISTOL, ENGLAND
FEBRUARY	1	PORTSMOUTH, ENGLAND
	2	BIRMINGHAM, ENGLAND
	4	MANCHESTER, ENGLAND
	5	SHEFFIELD, ENGLAND
	6	LIVERPOOL, ENGLAND
	8	NEWCASTLE, ENGLAND
	9	GLASGOW, SCOTLAND
	12	LANCASTER, ENGLAND
	13	LEEDS, ENGLAND
	14	LEICESTER, ENGLAND
	15–28	VACATION, RECORDING, AND REHEARSING
APRIL	1–21	VACATION, RECORDING, AND REHEARSING
	22	JOHNSON CITY, TENNESSEE
	23	LOUISVILLE, KENTUCKY
	24	DAYTON, OHIO
	26	WHEELING, WEST VIRGINIA
	27	RICHMOND, VIRGINIA
	29	CHARLOTTE, NORTH CAROLINA
	30	FAYETTEVILLE, NORTH CAROLINA
MAY	11	COLUMBIA, SOUTH CAROLINA
	13	GREENSBORO, NORTH CAROLINA
	14	SAVANNAH, GEORGIA
	15	DOTHAN, ALABAMA
	17	ATHENS, GEORGIA
	20	LEXINGTON, KENTUCKY
	21	KNOXVILLE, KENTUCKY

	23	MOBILE, ALABAMA
	24	COLUMBUS, GEORGIA
JUNE	11	PHILADELPHIA, PENNSYLVANIA
	12	CHARLESTON, WEST VIRGINIA
	14	PORTLAND, MAINE
	15	SPRINGFIELD, MASSACHUSETTS
	16	HEMPSTEAD, NEW YORK
	18	HYANNIS, MASSACHUSETTS
	19	BUFFALO, NEW YORK
	26	DENVER, COLORADO
	27	SALT LAKE CITY, UTAH
JULY	2–4	OAKLAND, CALIFORNIA
	3	TULSA, OKLAHOMA
	7	MADISON, WISCONSIN
	8	SPRINGFIELD, MISSOURI
	10	CHICAGO, ILLINOIS
	12	POUGHKEEPSIE, NEW YORK
	13	ASBURY PARK, NEW JERSEY
	18–21	VACATION, RECORDING, AND REHEARSING
AUGUST	1–22	VACATION, RECORDING, AND REHEARSING
	24	FRESNO, CALIFORNIA
	27	ANAHEIM, CALIFORNIA
	29	LAS VEGAS, NEVADA
SEPTEMBER	1–30	VACATION, RECORDING, AND REHEARSING
OCTOBER	1–12	VACATION, RECORDING, AND REHEARSING
	13	STATESBORO, GEORGIA
	15	MIAMI, FLORIDA
	16	ST. PETERSBURG, FLORIDA
	18	LAKELAND, FLORIDA
	19	GREENVILLE, SOUTH CAROLINA

LYNYRD SKYNYRD

SOURCES AND ACKNOWLEDGMENTS

Written during a period of about two years, *Lynyrd Skynyrd: Remembering the Free Birds of Southern Rock* is based upon the author's memories of his friendship and travels with the late Ronnie Van Zant and other members of the band; interviews with their families, friends, and associates; reviews of hundreds of American and British newspaper and magazine articles, and of hundreds of pages of civil and criminal court documents; and the books *Backstage Passes and Backstabbing Bastards* by Al Kooper, *Lynyrd Skynyrd: An Oral History,* edited by Lee Ballinger and Dave Marsh, and *Midnight Riders* by Scott Freeman.

I appreciate all of the many significant contributions of everyone who helped make this project possible, but I am especially grateful to those who gave so generously of their time to share their extensive, intimate memories, which have greatly enriched this book. As one of Ronnie's closest friends who spent countless hours with Lynyrd Skynyrd, pre- and post-stardom, Bill Ferris helped reconstruct the major influences that helped guide Ronnie's life. Larry Steele, who spent many years with the early band and briefly joined the group, provided many historical details about the band that no one else could recall. Dorman Cogburn provided valuable musical insights, Kent Griffith offered his extensive collection of news articles and his memories of an ailing Allen Collins, and Ed Mangum described the background for the drug bust that followed the funerals for Ronnie, Steve, and Cassie.

I am grateful to Joe Barnes, Kevin Elson, and Craig Reed for their vivid recollections of working for the band, and I appreciate the assistance of musical artists Charlie Daniels, Pat Boone, and the late Leon Wilkeson.

I also owe a debt of gratitude to others who contributed, including Bill Babcock; Mike Basford; Tony Beazley; Rick Broyles; Tony and Jennifer Bullard; Jerry Casey; Donald Chase; Bill Chester; Dorman Cogburn; Jim Daniel; Jeanne Marie LaSala Dorman; John and Robin Eastwood; Carl, John, and Tom Ferrell; Mitch Gilbert; Kent Griffith; Justin Guyton; Randall Hall; Ollie Mae Hamner; Vernon and Michele Hamner; Marie Darsey Harris; Leslie Hawkins of the Honkettes; Randy Herrin; Larry Junstrom; Ed King; Harley Lamoureaux; Don Lindstrom; Ronnie Maggart; Theresa Mellon of the National Archives and Records Administration; Wayne Minter; Nick Nicoll; Charles Odum, Jr.; Bob "Slim" Rader; Teresa Gaines Rapp; John Rodgers; Darren Ross; Bobby Sanders; George Sardos; Jennifer Sieck; Leonard Skinner; Glenda Hamner Slenk and Rick Slenk; Eva Strunk; Ben Upham; John Winslow; Jay Zienta; and Nick and John Zingaro.

And I especially want to thank Karen Harlow and Scott and Susan Carraway for their support and Tom Saunders for all of the hours he spent scanning photos for this book.

Grateful acknowledgment to the following for permission to use photographs: Mike Basford, Tony Beazley, Rick Broyles, Tony and Jennifer Bullard, Jeanne Marie Lasala Dorman, John and Robin Eastwood, Joe Farley, Kent Griffith, Ollie Mae Hamner, Bob Rader, Teresa Gaines Rapp, John Rodgers, Darren Ross, Bobby Sanders, George Sardos, Larry Steele, Eva Strunk, and Ben Upham.